P9-DNP-931

Forever Yours, Faithfully

Forever Yours, Faithfully

My Love Story

Lorrie Morgan

with George Vecsey

Ballantine Books
New York

 Published
in the United States by Ballantine Books, a division of Random
House, Inc., New York, and simultaneously in Canada
by Random House of Canada Limited, Toronto.

http://www.randomhouse.com

Library of Congress Cataloging-in-Publication Data
Morgan, Lorrie.
Forever yours, faithfully / by Lorrie Morgan with George Vecsey.—1st ed.
p. cm.
ISBN 0-345-41297-4 (hardcover)
1. Morgan, Lorrie. 2. Country musicians—United States—Biography
I. Vecsey, George. II. Title.
ML420.M6174A3 1997
782.42'1642'092—dc21
[B] 97-24008
CIP
MN

Text design by Holly Johnson

Manufactured in the United States of America

First Edition: October 1997

10 9 8 7 6 5 4 3 2 1

To Morgan and Jesse, from Mommy.
"May the truth always set you free."
You are my life.

Acknowledgments

My special thanks to:

My family: Mom, Candy, Beth, Liana, Marty, for always loving me unconditionally.

My children, Morgan and Jesse, for being the beat of my heart.

Mike and Loren, for allowing me to chase my dreams and for loving my children.

Susan Nadler, my manager, for her vision and belief in me.

Ruthie, for being the cornerstone of my life.

My office staff, for their hard work.

All my loyal fans, who remind me why I love what I do.

The members of my Slam Band, who protect me on the road—and play good music, too.

Last but not least, George Vecsey, for capturing the love in my life, and being able to translate it into black and white.

—Lorrie Morgan

Thank You

Peter Gethers and his associate, Amy Scheibe, for making this book a reality.

Esther Newberg of International Creative Management for putting the deal together.

And all the others who helped with interviews and information and the logistics of putting out a book:

Mary Bailey
Lieutenant Harry Bell
Mike Chamberlain
Ralph Emery and his staff
Joe Galante of RCA and his assistant, Teresa Russell
Mindy Harrison
Kay Johnson, Loretta Johnson, Loudilla Johnson
Don Light
Jack McFadden
Raymond W. McLain
Blake Mevis
Lane Palmer
Ronnie Pugh of the Country Music Foundation, a wonderful resource right on Music Row
The people in Sandy Hook who care about Keith Whitley
Dianne Sherrill
Evelyn Shriver
Lynn Simpkins
Ricky Skaggs
David Skepner
Mary Lou Turner
Faye Whitley
Curtis (Mister Harmony) Young

—George Vecsey

VOICE

There was pain in his voice,
Pain from back in the mountains,
Pain from deep in the soul.

Low voice, resonant voice,
Big voice for such a pretty man.

Our music is all about heartache.
Keith lived it.
Hear him once, you knew,
This was no kid come to Nashville,
Looking to be a singer.
He was an artist.

Torment inside.
Sang to let it out.
There was pain in his voice,
No one knew what.

FOREVER YOURS, FAITHFULLY

CHAPTER ONE

I was in love with his voice before I saw his face.

You hear a lot of voices in Nashville. Voices on the car radio. Voices in the clubs. Voices on the tube, in the elevators, on intercoms. Voices in the music stores. At the Opry. Voices at the Ryman Auditorium. Voices from the back studio.

His was the most gorgeous voice I had ever heard in my life, soft and gentle, low and powerful, a bit of mountain twang to it, so subtle, so practiced, so perfect.

I was working at Acuff-Rose, that venerable music publishing institution. During the day, I would sit at the front desk, a receptionist greeting other singers, other songwriters. In the evening, I recorded demonstration tapes of other people's songs.

We were all trying to catch a break.

One day I heard this gorgeous country voice coming from the back studio.

"Who"—I blurted—"is that?"

One of the producers, Ronnie Gant, was walking with me in the corridor. I had gone out with Ronnie once upon a time, and he understood my moods.

"That's Keith Whitley, out of eastern Kentucky. He used to

sing bluegrass," Ronnie said. "My brother Don is producing him."

Ronnie suggested we duck into the control room and watch the session.

Through the soundproof glass I could see a singer, slender and lithe and curly-haired, gentle, with a touch of shyness. His face was divided into a laughing smile and sad eyes.

Keith Whitley was making a demo tape of a song called "Does Fort Worth Ever Cross Your Mind?" The words were great, but the voice was even greater. It made you want to cry over lost loves and missed opportunities.

I was no novice. Twenty-seven years old, I had been singing in this town literally half my life. I was George Morgan's daughter. I knew talent when I heard it, and there was talent coming from the studio.

The music stopped, and Keith Whitley walked into the control room where he was met by a few Acuff-Rose people and a woman. I made sure I got an introduction.

"I know you," Keith Whitley said in a voice as soft as silk. "We met a few months ago. You were doing Ralph Emery's morning show on WSM, and somebody introduced us. Remember? This is my wife, Kathi. She was there, too."

I said hello to a sensitive-looking, pretty brunette. A definite wife.

I could not remember meeting Keith Whitley before. Ralph's show was at four-thirty in the morning, and I tended to block out anything that early. I had even blocked out this man with the beautiful voice, but he was bemused, not annoyed, that I did not remember him.

"I heard the recording you made of that Supremes song, 'Someday We'll Be Together,' " Keith said. "I really liked it."

Now I had two thoughts, both of which I kept to myself. One: This is not only the most gorgeous voice I have ever *heard* in my life, this is also the most gorgeous man I have ever *seen* in my life. Two: This man is married, let's get out of here. Which I did. I had just broken up my own marriage and did not even want to think about any other marriage going wrong. There was enough of that all around me.

I was all for the old ways of Dad and Mom staying together till death did them part, which, unfortunately, it had done with my dad, far too early. Looking back, I already knew that Keith could be the mad passion every woman knows is possible. I'm not saying I willed it to happen. I'm not saying I did anything. Rather, I saw this lithe, bearded man, fixing his smile on me, and I knew we would meet again.

When I talk about my love affair with Keith Whitley, I often refer to *Romeo and Juliet*, which I studied back at St. Bernard Academy in Nashville. The Franco Zeffirelli version is one of my all-time favorite movies, with those two beautiful young people playing the lovers. I can quote passages verbatim from Shakespeare:

> "See! How she leans her cheek upon her hand!
> "O! that I were a glove upon that hand,
> "That I might touch that cheek!"

That is how I felt about Keith Whitley, immediately—the mad passion that made me want to be the glove that touched his cheek, the shirt on his back, the jeans on his body, the cap on his long, flowing hair.

Is it fair to compare the two of us to Romeo and Juliet? In Shakespeare, the lovers are kept apart by the rivalry of their two feuding families, the Montagues and the Capulets. They feign their own deaths, so they can flee together. When their plot goes wrong in a gloomy tomb under the ground of Verona, Romeo kills himself with a deadly poison.

"Here's to my love! O true apothecary!
"Thy drugs are quick. Thus with a kiss I die."

Keith died in our bed in Goodlettsville, Tennessee, from a huge and gruesome cocktail of alcohol, while I was thousands of miles away.

When she sees her love, dead on the ground, Juliet wastes no time.

"Yea, noise? Then I'll be brief. O happy dagger,
This is thy sheath; there rust, and let me die."

Instead of choosing death in a hidden vault, I chose to survive, to raise our children, to play the *Opry* the night after my husband's funeral. I have sold millions of CDs and cassettes, and I have made videos wearing sultry red dresses. And I love again.

Still, with all due respect to William Shakespeare and all who are touched by words, I do compare Keith and me to Romeo and Juliet.

We came from different backgrounds, he from the hills of eastern Kentucky, I from the suburbs of Nashville. People said we were not right for each other, people even warned me that he was an alcoholic with a sorry future. But for a brief (and I would say a tragic) time, we loved each other as intensely as two people can love. I call us Romeo and Juliet not because of his death but because of the life that flowed between us, the short and furious love that I feel every time I watch the Zeffirelli film, two young people looking at each other and saying, "Yesssss."

I do not recommend this mad, impetuous love for anybody else, not for my own children, but we all know it exists, that it is an ideal. You can be Romeo and Juliet at other stages in life. I am just discovering that.

I have been waiting to write about Keith Whitley since the day he died, May 9, 1989. I have wanted to talk about the man who was my husband, who was my inspiration.

My life goes on. I've had a bit of notoriety as the singer who dated a quarterback and a senator and a famous country singer, yet never stopped thinking she could find the stable love she had wanted with Keith.

Keith Whitley is a legend now: Extremely talented mountain man who drank himself to death. Keith was one of those artists who goes unappreciated while he is on the earth. How many paintings did van Gogh, another tortured soul, sell while he was alive? I think it was one—to his own brother.

It would have been nice if people had recognized that Keith was unique while he was alive. It's the same way with my father. People talk about his beautiful, mellow voice now. Where were they when he was driving hundreds of miles to make a few dollars?

I have wanted to tell people that Keith was not some country-music drunk, that he was a good man, that there was heart and soul inside, behind the voice. I have also wanted to tell people that there was more trouble to Keith than anybody knew, including myself.

I have something to say to people—women in particular—who love somebody with a problem. Since Keith's death I've learned a few things about what to recognize, what steps to take. I wish I'd known them while Keith was alive.

I've held most of this in for years, but now it's time to talk about it. There are still mysteries surrounding Keith's death, mysteries I kept encountering as I worked on this book.

There are also some things I'd like to tell people about survival—about looking at your darkest day and knowing that somehow you can get through it, and then take care of tomorrow. I've been there. More than once.

CHAPTER TWO

In those early months of 1986, Keith Whitley's voice was in the air in Nashville, this tiny village of country music, where everybody knows everybody else, where the singer on the car radio is walking down Music Row as you drive past.

Much of the world had not yet discovered him. They were still listening to the dandified one-hundred-and-one-violins sound of urban country music that was the rage back in the early eighties, but here was this real-life country boy from the back hills of eastern Kentucky, singing to me out of every speaker.

A few days after hearing his voice in the corridor of Acuff-Rose, I was on the road with my leased bus and my little pickup band, consisting of whoever happened to be available at the moment. I was somewhere on that long highway between being George Morgan's little girl and being Lorrie Morgan herself.

While we rolled across this huge country, we were listening to a bus tape, one of those cassettes that keep us going on the long hauls—maybe a taped prank phone call or a comedy routine or somebody's new song—and that gets passed from bus to bus: "Hey, have you heard this yet?"

The tape of the day was bluegrass, provided by my drummer,

Rick Vanaugh. I hope I don't offend anybody, but I am not a big bluegrass fan. My dad, with his smooth country voice and the soul of an Irish tenor, used to say, "Have you ever heard a happy bluegrass song?"

Coming over the speaker in our bus was a tape by J. D. Crowe and the New South, a bluegrass band out of eastern Kentucky, and the lead singer had a haunting voice that managed to overcome the twanging banjos and wailing fiddles. The voice penetrated me, right down to my toenails. I asked who it was, and they said, "It's this new guy, Keith Whitley."

It seemed as if Keith Whitley was everywhere. One day I was watching *Nashville Now* with one of my best girlfriends, the very talented Mary Lou Turner, who used to sing with Bill Anderson. The guest on Ralph's show was—you guessed it—Keith Whitley.

"Who is that?" Mary Lou asked.

"Oh, you'd like him," I said, trying to be blasé.

"He sounds wonderful," Mary Lou said.

"He's married," I said dourly.

After Keith's segment was over, we turned off the television and went out to the mall. Mary Lou wandered into a pet store, and found herself peering into cages, right next to—yup—Keith Whitley.

You have to understand something about Mary Lou Turner. She is cool. She is part of establishment Nashville, a singer out of Hazard, Kentucky, and Dayton, Ohio, who came to town and made it. She doesn't go around gawking at celebrities because, well, she wouldn't put it this way, but she's a star herself. Nevertheless, she was struck by the incongruity of seeing Keith in such a strange location, so soon after we'd been discussing him.

"I just saw you on television," she said. "I was over at Lorrie Morgan's. Lorrie's right around here somewhere."

Keith was polite, and they chatted for a few minutes, and then Mary Lou wandered off to find me.

"You'll never believe who I just saw in the pet store," Mary Lou said. "Keith Whitley. Come on, he's still in there."

"I've got a lot to do," I said. "Let's get going."

I did not want to go chasing a man into a pet store. Not that man, that *married* man.

A few days after that, Mary Lou and I were up in Dayton for a show, and we were listening to tapes. Donnie Collins, another singer, played one tape with songs like "I'll Be Your Stepping Stone," and "Gone, Gone, Gone," and "Tennessee Blues."

The voice was Keith Whitley's. What was going on here? I just loved that tape, and asked Donnie to make me a copy for the ride home. Mary Lou remembers me driving down the interstate in the pouring rain, playing the tape over and over again.

Keith had been in Nashville only a short time, but already he had established himself as a country singer's singer. He was a throwback, with an authentic throb in his voice that spoke of small towns and winding roads and lonely times, the real life out there, just like Hank Williams and Johnny Cash.

The singers knew about Keith Whitley's talent, even if the general public did not. They were listening to his records; they were packing his tapes on their buses and in their sound systems at home, the highest compliment of all.

Now for the next coincidence. An old friend of mine named Dean Dillon had pitched me a song he had written called "Miami My Amy," about a man from Los Angeles who falls in love with a woman in Miami, and how he catches the first plane back to see her.

The song would not have worked for a female singer—not this female singer, anyway—but I loved it, and I used to listen to Dean's demo tape on my car cassette player.

I knew this song "Miami My Amy." I knew what the right male voice could do for it.

On Saturday evening, April 12, 1986, I was driving in from

Mom's house in Madison. I was a member of the *Grand Ole Opry* and appeared on it almost every Saturday night.

As I drove, the radio played a new recording—"Miami My Amy." The disk jockey said it was "by a gentleman named Keith Whitley."

Not only that, the disk jockey said, but Keith Whitley was going to appear on the *Opry* that night.

I pulled my car onto the shoulder of Briley Parkway, all flushed, knowing I was going to run into Keith that night.

I had never felt like this before. The first time I sang on the *Opry*, when my dad introduced me at the age of thirteen, I had been so shaken that I thought I was going to faint. That was kid stuff. As I sat in my car on the edge of the road, I could not get my legs and hands to drive the car. I was turned to jelly. This was grown-up stuff. My life was about to change, and I knew it. I really did.

Somehow I got to the Opry and worked my way backstage. The guys in my band knew I liked Keith's music and they were always ribbing me about him, but we had never appeared on the *Opry* on the same show.

I was darting around backstage, just trying to work off my nervous energy, when I ran into him. I just froze. The only thing I could think was, He is so incredibly gorgeous. He was talking to me, but I felt I was inside a glass bubble, vaguely hearing him talk, but so far away, so removed, that this was happening to somebody else.

I stuck out my hand and I said, "Hi, I'm Lorrie Morgan," and he said, "I know who you are." Once again, he was bemused. This was the third time we had met, and I was still acting like a tourist, a civilian.

I could have shaken his hand forever, just held on to it. Nothing else was working right. Then I heard him say: "I just got divorced. Maybe we could get together."

What happened to that nice-looking wife? I didn't ask.

I did not offer my phone number or comment on the invitation he had just made. I just faded backward, feeling my way along the walls of the corridor like some kind of sleepwalker, until I got to the rehearsal room.

"You look like you've just seen a ghost," somebody in the band said.

"I don't know what just happened to me, but I don't want to talk about it," I replied.

Things were getting complicated. The very next morning, I was supposed to move back in with Ron Gaddis, my ex-husband, whom I had started seeing again. We thought it would be the best thing for our daughter, Morgan, and maybe for both of us, too, but now I found myself standing in the wings of the *Grand Ole Opry* with what could be mildly described as a raging crush on Keith Whitley.

To this day, I do not remember what I sang, or whether I made a total fool of myself. Then I stood there, gaping, as Keith sang "Miami My Amy," and then I thought the very best thing for me to do was get out of there. Just get out. I ran to my Camaro, turned on the car radio, and headed back out along Briley Parkway, crying, so emotional, so torn between doing the right thing for my family, and the right thing for my heart.

My heart won. I turned the car around and drove back to the security station at the Opry, where I spotted Tim Atwood, a piano player I knew.

I wrote down my phone number, and I said, "Tim, this is really important. Please give this piece of paper to Keith Whitley as soon as you walk through this door." He said he would do it, so I turned my car around and went home to Mom's house, the house where I grew up, the house where Morgan and I were living at the moment.

I tried to sleep but I kept thinking: What am I going to do? The next morning I was going to the eleven-thirty Mass, and just as I was leaving I heard the phone ring. I let the answering machine pick it up, and it was my ex-husband saying, "Hey, it's me, give me a call."

I did not pick up.

Instead, I called up Mary Lou and said, "Guess who asked me out?"

"Shotgun Red," she said, meaning the homely puppet on Ralph Emery's show.

"No, Keith Whitley," I told her.

"If you don't date the man, I'm going to," she said. And she is married.

Then I went to church and prayed. Our family is devoutly Roman Catholic. Dad had converted when he married Mom, and we had said prayers together, all five kids, even if we sometimes pinched and elbowed each other. We loved the mystery and the ritual of our church. Now I was on my knees, hoping for an answer. I did not want to hurt anybody, but I was having some serious doubts about moving in with Ron that afternoon.

I got home at twenty to one, and there was another voice on the machine. It was Keith Whitley's voice, saying, "It's eleven-thirty, and I thought we could go to the park." I felt my heart stop beating. I do not know if God takes any interest in affairs of the heart like this. I do not know what God thought about my breaking a promise to Ron. I only knew what I had to do.

I dialed the phone and said, "Ron, I can't do this. It just doesn't feel right." He was upset with me, more than a little, and I owed it to him to listen to his anger and his sadness. Then I called Keith and missed him, but he called me back around two, said he was going out of town that evening, but asked if I'd see him that afternoon. I said I would.

I had been through a lot in the last twenty-four hours—meeting Keith at the Opry, wrestling with my conscience about Ron—and now I was a nervous wreck. What should I wear for my first date with Keith? Should I get all dressed up, or be casual? What was the message? Because it was getting to be spring, I finally decided on a one-piece shorts outfit, Hawaiian-like, a black background with lime green and orange flowers, real short, buttoned in the back, with a little triangle cutout in the back. And sandals, with a bit of a heel. I have to admit, I was looking good.

He was living at the Magnolia Apartments right off Wedgewood, not far from Music Row. I can't remember why I went there first. My legs could hardly walk up the steps to his second-floor apartment, and when he opened the door, his first words were, "You look beautiful."

We drove to a Wendy's drive-through, bought hamburgers, and went over to Centennial Park out on the west end of town, with a huge replica of the Parthenon, like the one in Athens, and its large round columns.

Keith and I sat by the pond, ate our hamburgers, and chatted away, just getting to know each other. He was so cute in his blue jeans and sneakers and a yellow T-shirt with long sleeves and three buttons.

I made sure he knew I had been married and had a daughter. I talked about Morgan's dancing class, my high hopes for her. I always wanted people to know that Morgan and I were a package, for life.

"I used to cut classes in high school and come over here," I told Keith. "My best friend, Ruth, and I would stop at the Krystal for a coffee and a doughnut, and then we'd come over here for a cigarette and feed the ducks.

"Oh, yeah," I said. "Father Ryan High School is right over there. That's where all the boys went."

Keith wanted to know about my friendship with Ruth.

"She tries to be practical, and I'm the one with the schemes," I said. "You get the two of us together, we're crazy."

"Crazy?" Keith said.

"Not the way you think," I said. "Corny, almost. We have this special vocabulary. We describe everybody with the word 'Mc' in front of it. This goes back to grammar school, before McDonald's had McNuggets and all that. We just came up with words to describe things. A McGriffin was a fat person. A McMillan was a cigarette. Don't ask me why. It just was."

Keith was laughing at our secret little language, and said he would like to meet Ruth. I said she was living in Florida.

We talked about our families. He knew about Dad, of course, and I told him about Mom and my three sisters and my brother.

"Tell me about your family," I said.

He began talking about his father and mother, a sister and two brothers. Then he paused and said his older brother, Randy, had died in 1984, when he was riding a motorcycle and was hit by a truck.

Many times in our life together, I would see Keith cry over the death of his brother Randy, but on this spring day in Centennial Park, he told me matter-of-factly. We were skimming the edge, staying away from emotions. We were not thinking about tomorrow.

We got up and took a walk around the duck pond, with Keith holding my hand, gently, and giving me a sweet little kiss, and I knew I was just head over heels for him.

We got back to his apartment around five o'clock, and I noticed that, for a man, he was very neat. Not compulsive or anything, just clean. We sat down on his couch and started kissing, and he tasted just perfect. His beard and mustache were soft, he smelled great, and his skin was smooth. He was gentle, too. Nothing urgent, just being there, letting me get to know him, letting me know the choice was mine.

I started to think, Do I make love with him—or not? If we made love that day, he would think this was my way with everybody I met. How could I tell him that I had wanted to make love with him from the moment I first saw him back at the studio, that I had been imagining where we would be, when it finally happened? Now I understood that it must not be today.

I could not say I didn't want to, so I lied and said I was on my period, and he said, "I understand, I totally understand." Then I said I really needed to get back and spend some time with my daughter, and he said he understood that, too. I got in my car and turned on the radio and there was Elton John singing "Blue Eyes." I think I cried all the way home.

Keith was leaving town to play a show in Alabama, but he called and said he would love me to see his next show in Atlanta. I asked Mary Lou to drive down with me.

I need Mary Lou the way Lucy Riccardo needed Ethel Mertz. I've got a few girlfriends and sisters who will claim they have a Lucy-and-Ethel relationship with me, and they're all correct. I'm the one with the wild schemes, and Ethel's always the one shaking her head saying, "I don't know if we should be doing this," but in the end, Ethel comes along to keep me out of further trouble.

Mary Lou was riding shotgun on this trip—"Thelma and Louise, except we didn't rob any banks," is how Mary Lou remembers it.

I packed my best white outfit and about half an hour outside Atlanta we stopped in a grungy gas station along the highway, where we could change out of our blue jeans and into our club clothes. The bathroom was so dirty that I had to put my blue jeans down so I wouldn't touch the floor, but I managed to get into my white jeans and white shirt and black boots without being contaminated.

When we got to the Buckboard, we were escorted to the

best table. Onstage, Keith seemed to be singing just for me and Mary Lou. He loved being up there, and he had so much talent.

After the last set, the promoter invited Mary Lou and me to stay at his home, where Keith and his two musicians were staying. First we went out to another club and listened to Steve Wariner, then we went back to the promoter's house, where he made sandwiches. We all stayed up late, talking and singing. The next morning, real early, Mary Lou and I drove back to Nashville.

I knew I was infatuated with this man. Whatever I did, at work, at home, I heard his soft voice, saw his soft smile.

Now he would have to pass two more tests. Any man I could love must first love hot chicken and my daughter, not necessarily in that order. The hot chicken is a family tradition going back to Dad's stopping at Prince's on Trinity Lane every Saturday on his way home from the Opry. He would bring home a sack of spiced chicken so hot you had to drink cold milk just to cool down. We were raised on that chicken. My taste buds have been trained to love spicy food. What if Keith Whitley were a peanut-butter-and-jelly guy? He said that he liked hot food, and I told him, rather haughtily, that we would find out about that.

More important, what would he think of Morgan? My daughter, who was five years old, had gone through hard times with my marriage breaking up. She was and is a very bright and sensitive young woman—we are very attuned to each other—and I knew I could never be involved with somebody who did not get along with her.

Morgan and I brought the chicken over to Keith's apartment. It was nuclear that day—white pepper, black pepper, you name it. For all his brave talk, Keith took his first bite and started sweating; then he said, "I think I might take some of that milk." But after a while, he seemed able to handle it.

When we were finished eating, Keith asked Morgan if she

liked to play hide-and-seek. You wouldn't think there would be many places to hide in a one-bedroom apartment, but Keith found all these great places—closets, the balcony, behind furniture. I watched the two of them running around the apartment, and I was thrilled to see my daughter having a good time.

Now it was getting serious. Keith also had people he wanted me to meet—his band. These were the guys who traveled with him well over a hundred nights a year, who rehearsed with him. A band is a family, too. And families have their own standards. Keith asked me to meet the band at the San Antonio Taco Company, and he told me to wear sneakers because we were going bowling afterward.

He was so cute, wearing his New York Yankees baseball shirt while he bowled. Is there any significance to a boy from eastern Kentucky wearing a Yankees shirt? None that I can find, other than that he just loved the Yankees.

All that evening, I could feel the five musicians and their wives and girlfriends inspecting me. The band members were reserved; a few of the women were downright hostile. They could see that Keith had an interest in me. They also knew I was part of the Nashville family, that I had my own little band, that I had made my own forays into the recording business. Whatever came along, I was not going to be a cheerleader on the sidelines. I was part of the business. I was a threat—and, boy, did I feel it.

When we all parted company that night, Mike Chamberlain called me "Kathi."

Well, he had a point.

I was going home with Keith.

We went back to his apartment, and this time we both knew it was time for love. I was not some honey he had picked from the crowd outside the stage door. We were already joined, already bonded. At first, he handled me as if I were a porcelain rose, gently, almost daintily, giving me every chance to change my mind again. But we were ready. He was perfect in every way, in tune with what pleased me. I felt like it was my first time. I loved the way he smelled, the way he moved, the way he sounded. We made love for hours, and I knew this was nothing I had ever experienced before.

I had been around. I knew a thing or two about entertainers. I knew they could have sex at any moment of the day, just by picking up the phone or waving to somebody outside the bus. But I knew this was not Keith enjoying himself with a stranger. We were wonderful together. With tears in his eyes, he kissed me. He was so thoughtful. Afterward, when most men just fall asleep, he wanted to know if I wanted something to drink.

I knew I should be going home, but I wanted to spend the night, and that's exactly what I did, calling my mom and making up some lame excuse for not coming home, which my mother did not appreciate.

The next morning Keith made me coffee in bed; then I put on one of his T-shirts, and we sat in front of the television and watched tapes, talking and laughing and making comments about the other singers. He was a very romantic man, and he smelled so good, always using cologne and baby powder, very conscious of his teeth being clean. We watched a tape of "On My Own," with Michael McDonald and Patti LaBelle, the big hit of the season, then Keith made love to me on the floor.

Eventually, I knew I had to go home, but my heart, and my life, was committed to Keith Whitley.

CHAPTER THREE

I could not stand to be apart from Keith. We tried to see each other every night he was in town, but I had to be a little creative with my stories. One night I told Mom I was spending the night at Mary Lou's, although I neglected to mention that Keith was there, too.

But Mom got the point the next weekend when Keith asked me to go meet his family in eastern Kentucky. This was a clear signal that we were serious about each other.

Keith was from Sandy Hook, a small town in eastern Kentucky, about six hours from Nashville. I was a suburban kid who had known the quaint alleys of downtown Nashville and the private back doors of the *Opry* since I was a child.

I had been through the Appalachian Mountains with my dad, mostly along the interstate or the main highways, and I had seen enough to know it was very different from Nashville.

Eastern Kentucky was the core of Keith's existence. In the few weeks I had known him, Keith was lovingly telling stories about his friends in Sandy Hook the way Minnie Pearl talked about Grinder's Switch, her mythical hometown. He was always talking about the Frosty Freeze, the little luncheonette where everybody congregated, just down the street from his house. Now he was taking me there.

I could feel the mood change as soon as Keith pulled off Interstate 64 in Morehead. I caught a glimpse of the university and the downtown, but soon the road curved in the contour of the mountains, giving you the feeling you were going deeper and deeper as the hills rose up on both sides.

There were nice modern homes as well as shacks with cars and junk piled up outside. There were farms nestled on the hillside, some cultivated carefully, others in disarray. Great beauty and squalor side by side. Old stone general stores, no longer in use, sparkling new mobile homes. Wrecked cars. Satellite dishes. It was so different from bustling, metropolitan Nashville.

"Can you imagine that I got away from here?" Keith said, over and over again. He was not judging his hometown, merely commenting on the distance between rural Kentucky and Music Row.

Every so often, a gravel truck from one of the quarries would hurtle around a curve, taking up more than its share of the road.

Keith talked about the wrecks in the hills, alluding to a couple he had been in, plus the motorcycle wreck in which his older brother, Randy, had died.

We turned onto another road and went through Laurel Gorge, a beautiful rocky pass, carved out by an ancient river. Then we were in Sandy Hook.

His parents lived in a double-wide mobile home they had fixed up on a nice plot of land, just off Route 7. His mother, Faye, was precious, a slender redhead with glasses, very bright, very well spoken, who helped put out the weekly newspaper in Elliott County. You could just see her glow as she hugged Keith. She said Keith called her practically every day, no matter where he was. Most boys do not call their moms regularly to chat with them as they get older, and she was obviously very close to Keith.

His father, Elmer, seemed much older, a little remote, and not in such great shape, physically or emotionally. Then I noticed a photograph of him taken five years earlier, and saw that he had been quite handsome and robust. I realized Mr. Whitley had never recovered from the death of his oldest son.

Later, I would hear from Keith and other people that Randy had been drunk at the time of the wreck. Their father had been called up the hill to the scene, and he saw where Randy had been dragged across the highway, his broken body lying by the side of the road.

Mr. Whitley had been so distraught that he had rushed to his car to get the pistol he usually kept in the glove compartment, and Mrs. Whitley was afraid he was going to do something violent. Fortunately, the pistol had been left home that day, so there was no further bloodshed.

However, Randy was a constant presence, a terrible sadness in the Whitley family. I didn't get the feeling that Keith felt guilty about surviving while his brother had died, but he definitely had looked up to Randy, and missed him terribly.

"Every family has one person who's special, and he was the one in our family," Keith once said. "We were really devastated, and that's one reason that success came for me at a good time. My family was so happy for me. . . . It helped everyone through the bad times."

According to Keith, his father had been a heavy drinker for years but one day had just decided to stop, and did. Keith was so nice with his father, talking politely to him, asking how he was doing. I kept thinking about how all the Morgans had loved our dad, and I felt very much at home in the Whitley household.

Mr. Whitley was missing most of his left hand, the result of an injury while he was in the service, but despite his handicap he had continued to work as an electrician, first in Baltimore, and later when they returned home to Elliott County. He could handle nails, wires, screws.

You could feel the love Mrs. Whitley had for all her kids—Mary, Randy, Dwight, and Keith—and clearly they were happy for Keith's success.

Just like my family, the Whitleys had a musical background. Mrs. Whitley liked to tell about her father, Lewis Ferguson, who had played banjo at square dances, and how she had "picked a little" when she was younger. The way mothers love to do, she told how Keith had been a child prodigy. She knew Keith was musical as early as two years old, when she was singing a song to him and he put his fingers to her lips and finished the song himself.

At the age of eight he had won a talent contest right in this town, wearing two toy pistols and singing Marty Robbins's song, "Big Iron." When they asked him to sing an encore, he had unbuckled his holster belt and let the guns drop to the floor, before he sang a hymn. They talked about how Keith had gone from there to Buddy Starcher's radio show.

They showed me the garage out behind the house where Keith, Dwight, and Ricky Skaggs had played music when they were younger.

"I had this grill out by the garage, and while the boys were practicing I would cook hamburgers," Mrs. Whitley said.

You could feel that in a way she wished she could roll back the days to when Keith was living at home and Randy was still alive. And who could blame her?

They loved telling me the old family stories, but I could tell it was rough on Mrs. Whitley, having another woman come along soon after Keith's divorce. I got the feeling that Mrs. Whitley was fond of Kathi, his first wife, who came from Grayson, just a few miles away, but Mrs. Whitley treated me as myself and made me feel comfortable.

They told me how they used to live on this very same spot in a two-story home, but one night when Keith was around twelve they got a telephone call from a neighbor that there was smoke on the second floor. They grabbed a few things and rushed out of the house just in time to watch it go up in flames.

"Randy never even got to take a pair of shoes or a stitch of clothing," Mrs. Whitley said sadly.

There had been no homes available in Sandy Hook, and they had not wanted to leave their spot by the main road, so they had bought a couple of mobile homes and created a double-wide out of it.

"The first time it rained, Elmer said he couldn't stand the sound of rain on a tin roof," Mrs. Whitley said. "So he put up the peaked roof by himself."

She smiled proudly at her husband and I thought of my Grandfather Morgan, with his missing leg, so animated and smart. The Whitleys reminded me of the way I was brought up. I knew I had made the right choice in falling in love.

But there were troubling moments, too. Even early on.

Keith drove me all around Sandy Hook, the seat of Elliott County but not much bigger than two streets coming together at a right angle. On the main drag was the post office, the library, and a few dozen stores, half of them boarded up. Behind the old stone school was a more modern high school that Keith had attended.

We doubled back near Keith's house and stopped in the Frosty Freeze, the meeting place for the town, maybe six tables, where people sat, watched television, and greeted each other. There was a bulletin board up front with Keith's photograph and posters of his last concert in Kentucky.

I was delighted to meet some of the people, until I began to realize that alcohol figured in many of the stories.

Keith told me about the time he was drunk and was sitting in his car in the open town square. His nephew Bobby, who is just about the same age he is, asked what he was doing.

"I'm fixing to jump the Frosty Freeze," Keith told Bobby, gunning the engine a little bit. Maybe he thought he could do the Starsky and Hutch trick-car thing, but Bobby had talked him out of it. I had not seen this daredevil streak in Keith. Maybe he was enjoying showing me the wild side of his life in eastern Kentucky.

We drove out into the countryside and he showed me the bridge he had driven off when he was nineteen. Yes, he admitted, he had been drunk and had rolled down a one-hundred-foot embankment into the river. Later I found out that a passerby had seen Keith and had called the paramedics, and when Keith came to in his car, he started fighting the paramedics. He had suffered a broken collarbone but was otherwise unhurt.

This all came on top of the stories about Randy. The death of his brother had not dampened Keith's love for motorcycles. You could see it in his eyes as he talked about them. He had his first one as a teenager, barely old enough to drive, "a beautiful 1962 Harley, built from scratch, but I had to sell it to finance my move to Nashville, and I haven't gotten another one."

Then Keith told me about being in a car crash with a friend of his who lost his life after they had been drinking.

I was a little unnerved by these stories, but I put them down to youthful hijinx, before Keith got serious about his life and his work. At least, that's what I wanted to believe.

Then there was the soulful, caring side of him. He took me for a drive to his uncle Henry's house, way out in the country—"in the head of the holler," the country way of saying "hollow," where two mountains come together, up high, very private.

You could see Uncle Henry loved Keith, because he started taking out old photos and familiar objects and showing them, reminding the two of them of the old days. Uncle Henry was getting old and having trouble getting around, and Keith was upset to see that. He had tears in his eyes as he hugged Uncle Henry and promised to come back and visit him soon.

Keith also took me to meet Big Rob, who was in his forties but still talked and thought like a child. Big Rob got his nickname because he used the name "Big" before everybody else's name. He had the run of the town and everybody looked after him. You could tell that Big Keith loved and protected Big Rob. There was not a mean or violent side to Keith, and he never showed any need to drink the whole weekend. Never touched a drop.

His parents knew we were in love, and they seemed pleased to let us stay in the same bedroom—"Keith's room." You know how parents are when their children have grown up and moved away. They keep the room the way it was—just in case the "child" decides to come home and have everything go back to the way it had been a decade earlier. This was the first time we had ever spent the night together without making love.

The next morning, Mrs. Whitley was bustling around early, making chocolate gravy, Keith's favorite with his breakfast biscuits. She and I had coffee in the kitchen; then she took Keith his breakfast and coffee—with Sweet 'n Low and cream—his cigarettes, and his ashtray, and she talked to him for a while.

I could see how much it meant to have her sweet and gentle son back home again, so I stayed out front to let her have some time with him, until I heard Keith calling, "Where's my baby?" I could not have felt more at home than I did with Mr. and Mrs. Whitley.

We left that afternoon to visit his sister, Mary, and her first husband in Ashland; then we headed west again, out of the mountains.

I could almost feel Keith relax. A lot of people are glad to escape their childhoods, glad to reinvent themselves somewhere else, which is why people head for Nashville, or New York, or LA, or Europe, or Kathmandu, or wherever their next place is. But I had the feeling that Keith had some extra burden that he wanted to leave behind.

"It's a wonder I ever got out of here," Keith said as he drove. "All you ever had to do in Sandy Hook was drink."

That first weekend in eastern Kentucky sent a tremor through me. Some people talk about alcohol as a way of having a good time, relaxing, but Keith linked alcohol with painful memories. I looked at him as he drove. The big smile was still on his face, as if it was fixed there, but his eyes were pensive and sad. He was dealing with some inner feelings I could not imagine.

As soon as we saw the bright lights of Lexington, we stopped for some pizza. He went into a Wal-Mart and came back with a tape by the group Journey.

"There's a song on here you've got to hear," Keith said. "I want you to listen to the words real carefully."

He popped the tape into the cassette player and put on the song "Faithfully," sung by Steve Perry, and written by Jonathan Cain, about a performer. I had heard the song before, but I had never paid that much attention to it. Knowing that it meant something to Keith, I paid close attention to it this time.

The singer says that the life of a music man is not ideal for a family, but he hopes maybe the woman needs a clown to make her smile, and then he confesses he would be lost without her. And every chorus ended the same way: "I'm forever yours, faithfully."

We listened to the song as we drove along the Bluegrass Parkway; then Keith pulled the car to the side of the road, turned to me, and I could see he had big tears in his eyes as he kissed me.

"I want you to always remember these lyrics," he said.

I felt Keith was putting his entire soul in front of me. He was so sweet, so vulnerable. We didn't talk about future plans that night, he didn't propose to me, nothing like that, but from that night on, I became Keith Whitley's companion, forever and faithfully.

Chapter Four

Back in Nashville, I had the vague sense of danger, after hearing Keith's stories about drinking.

Alcohol was not a priority of mine, and Keith would bring home nonalcoholic champagne for the two of us. We bought nonalcoholic beer when we were alone, but that only made him want the real thing, so we stopped.

I was not totally naïve about the problem. I had a few relatives who were alcoholics, and a few brothers-in-law, too. I had seen them unable to attend a family gathering without a drink always in their hands. They were openly preoccupied by drink—who was serving as bartender, who would open the next bottle, who was buying, come on, everybody have a drink. And sometimes they would get boisterous or mean, depending on the demons inside them.

Keith's demons were harder to read. He rarely drank socially, so it was hard to get a sense of the problem, but I found myself worrying about him.

My sister Beth remembers the first time I brought him over to visit her and her husband, and she offered Keith a drink. He accepted, but his behavior did not seem to change.

One day I was about to work the matinee at Opryland, and

tried calling Keith at his apartment. There was no answer. My face must have showed my concern. We always say a prayer before each performance, and I always ask one of the musicians if he will lead us, and this time I asked Dave Fowler.

For the first time, Dave acknowledged my new relationship, praying to God to watch out over Keith.

After the show, Keith's phone still did not answer.

I called a good friend of Keith's, Don Cook, the songwriter, who is now in charge of creative development at Tree.

"He was here drinking," Don said. "You know he has a serious drinking problem, don't you?"

This was the first time I had ever heard anybody say this. I began to worry that something was wrong, so I asked Don to meet me at Keith's apartment. Sure enough, his car was there, but when we banged on his door, there was no answer.

Keith's apartment was on the second floor, right on the corner, sharing an outside balcony with the next apartment. Don and I knocked on the next door, and two men answered—Iranians, if you can imagine. We tried to explain that we needed to get into the next apartment, but both just threw up their hands and said, "I don't understand. I don't speak English."

Don brushed past them into their apartment, walked out onto the balcony, and climbed over the low railing to Keith's balcony. He opened the door, with me right behind him. Keith was passed out in the recliner, his breath very shallow.

We both shook him but we could not wake him up. In desperation I called Vanderbilt Hospital, which is only five minutes away, and said, "We're bringing in somebody who is overdosed." They said they would be waiting for us outside the emergency room. The Iranians helped us carry Keith downstairs to the car and I sat in the front bucket seat, cradling Keith alongside me while Don raced to the hospital.

Just before we got there, I could feel Keith's body go motionless, his breathing completely stopped. I had never seen anybody die before, but I had the terrible feeling that my new love was dying in my arms.

I started banging on his chest with my two fists, shouting, "Don't die on me, you son of a bitch! Don't die on me!" I was so scared, and so angry, that I put all my emotion into pounding his chest.

Just then we got to the hospital where the nurses and doctors were waiting outside, as they had promised. They ripped off his clothes and started giving him an IV, then rushed him on a gurney into the emergency room. Don and I could do nothing but wait.

Forty-five minutes later, a doctor came out and asked, "Who is here with Mr. Whitley?" When we responded, the doctor said, "Do you have any idea how much he had to drink? He's alive—but barely. The amount of alcohol he drank was almost lethal. I've been a doctor for twenty years and I have never seen anybody drink that much alcohol—and live."

I asked if I could see him, and they led me into the emergency room. Keith was hooked up to the pumps and the IV tubes, but he was starting to come out of it, his face showing his shame.

"I'm really sorry," he said, as hapless as a little boy who has had an accident. All my anger was gone.

Later, I remembered Dave Fowler's prayer in the dressing room back at Opryland, and I gave thanks to God for the power of prayer. To this day, I believe Dave's prayer, and God's will, saved Keith's life.

Keith said he wanted to go home, but the staff told him he would have to spend the night. I called my mother and told her I was going to stay with him; then I called his mother and sister and told them that he had almost died. As I look back now, they did not seem surprised, nor did they volunteer to drive over from eastern Kentucky, which made me mad. I mean, he and I were only starting to go together, and they were his family, but they just said, "Let us know what happens."

I slept in the hospital. Sometime during the night, Keith woke up and said, "Get me out of here." I told him he couldn't leave because they had a catheter stuck in him, so I got some soap and water and a washcloth and washed some of the blood and dirt off his face, trying not to notice the big tears in his eyes.

In the morning, I woke up and heard him rustling around in the bathroom. I jumped up and discovered he had yanked the catheter right out of him—with blood splattering everywhere. Now he was getting dressed and getting ready to go home, that's all there was to it. He was not angry or belligerent, the way some men are when they are drunk or hung over, but his mind was made up. A nurse came in and noticed that he was detached from the catheter and she ran off to get some help. That was all Keith needed.

"Look, I'm going home," he said. "Are you going with me?" So we left.

Fortunately, he suffered no damage from leaving the hospital so prematurely. I took him home to his apartment and made sure he was safe.

I had many questions about his drinking, but Keith would not discuss what had happened. When I tried asking, he just clammed up. Now, I recognize that as the defense of the alcoholic, and I know that people must not let it intimidate them, but at the time I respected Keith's claim on privacy and secrecy.

However, I did notify Don Light, his manager at the time, that Keith had nearly died from alcohol poisoning. Don informed me that Keith was supposed to take a pill, Antabuse, that would not allow him to drink.

"You must be sure he actually swallows it," Don said. "He'll tell you he swallowed it, but he won't."

This was the first time anybody had ever explained the devious ways of an alcoholic. I had always taken people's word. When they were wrong, they were wrong. When they were sorry, they were sorry. When they promised, they meant it. I had a lot to learn.

Don told me that Keith had to wait twelve hours after his last drink before taking the pill, or else he would become ill. One leading book on addiction lists the response to Antabuse and alcohol as: "facial flushing, a rapid heart rate, decreased blood pressure, nausea and copious vomiting, chest pains and shortness of breath."

The pill, also known as disulfiram, has been used on alcoholics for over thirty years. According to Dr. Gary I. Wadler, one of the authors of *Drugs and the Athlete*, anybody using Antabuse "must be participating in other forms of therapy, for instance, psychotherapy and/or self-help groups."

Keith was not involved in any program, was not seeing anybody. He wouldn't even discuss the problem with me. The only concession he made to his terrible problem was that he would swallow the Antabuse—if it was shoved down his throat. In the weeks and months to come, I would literally take the pill, put it on his tongue, and tell him to swallow. Then I would tell him to open his mouth, and I would inspect his mouth and throat to make sure it had gone down. There would be days when he would fool me. On the days when he did swallow it, his position was that he was doing it only as a favor to the rest of us.

The good news was that the Antabuse did make him sick enough that he would not drink.

I did not see it clearly that day, but Keith's life depended on whether or not he swallowed that pill.

That day after I brought him home from the hospital, I felt it was safe to go home, after being assured he had swallowed the pill. I know now that I should have retained some of that anger to ask him what he had done to himself the day before, but I could not. I was not prepared for anything like this. Maybe we never are.

Now I started to look for clues. I already knew from Keith that his father and brother Randy had an alcohol problem. It bothered Keith a lot that Randy had died, leaving behind a wife and kids. Sometimes Keith would cry and talk about how much he missed Randy.

He also knew that his idol, Lefty Frizzell, had worn himself out with hard living, and died of a stroke at the age of forty-seven. There is a whole history of riotous living and early death in country music. Hank Williams wrote the song "I'll Never Get Out of This World Alive," and he drank so hard that he hastened the process.

Keith seemed attracted to that way of life like a magnet. I don't think he was strong-willed enough to say, "It won't happen to me."

He would stay sober for weeks; then he would just get smashed, with no warning. I must say this: Any time Keith was drunk, I never heard an abusive word toward me. He never yelled at me, was never physically or verbally mean.

I learned things about Keith in bits and pieces. It turned out that he had gone to several treatment centers before I met him. From what I gather, he had never cooperated with the counselors, thought it was all a waste of time. Finally, one counselor told him not to bother coming back. This was the only person who had challenged Keith. The rest of us, who loved him, who needed him, tried to work with him.

Keith did not deny that he had a problem. He understood how the Antabuse worked and tried to explain it all to me. He knew he could not afford to take a muscle relaxer because whatever was in it would trigger his need to drink. He could take an aspirin or Alka-Seltzer but nothing strong. If he had a toothache, you'd have to worry about what he took, or what the dentist would give him. He definitely had chemical problems, but still that did not explain his need to drink.

One day, not long after we met, Keith told me, "I used to be able to get drunk, then get up the next day and be about my business. But now if I started drinking, I can't stop. Once I start, I can't stop until I pass out."

I tried to be optimistic. I was always told that his dad, after thirty years of drinking, had just put the bottle down one day. I thought, Maybe this is something Keith is going to outgrow. One day we'll look back and say, "God, remember all the troubles we went through?"

I was young, I was full of hope, I would help him beat this. I was sure that all I had to do was to get to know him better. People who love alcoholics are too optimistic.

They think their love will be strong enough to save somebody.

CHAPTER FIVE

By the time I met Keith Whitley I was twenty-seven, with a daughter, back living at home after a divorce. Mom's house echoed with the love and vitality of the big family that once had snuggled under its roof.

All my hopes and dreams for this new man in my life were based on the warmth and security, the music and the laughter, in my family's house.

I knew what I wanted from life. I wanted to sing, but I also wanted a family and a home. I wanted a husband who treated me the way Dad had treated Mom.

I can still see Dad after twenty years of marriage, treating Mom like his first date. He'd have her sitting on his lap, calling her "Darlin'," never a cross word between them, ever.

But it could not have been easy, what with five kids. No matter how I remember Dad and Mom having fun at home, the fact is Dad was away half the time, out at nights working.

He wasn't one of those dads who got up in the morning, picked up the *Nashville Tennessean* off the front stoop, went to the office, and came home in the afternoon with the *Nashville Banner* under his arm, ready for supper. His life was irregular. Dad was a country singer. Dad was George Morgan.

Dad was known all over the country, in Canada and Europe, too, for his first song, "Candy Kisses," which he wrote when he was just starting out in the business.

The story goes that Dad was thrown over by a girl he was seeing, "and it occurred to me that my kisses meant less to her than the candy kisses my mother used to bring home had meant to me when I was a kid." He said it took him twenty minutes to write the words and hum the tune. He began singing his song on all the little radio stations in Ohio, and later he made his first record, his very first single, and it got to be No. 1 on the pop charts. Not the country charts but the pop charts. Dad had been twenty-four years old.

By the time I came along, the last of five children, Dad would go down to the *Grand Ole Opry* every Saturday night when he was in town. He would perform his signature song for people who had driven hundreds of miles, as well as for the radio audience sitting in living rooms and kitchens and on front porches all over America.

Dad had a clear, mellow voice, not quite what you'd expect to hear on the *Opry*. His favorite singers were Perry Como, Bing Crosby, and Eddy Arnold, who was the least "country" singer of all the men working in Nashville at the time.

They take their traditions seriously in Nashville. In their time, Dad and Eddy Arnold were sometimes criticized for not being "country" enough, and poor Keith, decades later, had to fight off the label of being "too country."

It was true that Dad's soul was closer to an Irish tenor, singing opera or folk songs or lullabies, than hard-edge country music, but because Dad was raised in northern Ohio, he gravitated to the stations, moved to Nashville, and became a regular on the *Opry* circuit. After "Candy Kisses," he would never again have a No. 1 record, but he earnestly went out every day to perform, and took as many bookings as he could get.

Not all country musicians have the reputation as a family

man, but Dad did. All the stories about him from that era emphasize how he lived for his family, couldn't wait to get home.

When he was on the road, he wrote Mom postcards and letters every day. Just recently, she showed me one he had written to her when I was born, another he had written when they were getting ready to get married, all these poetic and loving letters.

My earliest memories are of waiting for Dad, hours at a time, hoping he would call. The phones were not as accessible then as they are now—no cellulars in your car back in the early sixties—but Dad would find a pay phone somewhere, call, and say he was in Phoenix; then he would give us an ETA: "I've got seven hundred and forty-three miles to go, and I'll be there at five-oh-seven," or whatever, and most of the time he would hit it right on the nose.

Meanwhile, Mom prepared all day, going to the beauty shop to fix herself up, making sure the house was neat, cooking fried chicken and dumplings, his favorite dish. We'd sit by the front window and watch for hours before his car pulled up, and he always brought gifts, cute things for us, either a negligee or a robe or house shoes for Mom. He just loved her, and his love permeated the house.

I was so happy when Dad was home. I can remember his singing me lullabies when I was little, and thinking I was asleep, and then thirty minutes later I'd crawl into bed with him and Mom. I always thought of them as a unit, even if he wasn't always there.

It's probably like this in a lot of households. The father is away a lot, the mother does much of the work, yet people get all sentimental about the father. Life is not fair. Especially to mothers.

Just recently I was feeling very nostalgic about the old days, and I was missing Dad. I called Mom, with tears running down my face, and I said, "Mom, thank you so much for all you've done for me, all the pretty things you brought into my life, the religion and the love and the discipline."

Mom said, "Oh, that's your father's side of the family. I learned all that from him." Dad's family was very affectionate, but Mom's was not. She came from a family of nine children, and Mom once said, "I never heard my mom say I love you." But she certainly learned to demonstrate her love over the years.

I told her, "I appreciate what you're saying, but I had a great childhood, and it came from both of you."

Mom was always behind the scenes, making things work. She was the typical post-war mom, staying at home, raising the kids, making things fun and attractive. I never went to school once without breakfast. I mean, a *cooked* breakfast. Pork chops or bacon and eggs. We would come home from school and there would be these great smells of dinner cooking.

Plus, Mom was always beautiful. She was raising five children, yet somehow she always managed to look great—her hair, her face, her clothes. My friends would whisper, "Your mother is so beautiful." And they still do.

She did not have expensive clothes because most of the time we were very middle class, and if Dad had a good month, maybe slightly above. But she dressed like a lady and acted like a lady—and she did washing and drying and cooking and cleaning, too.

Looking back, I see a house packed with people, Mom and Dad, the five kids and their friends, our families and our friends, dozens of them, all over at once. Dad loved to cook, great recipes for green chili and other spicy things, and Mom would tease him because Dad would never clean up after he cooked. I can see them playing cards—rook or euchre or poker—people with nicknames like Lush and Clyda, the Beardens across the street, at the house until two or three in the morning. We grew up knowing how to treat company, my mom the perfect hostess.

My life has not taken me in the traditional path I had expected, but I still try to live up to this image of my own family.

My dad would have been a hero to me if he had worked in a factory or a bank, but of course I never could separate that he was a country star, a tall fair-haired man with a full pompadour that came back in style in the eighties with President Reagan. Dad's hair was always light, even before it turned silver. His nickname among the *Opry* musicians was "Whitey."

Dad was born with weak eye muscles that forced him to turn his head instead of moving his eyes. Several operations failed to fix it, and Dad often had a fixed stare to him, that made him seem austere, remote, but nothing could have been further from the truth.

His own early life is the stuff of country songs: hard times, pain, poverty. He was born George Thomas Morgan on June 28, 1924, in Waverly, Tennessee, out west of Nashville. His parents, Zachariah Valentine Morgan and Ethel Turner Morgan, had seven children, but one of them, Little Zack, died within a year.

I was lucky that I got to know my grandparents really well, and hear their stories of the old days. Grandpa Morgan had an artificial leg made out of wood from the knee down. We were transfixed by the sight of the wooden leg, and sometimes he would let us knock on it.

He wasn't shy about telling the story. When Grandma was pregnant with Dad, Grandpa was working in Tennessee as a farmer and also cutting ties for the railroad. Two weeks before Dad was born, Grandpa was out hunting groundhogs along the railroad tracks and the lace to one of his high, leather boots became undone, but he didn't get around to tying it. He was crossing the railroad tracks on some rural line, way out in the country, when the lace got caught just as the track suddenly switched.

Suddenly, Grandpa heard a train roaring down the line, he

realized he had no time to pull out the long laces of his boot. He had only one alternative—fall straight back, and break his leg to keep from being killed. He felt the leg snap as he threw the rest of his body backward, and then the train cut off his leg at the knee.

Whenever Grandpa would tell the story, he would reach into his pocket and dramatically remove a pocket knife.

"If I had this, I could have cut the lace," he would say. "I've never been without a pocket knife since that day."

He was a big man, very wise, very funny, and he loved playing practical jokes on people, which is where my father got it. By the time we knew him, Grandpa was able to get around quite comfortably, humming or whistling gospel music or country music, or just saying, "Yes, yes," to himself, the way Fibber McGee did on the radio. We used to sit and listen to "Fibber McGee and Molly," and "Amos and Andy," with Grandpa.

He had made something of his life, despite that terrible accident. Before he could afford an artificial leg, Grandpa had been forced to move to northern Ohio to get a job hauling coal with a horse and wagon. Later he went to work for a rubber company in Barberton, a suburb of Akron, and he brought his family up from Tennessee. Eventually, he acquired the artificial leg.

"I can remember times during the Depression, he would come home, take off that wooden leg, and the blood would be seeping out of that stumpstocking," Dad told Dixie Deen in a 1967 interview in the *Music City News*.

Growing up with the *Opry* coming from a big Majestic radio, Dad loved music. He quit high school in the eleventh grade—"like so many foolish kids," he once said—and in 1943 he made his first public performance. On New Year's Eve, somebody saw him with a guitar, asked him to sing in a restaurant, and he came away with five dollars in tips. Later he joined a band, playing harmonica with his younger brother, Bill, who had a great singing voice.

Dad did go into the service but was discharged because of his eyes. Bill joined the United States Marines, and his life changed forever on July 22, 1944, during the invasion of Guam. Storming onto the beach, Bill was hit by a bullet and was permanently paralyzed. He has spent the rest of his life in a wheelchair, which has not kept him from having a full life in the music business in Nashville, and from being friends with Hank Williams Sr. and Eddy Arnold, and staying close to Dad.

Dad started singing at WWST in Wooster, Ohio, opening up the station at five in the morning. He also performed at shows around northern Ohio, which is how he met Mom, Anastasia Paridon, when she was sixteen.

"I met George at Marshallville High School," Mom told me. "My dad didn't usually let me go to shows, but that night he did. After that, I listened to George on WWST and wrote him fan letters. I'd request songs from him."

Dad made a quick move to WWVA, the famous country station in Wheeling, West Virginia, but he missed Mom and moved back to Ohio. Around the same time, he made a demo of "Candy Kisses," sent it to Nashville, and was invited to sing on WSM and the *Opry*.

It had to be a tremendous thrill for Dad to sing on the *Opry*. That show was already a national institution, four hours of live music and comedy going into people's living rooms. The country was much more rural then, not many homes had television sets. People would sit around the radio on Saturday night, listening to the familiar voices of Roy Acuff and Minnie Pearl and Eddy Arnold.

The *Opry* was then situated at the Ryman Auditorium, an old Christian mission house turned into a music hall, hunkering right above Broadway in downtown Nashville. It was the temple of country music. People made pilgrimages there, in the dusty old days before the interstate, arriving hot and tired and staring up at the dark red-brick facade and a few windows, thinking they had arrived at the center of the universe.

According to Dad, he had trouble finding the center of the universe.

He liked to tell the story on himself that for his first appearance on the *Opry*, he stayed at a cheap room downtown and asked directions to the Ryman, but somehow had walked around downtown for twenty minutes without spotting it.

Knowing that show time was fast approaching, Dad felt a little desperate, so he walked up to two men standing on a corner and asked directions. According to his story, the two men were Eddy Arnold and Gabe Tucker, both members of the *Opry*, whom Dad recognized. Dad introduced himself and said he was scheduled to appear on the *Opry* in a few minutes.

"My name is Gene Autry and this is Hoot Gibson." Arnold said.

They thought it was hilarious that a man about to make his debut at the Ryman could not find it. In good country-boy fashion, the three of them gabbed for ten minutes without getting to the directions part.

Finally, Dad said, "Look, Eddy, I'm not kidding. I'm really lost. Where is the Ryman Auditorium?" He convinced the two men he was serious, because they turned him slightly and pointed at the red-brick building and said, "You're standing right behind it." And they pointed out the stage door, so Dad made his show in time.

On January 16, 1949, Columbia recorded "Candy Kisses," with Red Foley's band. It hit No. 1 on April 2 and stayed there for a month.

That was enough incentive for Dad and Mom to get married on August 9, 1949. They tried Nashville for a while; then he quit the *Opry* and moved back to Ohio. That same year, Columbia also recorded Dad's version of Tim Spencer's "Room Full of

Roses," which got to be fourth on the charts. In 1949, Dad was the fifth highest ranked country artist, according to record sales. It would be the best year of his career.

Dad was a big name at the *Opry*, and he was a draw out on the road, but he fell between the cracks of the raw-edged country boys like Hank Williams or Elvis and the smooth mainstream singers like Perry Como and Bing Crosby.

He recorded with Dinah Shore and Rosemary Clooney, he performed with the Nashville Symphony and with Helen Traubel of the Metropolitan Opera. He performed with a full orchestra on one album and was well known for his duets with Marion Worth, particularly the song, "Slippin' Around." He pursued his dreams, he made a living, he had a great time, and I never saw him despair or complain.

Dad was known around the *Opry* for his practical jokes, like clipping off somebody's tie just before he went out to sing. Dad had a list called The Top Ten Ugly List, which he was constantly revising, and guys would be proud to be on it.

Once Dad spent weeks going through the charade of convincing friends that he was feeling suicidal, just to set up the prank of being seen floating in the bathtub with ketchup splashed all over his chest. That sent a couple of his buddies screaming for help, before Dad arose from the water, miraculously cured.

They still tell the story about Dad in one of those old hotels with the ladder going to the top floor. He had a Frankenstein's monster disguise, and he would lumber around with his arms out. Apparently, a maid climbed up to clean the rooms, and saw the monster lurching around, and she never came back to that hotel again.

He and his pals would stage mock fights backstage, sometimes even out in public, and finally somebody would have to explain to the onlookers that Dad and Ernest Tubb were really not beating the living daylights out of each other, but just hacking around.

Dad was usually the instigator, but one time somebody got him back. Ralph Emery loves to tell the story about how he and Dad did their banking with the same man, Clarence Reynolds, whom they called The Hillbilly Banker because he was willing to do business with country-music guys.

Dad was often playing tricks on The Hillbilly Banker, whom he also called "Curls"—because he was bald. One time the man was in an important business meeting, and Dad tiptoed into his office, planted a big kiss right on his face, and tiptoed out again. That almost blew the deal, Ralph says.

But The Hillbilly Banker got Dad back. Dad was out in California, trying to cash a check one time, and he used Mr. Reynolds as his reference. That was not a good idea because The Hillbilly Banker told the California banker, "If that was me, I'd throw him right out of your office," which the man did.

Dad called Mr. Reynolds from a pay phone outside and he said, "Hey, Curls, what are you trying to do to me?" And The Hillbilly Banker said, "George, are you going to play any more practical jokes on me?" Dad promised he wouldn't, and he never did. But he had plenty of other victims.

The jokes were just Dad's way of telling people not to take any of this all too seriously. He knew that his marriage, his family, his religion, his friends, his fun, were more important than reaching Number 1 on the charts, not that he ever stopped looking for the next "Candy Kisses." But if not, well, Dad had his life.

Dad taught me everything about family, about affection, about love, about music. In some ways, he was much like Keith: very passionate, extremely sentimental. We'd give him birthday cards and he'd sit there and bawl. He truly loved his kids, and he loved having a house full of them.

The first child was Candy Kay, named after the song, of course. When I was a little girl, I thought Candy was the most beautiful woman I'd ever seen, especially with her long, brown hair. She was a terrific big sister, a great swimmer who taught me how to swim and how to dive.

Candy blazed the trails in the family. She was the first at St. Joseph's grade school, wearing the uniform, and then she was the first at St. Bernard Academy, the all-girls school across town in Madison that all four of us would eventually attend. I can see Candy in her summer uniform with the plaid skirt and the blue "popover" and white blouse, or the winter uniform with the pleated wool skirt and white blouse and blue blazer. She would drive Beth to school, and then Beth drove Gilly, and then Gilly drove herself.

Candy started out singing with Dad. He would bring her down to the Friday-night version of the *Opry*, the "Frolics," and she would play at some of the fairs or if he was singing at a Christmas show at prison or some other benefit. I can vividly remember her singing a folk tune called "Wolverton Mountain," and I was sure she would be an entertainer, but she decided it was not for her.

"I was too insecure," Candy said recently.

She fell in love with somebody she met near Mom's old home in Ohio, and she decided that singing was not what she wanted. In recent years, after a divorce, she has become a pediatric nurse.

The next child was Bethany Belle, who was Dad made over, a prankster, always with something funny to say. Beth had gorgeous, long blond hair down past her bottom. You could get away with a little more with Beth than with the others. We're big on nicknames in my family, and my dad used to call her his "Blue-eyed Macooshlah," or something like that, from an old John Gary song, which means girl or love in Ireland. So we started calling her "Coosh." Dad used to sit and laugh at Beth. She was the entertainment.

When I was young, Mom picked Candy and Beth as my designated playmates, and they would take turns entertaining me for hours, on the swings out in the backyard.

Liana Lee was the third girl, and she was definitely her own person, not anything like Candy or Beth. For some reason, Beth started calling her "Mrs. McGillicuddy," and it stuck, and then Dad called her "Cuddy" and the rest of us started calling her "Gilly" and that's who she is to this day. Gilly was very sensitive, somewhat of a loner, who had to have her own bedroom when she was young because Candy and Beth were allowed to stay up later, and Gilly needed to do her homework and get her sleep.

"I'm a middle child," Gilly told a friend recently, "and you know all about middle children. I used to say, 'I'm too young to play with the older girls and too old to play with the younger ones.' "

It's my impression that Dad always knew that Gilly was special. Even when Gilly was thirteen or fourteen, he would hug her and rock her more than the others.

"I remember a couple of the girls told Mom that Dad gave me too much attention," Gilly said recently. "Dad asked me if I thought that was true, which I didn't. Dad tried to make each of us feel important."

Then there was Matthew Martin, called "Marty" by everybody. He got his middle name after Marty Robbins, the great singer known for "El Paso" and auto racing, who was one of Dad's best friends at the *Opry*. Just a great guy. Whenever Dad and Marty would see each other, they would slap each other's face, big ringing slaps, echoing in the tiny backstage of the Ryman, and they would holler, "Let me have your face." With a pal like that, naturally you name your first son after him.

I always get a little emotional when I talk about my brother because I remember the great times we had when we were young.

Dad was more sentimental with the girls and a little more discipline-oriented with Marty. Boys were expected to protect girls. Boys were going to have to go out into the cold, hard world.

Marty grew up with extremely high respect for women. I'm sure that was instilled in him because Dad respected Mom so much. Marty always felt the two older girls picked on Gilly, so being the only boy, he felt it was his place to stick up for her.

One day Beth was snapping the dish towel at Gilly, the way bigger sisters will do. Marty had enough. He picked up a teakettle and said he would whack Beth over the head with it if she did not leave Gilly alone. Dad said he admired Marty's protectiveness, but did not think that would be a good thing to do, either for Beth or the kettle.

Marty and I used to play together. I was like his little brother. He taught me how to climb trees. How to run fast. How to whittle. How to whistle. How to fish. How to find crawdads.

When I was little, we lived on Devonshire Drive in the Bellshire section out west of Madison, an area that used to be old hog farms, and was still pretty rural, although suburbia was slowly creeping in.

We lived near the North Fork of Ewing Creek. As soon as the weather would allow, Marty would pack peanut-butter sandwiches and pickles and we would pretend we were cowboys on the trail. He taught me a lot about nature, being quiet, not disturbing our surroundings.

We would play in "the drop-off," a pool created by a culvert running under the road. Marty and Michael Baldwin and Brian Baldwin used to play in a tree house in a mock orange tree in our backyard, and usually they would include me and Lisa Baldwin, my best friend back then.

We were outside all the time, playing kickball in our bare

feet. All the families had a lot of kids, so we were always able to get five or six on a side.

At one point, right near the house on Devonshire, there was a huge excavation for a septic tank out back that must have been twenty feet long, ten feet wide, ten feet deep; and before they could install the septic tank, the hold filled with water. I was so terrified I was going to drown that I would not go anywhere near it.

Marty still likes to tell the story about Dad's hunting dog, a huge and ornery beast named Marvelous Marv, after the famously inept first baseman with the New York Mets, Marv Throneberry, who was from western Tennessee. (The dog and the first baseman had the same doleful expression on their faces.)

One day I was out messing around near Marvelous Marv's doghouse, and he got to tangling with me, and his long leash became wrapped around my legs, then he ran a few circles around the doghouse, lashing me to the doghouse as effectively as if he planned to burn me at the stake, which maybe he did, come to think of it. I screamed at the top of my lungs until Marty and the rest came out and rescued me from Marvelous Marv.

When I was ten, we moved to Madison, the same house my mom lives in today. Every time I visit Mom, I think about the good times there, how Dad decided that poor Marty would make a great target for his practical jokes.

Dad discovered how to call on the old-fashioned phone system from the extension in the back of the house to the extension in the front of the house. Marty answered, and Dad said, "Marty, would you bring me the phone book?"

Marty, never thinking that he had just seen Dad in the house, asked where he was, and Dad said, "I'm out in the driveway." So poor Marty went outside in the snow, carrying the phone book, with the rest of the family waving at him through the window.

Then there was the time Dad made a big show of locking all

the doors for the night, while Marty and Gilly were still downstairs watching television. Only Dad secretly left the side door open, with just a long security chain across it. Then Dad slipped out the back door, and came around the side, and stuck his arm through the opening, as if trying to break in.

Poor Marty ran up the stairs, leaving Gilly right there, and he was shouting, "A man is trying to break in!" Marty must have been terrified. He had been holding a pencil in his hand, doing homework when he had spotted the "burglar," and he had carried the pencil right up the stairs. It rubbed against the white wall all the way up, leaving a dark mark. Dad just loved to catch Marty like that.

But Marty was also Dad's huntin' buddy. Dad taught Marty how to hunt and feed the dogs, how to wash the cars, all the guy stuff, and Marty really looked up to Dad.

"I used to think he picked on me," Marty said recently. "But I realized he wanted me to be a man. After I grew up a little, I could really appreciate him. Of course, I got him with a few practical jokes, too. I'd call him up and disguise my voice and say I was from the service station. Beth and Lorrie and I got that from Dad."

Then there was me, fifth and last. They named me Loretta Lynn, and to this day, people think I was named after the great Coal Miner's Daughter. It would have been an honor—but it just didn't happen that way. The fact is, I was born on June 27, 1959, a full year before her first record, "I'm a Honky-Tonk Girl," hit the charts at No. 14 on July 25, 1960.

Nobody had heard of Loretta Lynn except in Butcher Holler, Kentucky, and rural Washington State, where she was living at the time.

I was Loretta Lynn Morgan on my parents' own good ear

for names. In a family of nicknames, I was soon known as Lorrie.

Dad was away when I was born, but there were plenty of hands to mother me. Mom says I had colic and cried for the first three months and that Candy rocked me and sang to me while Mom kept the household going.

"I can see Candy singing nursery songs to Lorrie," Mom has said. "Candy is a good singer, and she put her own tunes to the rhymes. They would sit in the swing set in the yard, and Candy would sing to Lorrie for hours, and Lorrie would say, 'More.' "

When Dad came home from the road, he loved to rock the babies, singing old-timey songs like "Santa Lucia," and "Way Down Upon the Swanee River," beautiful tunes for which his voice was perfect.

My earliest memories are of music. I loved my dad's voice, particularly when he sang the ballads, and in our household, people never put down other kinds of music by saying, "That ain't country."

My three sisters were into all kinds of music—the friends we admired at the Opry, Brenda Lee, Jean Shepard, Tammy Wynette, Jeannie Seely, but also the great Motown music, Dionne Warwick, the Supremes.

My favorite singer when I was growing up, my favorite singer of all time? Johnny Mathis. I know he ain't country, but I always loved the sensuous phrasing, the way he caressed a lyric, that soulful, sensitive voice. I loved his records long before I discovered boys—and once I did, well, Johnny Mathis on a car radio is just about as good as it gets. Many years later I would get to record a song with Johnny Mathis, and he would be as nice and beautiful as I had always thought.

There was always music in the house. Dad would sit on the porch, playing his guitar and singing songs, not necessarily country songs. Candy can remember us singing "When the Red, Red Robin Comes Bob-Bob-Bobbin' Along" as we drove in the car.

Every so often we would perform at home, all five of us. One of us would hold the flashlight, another would make the introductions, and we would take turns.

"Mom and Dad would sit and applaud," Liana remembers. "To me, it was very real. It was my parents' way of making us feel, 'I am somebody.' "

They all agree that I was the scene-stealer, the youngest child, the ham, from the time I was an infant.

"Did she tell you about the Tupperware glasses?" Candy asked a friend recently. "We had these large, colored Tupperware glasses, and Lorrie would put her feet in them when she was three or four. She could wriggle her feet down into them, and walk around the house like a ballerina. They were her 'point shoes.' She was hilarious."

Candy says I was always imitating my older sisters.

"She borrowed a razor from one of the girls and shaved her legs when she was only eight," Candy recalled recently. If she says I did, it must be true.

Dad was always bringing us presents back from the road. My favorite present was a new supply of false fingernails. I loved gluing them on, and playing grown-up.

Beth was my stylist, fixing me up in long dresses and a wig, makeup, a tiara, the whole works, and I would sing songs by the Beatles. Petula Clark. The Four Seasons. The Beach Boys. I knew 'em all. When my performance was over, I would charge everybody a nickel, and soon a quarter.

Marty and I would collaborate on songs. He'd write 'em and I would sing 'em, and we would perform them for the family. Dad would nod his head and say, "Well, that has promise" or "You're getting there." I always thought my big brother would make it big with his songs, and I made him promise to take me along with him.

"I didn't know she would go into the business," Mom has said, "but Lorrie always was center stage. She wanted to tell things, even dumb jokes. She wanted to be the center of attention. Her first song when she was nine or ten was 'Eyes of Green.' Her dad was amazed. The talent was there. But one thing about Lorrie, she hated to work around the house. When supper was over, she'd say, 'Oooh, I have to go write a song,' and she would disappear somewhere, and when she finished, the dishes were done."

Well, I had things to do. Everybody would fight over the dishes. If Gilly had to dry, she would put the dishes back in the sink if they weren't clean. Everybody was saying, "I hate you, I hate you," like all big families, but we were incredibly close.

I guess I must have been an argumentative soul. I'd make Dad play Barbies and I'd be the boss. He'd say, "I think I'll go to the grocery store," and I'd say no, and he'd just cackle. He'd say something was black and I'd say it was white, and after a while Dad started to call me "Fussbutt," which soon got shortened to "Fussy."

Early in the morning, I would pester Beth to wake up and play. I would make her go outside to the sandbox and make breakfast, called chow-chow—a scrumptious mixture of water and sand. When Dad was around he would pretend to eat it and love it.

I loved playing school at home, which was surprising, since I actually hated going to school. My mom likes telling the story about the day I wouldn't go to school, when I was in the first grade. Mom told me, "I don't care, I'm taking you to school, even if you're not dressed," and she tossed my clothes into the car and started driving. Finally I relented and changed out of my pajamas before she stopped the car.

"She walked into school," Mom concludes, "the nun came out to meet her and held her hand—and Lorrie bit her right on the hand."

I have no recollection of that incident whatsoever, as you might imagine.

Eventually, in high school, I would pay my friends a quarter or fifty cents to copy their homework. Miraculously, I never failed anything.

I got a lot of my education at home. Dad loved to stay home and cook and be with family and friends, like Bob and Dot Bearden, across the street. Dad called Mr. Bearden "Pal" and loved to hang around with him. Debbie, their daughter, was a few years older than me. When we first moved in, I told her my name was "Sam"—I have no idea why—and for a week or two she believed me. We were inseparable for years. We would do cartwheels across the street to visit each other's house.

Rob Bearden and Marty were friends. Dad used to call Rob "Lightning" because of the slow way he ambled around. Our families even traveled together. One time Dad and Little Roy Wiggins were playing in Gatlinsburg, and they provided housing for us, a big chalet. Debbie and I were playing in this little creek out behind our place, just a little water trickling down the stones.

That night there was a storm, and the rain just poured down the mountainside, turning that little trickling creek into a raging torrent—but we didn't understand how serious it was. Debbie and I went out to play in it; she was caught in the torrent and was knocked downstream. Marty rushed out and got the metal chains from a swing set, tied them around his waist and, with a bunch of other people, he waded out into the stream to grab Debbie off a rock where she was clinging.

Meanwhile, Rob—"Lightning," remember?—was still taking off his shoes, pondering the next move. Marty was a hero for days.

When I got into high school, I started hanging around with Ruth Ralph, now Ruth Spain, who works with me now.

"George Morgan was like a second dad to me," Ruth said recently. "If we were out somewhere and Lorrie asked for a new dress, George would say no, not unless he could buy the same for me.

"The Morgans always said grace before dinner," Ruth added. "If I forgot to make the sign of the cross, he would say, 'Now, Ruth, we're going to do this one more time.' You felt like part of the family."

Dad was a homebody, but he also liked to take us to good restaurants and teach us etiquette, how to place our napkins on our laps, not to eat with our elbows on the table.

We were not rich, by any means. Dad would come off the road with barely enough to pay the bills, yet he insisted on taking Mom and the rest of us somewhere nice. He would take us to the Hearth, which was then the best restaurant in Nashville, with real English and French waiters, and a menu that included oysters Rockefeller and oysters on the half shell.

I'd say, "I don't want to try it," and Dad would say, "Don't ever say you hate something unless you try it. There's nothing worse than somebody saying, 'Oooh, that looks gross, I'm not trying that.' " So I made him teach me how to eat oysters. The first time I couldn't get 'em down, but I learned to love them.

He taught us all to say "Yes, sir" and "No, ma'am" to people who were serving us, and he would show us how to tip the coatroom person and the person who parks your car. He even taught us to stop and give a dollar or two to somebody on the street who might be down on his luck.

Dad was strict not only about table manners. He had high standards for the way we acted—and the way we were treated.

My first boyfriend was nicknamed "Goo Goo," just like the candy bar that sponsors the *Grand Ole Opry*. ("Go get a Goo Goo. . . . They're goooood.")

One time Goo Goo called the house and said, "Is Lorrie there?" and Dad said, "Excuse me?" Goo Goo repeated his question, and Dad said, "I'm sorry, I thought you said, 'Is Lorrie there, please?' " Then Dad just hung up the phone. A few minutes later, Goo Goo called again and said, "Mr. Morgan, is Lorrie there, please?" And Dad said, "Just a minute."

My first date was for a school dance when I was just barely fifteen. Dad wasn't too crazy about my going, but I said, "Everybody's going," so he relented. When Goo Goo came to the door, Dad shook his hand, just squeezed it. Then Dad looked down at Goo Goo's shoes and said, "C'mere, boy," and took him to the bathroom and polished his shoes. Dad later said, "I judge a man by his handshake and the way he keeps his shoes polished."

Dad loved his children and his grandchildren. He sang at Candy's wedding, Beth's wedding, and Liana's wedding. One time, when Liana was married to her first husband, she dropped over at the house and Dad hugged her and he said, "I just hope I live long enough to see your babies."

That was Dad, an emotional husband and father, a gentleman, a country singer with old-time values. We were raised to believe in fairy tales and happy endings.

CHAPTER SIX

And then we joined the real world. When Beth was seventeen, she started going out with Lane Palmer, and before long she was pregnant. This was the first time anything like that had happened in the family, on either side. Because of our religion, abortion was certainly not an option, so Beth and Lane were married.

Lane was a very engaging character who ranged between charming and vicious, depending on what was coursing around in his system at the moment, unleashing those demons underneath.

It was no accident that he and Keith would become friends, years later, and that the two of them would collaborate on a forty-eight-hour comedy of errors that became a tragedy. Only in the course of writing this book would I come to understand Lane's role in Keith's last hours.

Lane is sober now, earnestly trying to make up for those lost years. Back then he was a potent mixture of alcohol and drugs, music and hard work, bullshit and blunt truth.

Even as a kid, I got a kick out of Lane. I have always loved him, and even trusted him. Only recently have I begun to wonder why.

"The Morgan women are attracted to men who are not good for them," Lane said recently, in his new recovering state.

I knew Lane was a tough customer early on, long before Keith arrived on the scene. One day a rough character came to the house looking for Lane. They went outside, started arguing, then the guy pulled a pistol and pointed it at Lane.

Lane did not hesitate. He purposefully walked up to the guy, raised the gun hand into the air, and just poleaxed him with the other hand, taking the gun away. Just like that. Before anything serious happened. Then Lane came back inside and resumed telling whatever story he had been telling. Lane always had great stories, whatever his condition.

Because I was so close to Beth, I practically lived with her and Lane at their rented apartment not too far out of town. For a ten- and eleven-year-old, it was great to stay over at their place, sit around, and play guitar with Lane. He had a lot of friends who drove motorcycles, and they would hang out and cook stuff and play music until two or three in the morning.

It was fun for a while, but Lane began getting violent with Beth. He drank too much and by that time—I found out much later—he was also developing a major drug habit. When he was high, his temper would flare.

By that time, they had a son, Jeremy, and I felt he was almost mine. I would sit and hold Jeremy and listen to Lane screaming and threatening Beth in the next room. Sometimes it would get physical. Jeremy would jump every time they would scream, and I would tell him I'd always be there for him and for Beth.

"This is going to sound weird," Beth said recently. "We should have been taking care of Lorrie, but she's always taken care of us. If you have a problem, you can always count on Lorrie. She'll help you solve it. It really should be the other way around because we're the older ones, but we lean on her a lot."

Nowadays Beth travels with me on the road, keeping me

happy and comfortable. She makes it clear that I was around for her, way back when.

"When I have problems in my life, she's the first person I call," Beth told a friend recently. "I didn't have the best of marriages, and I'd call on her. For anything.

"If I had a mouse running around on the floor, I'd be up on the kitchen counter and I'd call Lorrie, 'Come in here and get the mouse,' and she would take care of it. Or if I had troubles with Lane, I'd call Lorrie first. She was only ten or eleven, but she'd say, 'What's wrong?' She always knew when something was wrong. I needed her. I never had to be parental with Lorrie. She was always parental with me."

Lane went to school at night, worked at his auto-body shop during the day, but there was plenty of time for him and Beth to get into it. Numerous times I would call Dad from the house and say Lane was being mean to Beth.

Lane was a real tightwad who forced Beth to save her pennies for groceries.

"I remember one time I yelled at him," Beth recalls. "This was at Lorrie's house. I yelled, 'You've got all that cocaine up your nose, but all I want is that little TV set so I can watch while I'm cooking.'

"Lane was really mean to me, depending on how he felt. One year he didn't get me anything for Christmas and the next year I got a Rolex and a Cadillac."

When Lane was not having a good month, Mom and Dad would have to give money to Beth so she could buy food for her family.

One time Dad drove out to their house and just about cold-cocked Lane, gave him something between a push and a hit and knocked him down on the couch.

"If you ever touch my daughter again . . ." Dad snarled. He didn't have to say another word, his meaning was quite clear, as Beth and Jeremy packed up their things for a stay at Mom's.

The amazing thing was that Lane took it. He was a little intimidated by Dad, and he was polite to Mom. He knew that Dad would not allow anybody to mistreat his daughter. Dad was the only person to whom I ever saw Lane say "Yes, sir."

Dad wanted to protect his kids from sorrows like this, but some of it was beyond his control. Lane was the father of Beth's child, and it was the right thing for a Catholic girl to get married. We had to make the best of it. So Lane remained a visible part of our family.

CHAPTER SEVEN

Nowadays they have Take Your Daughter to Work Day. I guess Dad was ahead of his time because he took me to work when I was little.

Dad's work just happened to be the *Grand Ole Opry*.

My early memories of the *Opry* are being backstage and having the whole world of country music going past me—at knee level first, later face-to-face.

The Ryman was so tiny that everybody was thrown in together. It was a very democratic place, friends and family mingling with the stars because there were no star rooms, no places to hide.

Jumbled altogether in my memory are Johnny Cash and Roy Acuff, Chet Atkins and Marty Robbins, Ernest Tubb and Ray Price and Kitty Wells. And there was Dad's hunting buddy, Stringbean, Dave Akeman, with a customized shirt forming an artificial waistline somewhere around his knees.

You'd stand there and be staring up at Minnie Pearl, with her gaudy calico sundresses, the goofy straw hat with the price tag hanging down, the wide comedienne's smile on her face, and then you'd get close and hear her rich vocabulary, her wide knowledge. (She was a college graduate, a cultured lady.)

Need a bathroom? You might be standing in line with Dolly Parton or Loretta Lynn.

Through the chatter backstage, you might hear Earl Scruggs and Lester Flatt. Later, when I met Keith, he could do this uncanny imitation of Lester Flatt's drawl coming from the corner of his mouth, and I would be transported back to being a kid backstage at the Opry.

Dad would take me and a friend, either Ruthie Ralph or Debbie Bearden, and we would scamper around backstage. Sometimes we would even scamper *on* the stage. There was a bench right on the stage so the family could sit and watch the performance. One time I spotted Tex Ritter doing the show. I loved his deep cowboy voice on "High Noon" and other hit songs, and I absolutely had to have his autograph, so I got it just before he began to sing. I decided to sit on the family bench and watch him perform, but I started giggling with my friend. Right in the middle of his performance, Mr. Ritter turned around and said, "Tell those kids to be quiet." I was so offended that I tore up his autograph, right then and there. Now I wish I had kept it.

I thought it was fun, just being there at the Opry with Dad. On the way to our house, he would stop and buy a sack of hot chicken and take it home.

Dad did not check his mischievous sense of humor when he left the Opry. One night on our way home, Dad said he wasn't going to stop for chicken that night. I was really annoyed at the interruption of our ritual, and Ruthie was, too, except she was too polite to show it. I kept bugging him and Dad said, "I told you, no," so when we got home, I went stomping off to my room, with Ruthie following me.

"Are you hungry?" Dad asked, and I replied, very dramatically, "No!"

"Well, that's too bad because I have this sack of chicken to myself," he said. For some reason, he had arranged to have the chicken sent home and waiting for us—just to annoy me, probably—and now I had to back off my position that I was not hungry.

Much later, I realized these were not just idle nights accompanying Dad to work. He was teaching me the business.

He did not leave his music at the door when he came in off the road. There were songs he did not get to sing to country audiences, songs he wanted to try out, songs that belonged to him and not to the public.

His best friend, Bob Bearden, would come over, and the two of them would play their guitars and harmonize, with Dad singing songs he was born to sing—"Autumn Leaves" and "The Shadow of Your Smile" and "Shenandoah."

Other times we would entertain his two friends, the Scro brothers, who had an Italian restaurant in New York, a city Dad loved. (And so do I.) One of the brothers played a huge harmonica and the other a tiny one. They would come to the house and play the most gorgeous songs.

After a while, Dad would say, "Fussy, sing me a song," and I would join the music, just natural, no longer some little kid being shown off for company, but an equal. I always got the feeling that Dad accepted me, that he knew what I could do.

When I was around five or six, Dad would ask me to come along sometimes when he was doing the Ralph Emery early show. These men liked each other so much that it was like going to visit your uncle Ralph—except that it was five-thirty in the morning and you were on the air.

One morning, just before Christmastime, Dad sang one of those Christmas hymns that he did so well. Then he called me out and asked me to sing along with him, one of the songs all of us sang at home: "I'm Getting Nothin' for Christmas." Singing with Dad in front of Uncle Ralph was no big deal at all unless you remembered what that red light on the camera meant.

After that it became a ritual, just before Christmas, with

Dad bringing me down to sing one or two songs. Either Debbie or Ruth would spend the night with me, and Dad would wake us up at three in the morning, and we would drive downtown to the WSM studio. It was so comfortable being at the studio with Dad and Ralph that the boundaries blurred between backstage and the set.

Otherwise, I could have been back home, playing for Dad and Mr. Bearden or the Scro brothers. After Ralph's show, I would change into my parochial school uniform and Dad would drive my friend and me to school.

When I was around eleven years old, Dad called me into the living room and pointed to a Ventura guitar leaning against the couch.

"Fussy, play that guitar and see if you like it," he said.

I started playing it. I'd handled Dad's guitar before, but this was a new one, all tuned up and ready to go. It felt great in my hands.

"Do you like it?" Dad asked.

"I love it," I said.

"It's yours."

I was stunned. I had no idea he was asking me to try out my own guitar. I knew he would never tease me about something as serious as a guitar, so I hugged him and rushed off to master the instrument. I went out and bought every songbook I could find, cutting lyrics out of newspapers, just building up my repertoire.

He bought me a Mel Bay learn-on-your-own guitar book, and I would take it off to my room and play, particularly when I was supposed to be doing the dishes. I never thought of the music as lessons or practicing, just a continuation of family fun.

That was when Dad was home. A lot of the time, he and Jeannie Shepard and Stonewall Jackson and Flatt and Scruggs and Bill Monroe and some of the other Nashville regulars would be packaged on a tour, and they would pile into cars and take off. That's how they made their living.

Most of them did not have buses, like everybody does today, and occasionally they'd get to fly somewhere, but that was a rarity. Back then, the speed limit was seventy-five, but Dad and the others would go fifteen above that on the interstate, or else they'd never get to their shows. Or get home, for that matter. He'd still be doing eighty coming up the driveway.

One thing that kept Dad sane on the road was his Citizen Band radio. He was really into it. This was back in the early seventies when CB radios became popular with the "four-doors"—meaning, regular cars—and not just with the "eighteen-wheelers"—meaning trucks. Dad was right on top of it, totally hooked on CB radios. His handle was Whitey, his backstage nickname because of that silvery hair.

He had installed a base station at home, and this sucker could get Mexico. Dad had every amp known to the technological mind. He would sit up at night and talk to people eight states away. Or he would call us from the road to let us know how he was doing.

Mom's handle was Red Rose, from the country song, "Red Rose from the Blue Side of Town." Dad showed me how to operate the radio, particularly the channel where all the truckers were, and all his buddies with handles like Jack Hammer, T-Shirt, Black Cat, and Wild Horse.

Pretty soon, I was talking on the CB more than Dad. My handle was Songbird.

One night when I was thirteen, I was waiting for Dad to come home, real late, and Mom was in the back. Everybody else was in bed but me, and I was talking to the guys out on the interstate, all the lingo: "Give me a 10-36" and "Ten-four, good buddy" and "What's your 10-20?"

One of those old boys said, "Hey, Songbird, how about singing us a song over the CB?"

I did not need much encouragement. We had a microphone on a stand with a pedal for a key, and I worked it with my foot. I sang and strummed my guitar and sang about three songs, and when I was finished I heard a faint voice saying, "That was beautiful, Songbird."

"Dad," I blurted, "where are you?"

"I'm out here by Percy Priest Lake and I'll be there in twenty minutes." He was coming in off I-40. We all got up and Mom made him a scrambled-egg sandwich at two in the morning.

The next morning, it was as if he had never been away. Mom and all the rest of us launched into a higher gear because Dad was home.

All through the house you could hear Dad's distinctive cough, a kind of "Uh-HUH," as he cleared his throat, the reflexive response of a singer checking out his tools of the trade. In church, no matter where you were, you knew he was there, by the cough.

At some point, I noticed that the cough had gotten worse and worse. I was so in tune to Dad. The more he coughed, the more scared I got. I also noticed that he had developed a habit of rubbing his left arm, and I noticed that he was more winded than he used to be, didn't have as much energy.

He was only in his late forties, but his years were like dog years, what with the cigarettes and the eggs and the fried food and the long hours on the road.

One night soon after my little concert over the CB, Dad said, "Fussy, why don't you take out your guitar and sing me something?"

I sang the song that Roberta Flack had made popular, "First Time Ever I Saw Your Face," which I was teaching myself on the guitar. I did not think I had it down yet, but Dad seemed pleased. When I was finished, he fell silent for a minute, and then he said, "How'd you like to sing on the *Opry* with me this Saturday?"

Even with my appearances with Dad and Ralph on the

morning show, I had never imagined performing on the *Opry*. That was for Dad and his friends. That was for grown-ups. Now the mention of the *Opry* made my insides quiver.

"Really?" I asked, trying to sound cool, trying not to show the terror.

"Yeah," he said. "Do you feel you want to do it?"

"I guess," I said, "but what do I sing?"

"Sing that song."

Somehow I did not think I could do that song justice, not like Roberta Flack, and besides, I was not comfortable about playing the guitar and singing at the same time.

"I'm so nervous, I don't know if I can do it," I confessed.

Dad was relaxed about it. "Anything you want to sing, sing. Think about it."

I decided I could handle Marie Osmond's song "Paper Roses," so we went out and bought a copy of the forty-five. Dad would come in at night and listen to me sing along with the record; then he arranged for me to sing on his portion of the show that Saturday.

Meanwhile, Mom had dug out the dress that Beth had worn in a wedding—cream-colored, empire-waisted, little ruffle to the bottom, maroon top, sparkly stuff through it, ruffle around the sleeve and at the wrist, very feminine, very girlish. She bought me a pair of black, strappy high-heel shoes, and although I loved playing dress-up, this was the first pair I had ever worn new.

On Saturday afternoon, my nerves were so bad that I had a severe stomachache. It was so bad that Mom gave me a half or a quarter of a nerve pill. She wasn't going to hear me because she was needed at home, but Debbie Bearden was keeping me company.

We got down to the Ryman, and Dad took me into the back room where I could rehearse with the *Opry* staff band. Leon

Rhodes, the guitar player, and Dad's other friends ran through "Paper Roses." They told me I was all set. I was all tense, but I was still ham enough to ask Leon what to do if I got an encore.

"Well, you won't," Leon said, "but in case you do, just come out and sing the chorus again."

The time was getting closer. Debbie had been as nervous as I was, both of us with diarrhea, both of us scared that I was going to mess up in front of a live audience and a worldwide radio audience.

Now I couldn't even find Debbie. She had totally disappeared. It was just Dad and me—and the millions of people.

At the commercial break, Dad came over and said, "How are you?" He could see I was shaking badly, even with the nerve pill Mom had given me. I was a wreck.

"I'll tell you what," Dad said. "Before I introduce you, I'll look over. If you want to come on, you nod yes. If you don't feel you can do it, shake your head no."

Backstage, people were talking to me. These were my father's friends, people I had known all my life, and they were just trying to encourage me, but I was afraid I was going to be sick. Lonzo or Oscar, or maybe both of them, came over, and I can remember thinking, Shut up, I'm trying to remember the words.

Suddenly, I saw Dad looking over at me, slightly quizzically, as if to say, "Well?" I couldn't work up any gesture more definitive than a shrug, my palms out, so Dad turned away from me and faced the audience.

"I want to introduce someone to you. She's making her first *Opry* performance, please help me make welcome Lorrie Morgan."

The band started playing, and Dad stood by the piano, off to the side. Out of the corner of my eye, I could barely see him, in his white suit, but I could tell he was crying and smiling at the same time. I was so petrified that I stood in one spot and sang "Paper Roses" without ever moving my body. A singing statue.

After the song was over, the whole audience stood up and Dad stepped up and hugged me and cried; he gestured to the audience and said, "Sing it again, Baby." I was crying, so happy that I had not let him down, and I sang the chorus again—take *that*, Leon Rhodes. I took my bow and Dad said, "Lorrie Morgan!" and it was over. I had survived.

Dad came offstage, picked me up, held me, and said how proud he was. I will never forget that moment, when the whole audience was personified in my crying-smiling big emotional father, the one person I wanted to please.

Then I went looking for Debbie. I found her in the tiny dressing room that all the women backstage had to use. Dolly. Tammy. Dottie. Loretta. Skeeter. Whoever was in town that night would hang up their fur coats and their leather coats, side by side, and use the same tiny makeup area. Debbie had spent my debut burrowed into the pile of coats in the corner, hiding in perfumed safety, just in case I made a total fool of myself. She heard my song on the speaker in the dressing room, and now she figured it was safe to come out.

On the way home, Dad stopped for the hot chicken, and Debbie and I wolfed down double portions. The crisis was over.

Through it all, I had this image of my father, so poised, so professional, just standing there onstage encouraging me. Little did I know. Years later I came upon this quote from Dad about my first appearance on the *Opry*: "If a performer thinks they get stage fright before they perform, wait until their child makes their first performance and you are watching."

He certainly fooled me.

From then on, occasionally I'd go on the road with Dad in the summer or on weekends, and he would call me up onstage to sing a song or two. I was still nervous, but somehow I would get through it.

I was there for some milestones in Dad's career. On March 15, 1974, he was the last singer to perform in the *Opry* on the stage of the Ryman. Country music was going big-time. The powers that owned the *Opry* had built a new amusement park out east of the river and named it Opryland, and now they were opening the new theater for the *Opry*. It even had multiple bathrooms and dressing rooms and a green room where the performers could wait.

The very next night, they opened the glitzy new palace. President Nixon (who only the day before had been named a coconspirator by a special grand jury investigating the Watergate break-in) came by to play the piano and take a yoyo lesson from Roy Acuff. Dad was the first singer on the night's program, an honor for him, to let *Opry* fans know the circle remained unbroken.

Dad was always there for me. I remained an indifferent student in high school because my life at home and my music mattered much more than schoolwork.

One time, Dad went with me to a parent-teacher conference, and the teacher said I was not doing very well. I started to cry because there was nothing I hated more than letting Dad down.

He was silent as we walked out of school, and I figured I was really in trouble. He never spanked me, never once, but he had a way of looking at you that let you know you had done something wrong.

He took my hand and he said, "You know, Fussy, I can't tell you I'm happy with your grades, but I want to tell you that I think you are very smart and you are going to go far in this world with your common sense.

"I'm not saying I'm giving you permission to have bad grades. But don't break yourself up over not knowing algebra or science, as long as you try."

At that point, I actually started to do better in school. Dad gave me confidence.

Dad had promised to bring me to the celebration of his twenty-fifth anniversary on the *Opry*. It would turn out to be more of a milestone than any of us could know.

On May 26, 1975, a month before the anniversary, Dad was putting up a new CB antenna on the roof. Home repairs were not exactly his strength, and Mom made him promise that he would leave the heavy work to his buddies, T-Shirt and somebody else.

"I ain't going up there," Dad promised Mom.

I was standing in the living room when I spotted Dad climbing up the ladder, but I figured he was just supervising, so I did not worry.

Suddenly, T-Shirt came running inside, shouting, "Anna, you need to call 911. George just had a heart attack up on the roof."

We lived across from the hospital and the paramedics came right over and went up on the roof, where they hooked Dad up to the EKG, which sent the signal to the hospital. I don't remember how they got him down off the roof because Mom made me go inside, but they rushed him to the hospital and ran tests on him.

They released him that night and said it had not been a heart attack but rather congestive heart failure. It turned out that Dad had already suffered one congestive failure going up the steps of the Capitol downtown. Never mentioned it to anybody. Just kept going because he had an appointment.

Now they began the long process of testing him at Baptist Hospital, a pioneer in cardiology in Nashville, and it was determined that Dad needed bypass surgery. Nowadays, bypass surgery is common. People have it in every city, every day, but in those days it was still being developed, and the procedure was just being started in Nashville.

Dad asked the doctor if he could perform for his twenty-fifth *Opry* anniversary, which was on his birthday, June 28. He received permission. I performed on the early show, and Dad also played the second show. After that his buddies gathered around, sang "Happy Birthday," and everybody had a piece of birthday cake onstage.

The very next day he went in for tests before the open-heart surgery. They discovered his condition was worse than the doctors had thought. All my relatives came in from Ohio and joined Mom in a big suite in Baptist Hospital. On the morning of the surgery, we all kissed him—his family, his friends, his record people. Mom has told me many times that one of the last things Dad told her was, "I love you, and make sure Lorrie gets her chance."

He came through the surgery and we all fell on our knees and prayed. He was taken to the recovery room, and everybody got to see him. We were warned he would not look that good with all the tubes in him, but the next day he sat up, writing silly notes to the doctors and the rest of us.

On the morning of July 7, Mom saw a nurse running down the hall, in full emergency mode. Mom knew Dad was the only patient in that wing who might need that kind of urgency.

It turned out that during the night, some of the nurses had not turned him properly from side to side. As a result, his trachea tube became clogged, and he went into a coma. In my mind, there has always been a question of whether they knew what they were doing. Open-heart surgery was so new, they were still working on the procedures. I genuinely believe that if my dad had had the same surgery just a year later, he'd be alive today.

We all gathered in his room and we watched the lines on the respirator slow down, watched him fade away, this big vital man who loved life so much. I looked over at my mom, who was taking this loss with so much dignity. I had no idea what she was going through, and I never would until the day I lost Keith. In the moments after Dad died, I tried to take my cues from Mom. Somehow we would get through this.

At the funeral home, I needed all the help I could get. I stood up next to Dad's casket and motioned for my friends to come up there. Ruthie remembers my brushing Dad's hands and kissing him. It's all a blur to me now.

The funeral was held at our church, St. Joseph's. I looked around and saw all the friends from country music who had come to pay their respects to Dad. I don't remember a word anybody said, so I have gone back to the old clippings just to remind me of that day.

"George Morgan never had a selfish, self-centered thought in his life," Johnny Cash said at the church. "He was a man of charity, a man of love. His first concern was always his home and family."

June Carter Cash recalled how Dad had sung at her wedding, and she said, her voice breaking, "I'll remember George as one of the truest, finest gentlemen I've ever known in my life."

Little Jimmy Dickens was there, and he said, "George and I started at the Opry on the same night and had hit records at the same time. I think he'd like to be remembered as a fun guy, a fine man and the family man that he was."

Mom had asked me to sing at the funeral. I did not know if I could, but she said, "If you can, you know your dad would love it."

All my life, Dad had stood by me. I would stand by him on this day. I held the guitar Dad had bought for me and I sang the Cat Stevens song "Morning Has Broken," which is really an old hymn, praising the peace and beauty of every new day given us by God.

As I sang, I imagined my dad up on the stage of the old Ryman, wearing his dignified white suit, so proud of me. I sang for my dad at his funeral, and I sing for him still.

CHAPTER EIGHT

I missed Dad, missed him terribly. There were times when that sorrow weighed down on me, made me think my life had been ruined, my luck had run out. Then I remembered I had a good family, that we all hung in together.

The usual ways of self-destruction were not for me. I didn't drink much, never have touched cocaine, tried pot a few times, like everybody else, but not to the point where it mattered much. For the record, I was a virgin when I graduated from high school. I was brought up to believe that you go to hell if you break the rules, and I take my religion seriously.

I was a little crazy at times, but I did not run wild. I saw no sense in that. Was I normal? Hell, no. I felt a little distant from the kids at school because I was already playing music and going out at night.

After Dad passed away, I was hired for the bluegrass show at the Martin Theater at Opryland, on a little outdoor stage for the fans passing through. I couldn't quite figure out why they had put me in the bluegrass show, but it was good money for a seventeen-year-old, so I didn't complain.

They put me in the same band as a very talented fellow named Dean Rutherford, who was always writing songs and talking about getting them on records. He eventually wrote "Miami My Amy," which would figure prominently in my life, but that was after he changed his name to Dean Dillon.

I started to play at some of the clubs around Nashville. Dad's steel man, Little Roy Wiggins, and other *Opry* musicians like Joe Edwards and Leon Rhodes, would accompany me, and then there was Ray Kirkland, who had played with my father and who became a father figure to me, always there for when I needed advice.

Another supportive musician was Curtis Young, known as Mister Harmony because he could make any performance sound better. Curtis had been a great friend of my father's going back to the days when he sang with Wilma Lee and Stoney Cooper.

One night he was hanging around backstage at the *Opry* and heard my father rehearsing a song called "Elusive Dreams." He started harmonizing with Dad, who liked the sound so much that he said, "Hey, why don't we sing it together tonight?" After a while, Mister Harmony was singing on all Dad's records, and now he began singing with me at the Palace.

Sometimes Ray Kirkland backed me up in places like the Rodeway Inn, the Ramada Inn out by the airport, George Jones's Possum Holler, Jerry Reed's Country Palace, the Godfather and some of the clubs in Printer's Alley, the picturesque little block just above the Ryman.

It was in Printer's Alley that I first saw the singer who would become the role model for my career. Her name was Dianne Sherrill—"two *n*'s, two *r*'s, two *l*'s," she very quickly tells people—and she was just about the best entertainer I have ever seen.

Dianne is a good old southern girl from Alexander City, Alabama, who had just arrived in Nashville. She is a petite blonde, one of the first women in Nashville to favor short hair, and she knew how to talk and flirt with the audience.

"Sexy but not slutty," Dianne says with that appealing

southern laugh. "I always like to wear short, lacy, frilly dresses. I want the men to like me, but I don't want to offend the women, either."

I would watch her, show after show, and learn from her. She has a kind of lisp on the s's, which wasn't too great for records, but was really appealing in person. She was playing at the Western Room or the Carousel, and I was a regular.

Dianne had known my dad, going back to when she went out with Joe Johnson, who produced my dad's records. Her dad, Hugh, loved my dad's music, and Dianne had visited Dad at the hospital shortly before he died. From the first time I popped into her club, she and I got along great.

Wherever Dianne was playing, I would go watch her. She would lend me her clothes—I distinctly remember some aqua-colored spandex pants that I had openly admired. More important, she used to call me up onstage, a kid of seventeen, and ask me to sing a song or a duet.

Some women are uncomfortable helping a younger woman, but Dianne was not threatened by me.

"When I first came to Nashville, Dottie West and Sammi Smith helped me," Dianne said. "Sammi taught me how to sing 'Rocky Top.' There's always room for more. You should pass it on."

Nowadays, Dianne is still performing regularly, and she also has a business called The Stage Coach, teaching young people about being an entertainer.

Diane went on to say, "I once asked Minnie Pearl how she could always be so happy in front of a crowd, and she said, 'I just love 'em.' I try to be the same way. I love what I do. I make sure I change clothes between every show, even if I'm doing four a night. If somebody stays for two shows, I want him to see me in two different outfits. I want them to feel they are being entertained. I don't try to sing a song like anybody else. What kept me here is my own style. The best time for me is when I'm on the stage."

Watching Dianne Sherrill handle the crowds in those jammed little joints on Printer's Alley gave me an education. I became more confident in dealing with fans, many of them with a drink in their hand and two or three in their systems, wondering out loud if this little blonde had any talent or whether she was just George Morgan's daughter. Most of the time it was good fun, nice people, lots of friends and family, doing what I wanted, right in my hometown.

Things had changed a little at home. About a year after Dad died, Mom married again, an old friend of ours named Paul Trainor, who had been a priest for many years.

Paul and Dad had been friendly. They used to go hunting together, and Paul had baptized a few of the older kids. He'd heard Candy's first confession and gave her her first communion at Holy Rosary, the first church we attended. Then he had left the priesthood and was working at the funeral home when we buried Dad.

I was glad when Mom started going to lunch with Paul. I was happy for her when they decided to get married because I wanted Mom to have companionship as the rest of us grew up. But I'll admit I had trouble with the reality of his moving into our house. I found myself thinking, He's staying in there? In Dad's room?

It was very personal, having another man in the house, and thinking about Dad, because as the youngest, I was still living there.

Candy admits, "I was always afraid of him, maybe because of that priestly aura, but I was happy for Mom and he was good to her."

Paul was very book smart, was a good guy, and was quite fond of us, particularly of Beth and me. He was very good about helping me with my homework. But he was, well, different, that's all. Maybe it was because he had been a priest for so long, but he did not share our flippant show-biz humor.

The Morgans can make a joke out of anything, even death. Beth will call me on the phone and say, "Oh, guess what. Dad was up at the house for country ham and he said, 'Tell everybody hi.' "

We all understand that. In our hearts, Dad is still part of our lives, he's out on the interstate somewhere, talking into the CB, gonna be home in twenty minutes.

Last Thanksgiving, Mom got onto the subject of Dad's open-heart surgery, and Beth asked, "What was the outcome of that, anyway?" and Mom said, "Oh, girls."

It's hard to break into a weird family sense of humor like that. We tried to keep up the family rituals, like playing cards, but Paul hated to lose. When Dad lost, it didn't matter, it was all just social, but Paul took it seriously. He was a responsible adult; he tried to be a father; he would be there for any of us, and would tell you what he thought. But he just wasn't Dad.

I grew to love Paul over the years, but he was the complete opposite of Dad. He was not the kind of person to give compliments, to show affection, to tell Mom she looked pretty. I was thrilled she had her relationship with him. Mom used to say affectionately about Paul, "Oh, he's an old priest."

As I look back on it, Mom was tolerant of me, too. I was sixteen, I was full of myself, and there were times I would tell her, "You just don't get it," or whatever the saying was back in 1975 and 1976. We had our fights, with me telling her she was boring, but she knew I was not the kind of kid you could hold down. I was the last, and I was full of the dickens, and Mom gave me some space.

(I have always heard that mothers put a curse on their children by saying, "I hope your children give you a hard time some day." Morgan and I could not be closer, but there are times when she is giving me The Look and I remember how I used to glare at my mother. I've got it coming.)

I did not suddenly become a leading scholar at St. Bernard Academy. I almost blew off school in my senior year. Dad was gone and I was so tired from my real life outside that I started paying kids twenty-five cents a page to do my homework for me.

I'm afraid I was a bad influence on Ruth. I'd be sitting in class, daydreaming about what great adventures I could be having outside, and I would whisper, "Ruth, let's get out of here."

We would slip out of school, hop in my car, and both of us would light up a cigarette, the legal variety. I was really into smoking now. My dad had smoked, and a lot of the country people smoked. Smoking and drinking, that was part of country music.

Nowadays you've got a lot of people at the *Opry* who drink Evian bottled water, but not back in those days. Everybody seemed to smoke as a matter of course, and so did I. I ain't stupid. I know it ain't good for me, but it seemed like a cool thing at the time, so I started. It is a bad habit, an addictive one, and I do not recommend that anybody else start. But there we were, Lucy and Ethel, puffing away.

After our smoke and our coffee and our ritual with the ducks in Centennial Park, Ruthie and I would visit the old people at the senior citizen center over by Father Ryan High School.

I had discovered the center while I was working at Opryland. A group of us had been sent over to sing for the older people, and I found I liked it. I've always loved older people. I feel I can relate to them. I loved my grandfather and grandmother, all the history they had gone through, and I loved the senior center, too.

These people had been young and beautiful once, Romeo and Juliet maybe, and now old age had set in, but some of them were like kids again. There was a kind of innocence in them, just as in children, that just tears me up.

I would keep my guitar in the trunk of my car because you never know when you might feel like singing a song. I would grab it and Ruth and head over to the center.

"Now, Ruth, don't cry," I would say before going in. I had experience playing in front of an audience. Life is a performance. However, it was not that easy for Ruth, who was not blinded by the imaginary spotlights that are always shining in performers' eyes. Ruth saw that these old folks, most of them women, were senile or crippled or broken-hearted, and usually a bit of all three. That's just the way life is. Some of them thought we were their grandchildren, which was fine with us. I'd pull out my guitar and sing them something soft and nice.

Ruth and I would try to coordinate our stories before heading back to St. Bernard, but that didn't always work. Sometimes the loudspeaker would crackle, and there would be an announcement: "Would Ruth Ralph and Lorrie Morgan please report to the principal's office?"

The principal, Sister Serena, so imposing in her dark habit, would ask, "Girls, where have you been?"

We knew better than to lie to Sister Serena. She would know. Don't ask me how, she would know. So we would tell her we had been to the senior center, and she would say, "Well, girls, that's really nice of you, but don't skip school to do it."

Sister Serena enforced the rules, but I know she bent them a bit for me. She and the other sisters got me through high school by loving me and giving me the benefit of the doubt. They knew I would rather have been out there entertaining somebody.

(I saw Sister Serena a few years ago at a convent. She was exactly the same person—but she doesn't wear the bustling black habit anymore. I wanted to tell her, "You go right upstairs and get back into your habit," but I did not want to offend her. Not Sister Serena.)

After my graduation from high school, I took any date that Buddy Lee and his booking company would come up with. My mom was not pushing me into show business, but she did encourage me, partially to honor Dad's request just before his heart operation. She knew that Dad had always believed I could make it.

Mom was not a stage mother, but she was one loyal companion. She would travel with me to these modest little engagements hundreds of miles away.

One time we drove all the way to some town in Nebraska—I have blanked out the identity—and it was much farther than anybody had led us to believe.

This was during the terrible gasoline crisis of the mid-seventies when the major companies mysteriously seemed to run out of fuel, forcing the prices up. In the big cities, people lined up a dozen cars deep; sometimes they had to buy gasoline on odd or even-numbered days, depending on their license plate numbers.

Out in the country, the service stations ran out of gasoline and just shut down in the evening, which was not very helpful if you were driving cross-country to keep a date.

Mom and I took turns driving and somehow we found the occasional open station, out there on the flatlands, with the cows and the silos and the crossroad towns. We drove through thunder and lightning and tumbleweed blowing across the highway, just to make a few dollars and spread my name out there.

When we finally reached the little town, I was washed out. Just whipped.

"If this is show business, I don't want any of it," I told Mom. "I'm quitting; I'm calling Buddy Lee and telling him not to book me anymore."

Mom was Mom. The voice of reason.

"Wait until morning. You'll feel better," Mom said.

Sure enough, a few cheers, a few dollars, a few hours' sleep, and I found enough strength not to quit—although not by much.

Things started to happen, slowly. I sang with Floyd Cramer at a roast for Wesley Rose, and as a result, in 1979, I was signed by Hickory Records, the Acuff-Rose label. My first record was "Two People in Love" and "Tell Me I'm Only Dreaming," which had moderate success.

Somewhere in there, I discovered I was a woman. I had been a tomboy growing up, out by the creek looking for crawdads with Marty. I always loved playing with Barbie dolls, loved to dress them up, and I admired them for their figure, given that I did not have much of a figure. I always had a fairly big butt and big hips—the Morgan women do—along with a small head. For a long time I had a flat chest, which made me feel, anatomically speaking, somewhat like a pear.

While I wasn't paying attention, relatively late in my teens, this got rearranged a bit, and I began filling out my jeans and my sweaters. The record company did a bunch of photos of me, and one of them was down low, from the back, wearing jeans.

"Wait a minute, who wants to see my butt?" I asked their art director.

The answer was, a lot of people. And those same people now also liked my chest and my face, too, apparently.

I had never thought I was one of the prettier girls in any setting. I carried myself well and hoped my personality and intelligence would carry me, but now I discovered that people thought I was a looker. Came as a surprise to me, but I would take it.

CHAPTER NINE

The road trips did not make me rich, but they did give me something I will treasure the rest of my life—my daughter.

It happened this way:

I would put together a different band each time I went out, depending on who was available. My drummer, Joe Roden, had lined up Randy Parton, brother of Dolly, to play bass, but Randy was known to cancel, and cancel he did. Joe came up with another bass player named Ron Gaddis, who performed at the Western Room in Printer's Alley with none other than Dianne Sherrill.

Anybody who played with Dianne was good enough for me. I told Joe to book him.

I got to this town in Ohio and saw my band-of-the-day all sleeping in their cars, just waiting for me. We went to the theater and started to rehearse a little, but I needed one of them to open for me—you know, sing a little, introduce me, front man.

"Now, who can sing?" I asked.

The bass player could sing a little, he said. Ron Gaddis did a sound check of "Heart Over Mind," an old Ray Price song, and not only was he good, but he was downright handsome. Right then and there, I fell for him.

We moved on to Indiana in different cars, and when we got back to Nashville I would go down to Printer's Alley to watch Ron Gaddis perform with Dianne.

This was really Ron's first big break in Nashville, playing four shows, six nights a week with Dianne. She tried to explain her theories of entertaining to Ron—"You get paid to smile," plus it's important to wear clean clothes and look well groomed. Ron was into the music, and he felt that should be enough. They had their clashes, but Dianne also knew he had talent and needed to make a few extra dollars on the road.

I asked Dianne if I could borrow Ron for a few days.

"Just don't run him," she said with a smile, meaning, bring him back.

For a while, Ron flip-flopped between Dianne and me, but somewhere along the line, Ron and I moved from being singers to lovers.

And that—as the saying goes—is where the trouble started.

I always say that Ron and I never dated, we fought. He was a whirlwind, pretty wild, liked to party, and we were both headstrong, both temperamental. We just butted heads, which was probably part of the attraction in the first place.

I wound up getting pregnant, and told my mother and stepfather. I was not sure about getting married, and there was no way abortion would have been an option. Paul suggested that, before I started showing, I should go away for a while, give birth, and put the baby up for adoption, a time-honored tradition. That way I would not have to get married.

"There is no way I will give up this child," I told them. I had been put on this earth to have that child. No matter what else happened, that baby had been created at a moment of love between two people.

Ron and I made plans to get married on June 25, two days before my twenty-first birthday. Because Ron had been married before, we could not be married in the Catholic church, so we had the wedding at home, with Beth serving as my maid of honor. We went for a honeymoon at Montgomery Bell, a golf and cabin resort in the western part of Tennessee.

We fought through the honeymoon, fought when we got home. The only thing we did right was creating the child growing inside me. From the moment I became pregnant, I had been bonded to my child; boy or girl, it didn't matter. I wanted to honor Dad with my firstborn child, and "Morgan" was one name that would work either way.

I still did not know the gender as the due date approached, with Ron and me still fighting.

One night I ran out of the apartment, jumped in my car, and started driving. Didn't matter where. I was on Due West Avenue, heading toward Dickerson Pike, and I had this mystical feeling I could talk to my child.

"Morgan," I said, "no matter what, it's always gonna be me and you." I was so committed to that child; I poured all my love and energy and hope into that tiny form growing inside me.

When I went into labor, we discovered the baby was turned backward. They did not want to use a forceps because the baby was tiny, so they decided on a C-section. They gave me the anesthesia, and I was a little groggy, but I was still conscious. Suddenly, they were holding up a tiny girl, only four pounds, six and a half ounces, and I was ecstatic to finally know the mystery of Morgan.

She was sweet and intelligent and beautiful, from that first moment, and I felt close to her, as if we had been together all my life. I would know her moods, and she would know mine, and I would protect her as best I could, and teach her, and love her.

You know, many years later, that is exactly how I still feel about Morgan. She can be moody, as a teenager will be, but there is a closeness that began before she was ever on this earth.

In addition to a beautiful daughter and a friend for life, I also got a new job. Ron started working for George Jones, who was having trouble holding on to musicians because of a few odd habits—like fighting, trashing hotel rooms, not showing up for dates, and firing his pistol inside the bus. Other than that, George was a delight.

(George and Tammy Wynette had long since parted. It's hard to believe they were married only six years. Seems like a century to the rest of us.) Anyway, George had run through dozens of musicians, and he needed somebody young and reckless and female.

"Just try out," Ron said.

I have always loved George Jones, the man and the music, although not the antics. I knew I would never get the job, but I went to the audition and saw five other girls in this tiny recording studio. Ron and the band were at the microphones, with George lounging on a couch.

A couple of the girls got up and sang old Tammy songs—no, not "Stand By Your Man"—and George just reclined on that lounge, semiconscious at best.

When it was my turn, I had to choose a song.

"My favorites have always been the George-and-Tammy duets," I said.

"Get George up there with you," Ron said, goading me on.

George roused himself from his private dreamland and shambled over to me. I chose the duet "Near You."

George was staring at me with those piercing eyes that can scare you half to death, but I was not about to back down. My competitive nature kicked in. Plus, I needed the job. I stared right back at him, jaw to jaw, eyeball to eyeball, and we sang the song. He gave me the job, right then and there.

Our first show was in town, at Pee-Wee's, the club his best friend, Pee-Wee Johnson, used to have. The whole music industry was there, and we did all right. Then we went out on the road to Billy Bob's in Fort Worth, and on from there.

George was really bad in those days. He has told most of the bad stories in his book *I Lived to Tell It All*, with Tom Carter, but I've got a few he did not remember. Frankly, it's amazing he remembers any of them.

There was the Christmas when George called us all in the back of the bus and started passing out small, clear bags of white powder. Call me old-fashioned, but I don't think that's what Irving Berlin had in mind when he wrote "I'm Dreaming of a White Christmas."

I handed the bag back to George.

"I don't do that," I said. "And I never will."

It took a while for my words to penetrate. Like I say, George was pretty bad in those days.

"Damn," George finally said. "I'm gonna have to buy you a real Christmas present."

A couple of days later, he presented me with beautiful cowboy boots. Two pairs.

George will never lose the nickname "No-Show Jones," which he more than earned in those years. You just didn't know, with George. We would open for him, and his manager, Wayne Oliver, would stand on the side and say, "Y'all sing another song while I try to get him onstage."

Sometimes we would go forty-five minutes and people would be yelling, "Where's George?"

One time I told the audience, "I'm out here singing my heart out and you're yelling. Let me tell you, the longer you yell, the further you are from George Jones." About half of them cheered my spunkiness. The other half started throwing popcorn boxes and paper cups at me.

One night George didn't come out at all. They had to sneak us into the bus, but the fans got on both sides and were shaking it back and forth. Ron forced me down on the floor of the bus and put a pillow over my head so I would not be hurt in case the rocks broke the window. It was awful.

For all of that, I loved George Jones. You had to. He wasn't deliberately being a jerk. He was hurtin'. Something inside made him act that way. A lot of people only wanted him up on the stage, but a few people just wanted him to be okay. One of them was Nancy Sepulvada, the woman from Louisiana he had just met. She went through some hard times with him, but finally she helped get him into treatment, and straightened out.

There was a lot of fighting going on in those days. George and Nancy. Me and Ron.

My marriage was a combination of the last six country music songs you heard, particularly the ones about people who wake up one morning and find life is a little different than they had dreamed.

That is the appeal of country music. It talks about frustration and loneliness and heartache, toughing it out, drowning your sorrows, the everyday compromises so familiar to the blue-collar people out there.

Life is not all about "Surfin' USA," which is great for kids of sixteen—getting on your surfboard, riding the waves—but as you get a little older and wiser, working the swing shift, managing a baby and a husband, sometimes it's nice to know that other people are feeling emptiness or flat-out pain.

Country music is a therapy for people—but not necessarily for the people who sing it and play it.

After I had been married to Ron for a while, I began to have anxiety attacks, feeling the world was going to swallow me up. I would start hyperventilating, almost unable to breathe. I thought I was going to die on the spot. I was not getting along with Ron, but there was something deeper working at me.

How many women have ever felt like that? Just raise your hand. I thought so.

Ron took my terror as a personal affront and put his face right up into mine, saying, "You're crazy, you know that? You're fuckin' crazy!" Well, I already knew that. I went to my priest and I said, "Look, I feel like I'm dying." The priest knew right off it was anxiety and recommended I see a therapist, which was a huge step for me, for any of us. I did not want to give Ron the satisfaction, so I held off about that.

The last night was in Biloxi, Mississippi, when Ron hit me a couple of times. I called the hotel security and asked them to protect me while I packed; then I took a cab to the airport. While I was in the airport, I was paged. I picked up the phone and, of course, it was Ron, begging me to come back, but I just said, "Fuck you," and got on the plane. I arrived in Nashville, called Mom from a pay phone, and she came out to get me. I said, "Mom, I'm coming home."

I couldn't eat for days. I was no longer thinking about performing. I just wanted to live to be twenty-five. "I don't care if I ever become a star," I told Mom.

"That's your choice," she said, "but you don't have to give it up. Look at your dad. He wasn't driven crazy by it. You can have a career. It's up to you."

I wrote songs like "Happy Anniversary" and "Diamonds from a Willow Tree," but I wanted nothing to do with performing in clubs, or traveling, or recording.

At the same time, I did go see a therapist, but he only added to my anxiety. I would walk into his office and it would be so solemn, so sad, that my panic only increased.

I would just keep talking, and the therapist would be staring at me, and I would think to myself, Well, do something, man. I'm worn out from a bad marriage and sitting in a car eight hours a day to get to a road date, and wearing my voice raspy into a bad microphone in a noisy hall, to make a few dollars. Now I come home to Nashville and sit in this tomblike office and all you do is watch me?

His main activity was to put me on antidepressants, which I hated. I became lifeless, just a sack, flopping around. The longer I stayed in therapy, the more lifeless I became.

Finally I said, "What the hell am I doing? I can go out and tell my story to people at night, get paid for it, and know they're relating to me and what I'm going through in my songs. What do I need with a man who sits there and says, 'Uh-huh, uh-huh,' and probably has never been in a bar in his life, and has probably never experienced the things I'm talking about. How could this son of a bitch help me?"

I did go back for one more session, and this time I said, "Doggone it, say something."

He just cleared his throat and said, "I can't really tell you what to do."

Silently, I thought, The hell with you, I'll go and listen to George-and-Tammy records. So I never went back.

Country music would be my therapy.

Driving away from his office, I reached in my purse, found my antidepressant pills, and just flung them out the window. If I was meant to be nervous, so be it. At least I was alive.

Some people might disagree with me and say that therapists are trained to recognize things, to understand other people. That's probably true. Maybe the therapist was waiting for me to sound feisty again, worrying about how much this was costing me. Maybe he figured I was healthy enough to fly off the branch without getting hurt. Could be.

From talking in front of this sphinxlike therapist, I did find the strength to go through the divorce. I was just too young to be married, especially to Ron. To this day I like Ron, and I learned from him. Every man who's ever been in my life, I've learned from. Something good has come out of every one. A little more intelligence was born with every failure. But by then, I knew it was a failure.

At this time in my life, I did meet a new friend. It happened the day I was visiting Roy Tessier, who was doing some of my booking at the time. I mentioned how much I loved Mary Lou Turner's version of Bill Anderson's song "It's Different with You."

"Oh, I book her," Roy said.

When my meeting with Roy was over, I went into the lobby and Mary Lou Turner was sitting right there.

"I am such a big fan of yours," I gushed, introducing myself.

She seemed a little preoccupied. Actually, she was a total bitch, which I remind her about to this day. She looked at me as if to say, "So what?" It turned out that she was there to collect money from Roy, never a pleasant task for an entertainer.

She was geared up for battle, not in a great mood, but I persisted. I had seen her around the Opry, and we knew each other, but we had never really talked. I told her how much I loved her version of Bill's song and asked if she had a copy.

She seemed to soften, and she said she would bring it over to the Opry, which she eventually did. She also gave me her phone number and said, "Call me sometime."

There was something so straight about her that I wanted to be friends. She was about ten years older than me, and she had even sung with my dad at times. I was wondering if she was just being nice to me because of Dad, but I decided to pursue it.

I drove up to her house in my car, and I said, "Let's go for a ride." We became good friends right away. I would help her with her two teenagers sometimes, and she would help me with Morgan sometimes, and we both could count on the other at three in the morning, which is my definition of friendship.

Mary Lou was also the rare kind of friend who will listen to your worst fears.

"I'm never going to make it," Mary Lou remembers my telling her.

She will tell you that she did not want any more fame than she already had, that she was grateful for what she had done. I had not reached that stage yet. I said I was getting out of the business, yet at times I could feel this gnawing sense that I wanted to be a star.

Mary Lou comforted me, told me I had great talent, that it was just a matter of time.

In 1983, I went to work for Ralph Emery on his morning show. I'm sure he knew I needed the work, and I was very grateful to sing a couple of live songs for his radio audience. Because the show went on so early, five-thirty, we'd all show up and wing it.

As much as I love Ralph Emery, I had to butt heads with him about the material I would sing. I insisted on coming in with nice gentle ballads, and he insisted that you needed up-tempo songs to help get farmers up and out to feed the hogs and milk the cows, and to get teachers and office workers in the mood to get dressed and go to work. Sometimes I'd just barge ahead and sing what I wanted. It was live radio.

One time Ralph introduced me, and he must have forgotten we were on the air, because he said to me, "I sure hope you're not gonna sing one of those draggy-ass ballads."

I just looked at the band and said, "Did I hear what I thought I did?" Needless to say, Ralph was mortified that he'd done that on his own show. But he gets the last word on this story: "The funny thing is that nobody complained about my language," Ralph insists to this day. "But I did get a few letters saying they agreed with me about the ballads."

Maybe.

Another time, I was trying to prove my point about how good my material was, so I brought my boom box cassette player into the studio and started playing a song for the guys in the band. I must have had the volume turned up, because Ralph could hear it while he was trying to talk to the radio audience. When he went into a commercial break, he yelled at me. He says he doesn't remember yelling—but I sure do.

Being asked to be on Ralph's show was a break beyond my imagination. The cable age was just beginning, and Ralph's show became *Nashville Now* on the TNN network, which soon reached twelve million households around the country, bringing me to the attention of a lot of people who had never seen me before.

One day I got a message from somebody named Sandy Gallin. Never heard of him. Almost didn't return the call. Turned out, Sandy Gallin manages Dolly Parton, one of the most talented people in the world.

Dolly had seen me on *Nashville Now*, and she wanted Sandy to try to sign me. He flew me out to Los Angeles, but we did not hit it off. Mom had bought me a new dress for my interview with this big-time Hollywood man, and the first thing Sandy said when he met me was, "What a hideous dress. That has to go."

My wounded pride sprang right out of one of Dolly's most beautiful songs, "Coat of Many Colors," about a mother who sews a coat for her daughter, using many different remnants. My mom had chosen that dress for me, and I loved it because of her. Dolly from Pigeon Forge would have understood how Sandy Gallin hurt my feelings.

I did sign with Sandy for a while, but I was not an LA type of girl. I was all Tennessee.

I began to wonder if it was ever going to happen for me, even in my hometown. I used to say I was like "wallpaper"—people saw me but they didn't see me. I came with the building. I was part of the decor. I had been there forever. Hey, there's Lorrie, George Morgan's daughter. Well, heck, we'll catch her next time around.

Although I was close to many people at the *Opry*, I was not a member of the official cast. That was reserved for the long-time stars or for newer attractions who had a hit record. Hal Durham, the manager of the *Opry*, was a long-time friend, but he was honest with me. He said he had no problem with my being on the *Opry* but that he couldn't extend membership to me, or it would look like he was doing a favor because of my dad. He told me, "You have to prove yourself," and I could appreciate that.

Things looked better for me when I signed a record deal with MCA, but Tony Brown, the head man over there, thought I was "too country"—the most dreaded sin of all.

He told me not to appear so much on the Ralph Emery show, which was terrible career advice in Nashville. Plus, Ralph is like family to the Morgans. He had helped my dad and he had tried to help me. I was going to appear on Ralph's show as long as Ralph wanted me.

Tony Brown also told me to start wearing the long, black baggy clothes that were suddenly hip. I had just started being proud of my figure, and now somebody wanted me to hide it inside a sack? No way!

I did get another break in 1984 when Hal Durham invited me to join the *Opry*, even though I hadn't had a hit record yet. I think he realized I was dedicated and was here to stay, and I will always appreciate his faith in me. I chose Bill Anderson to induct me because he had always been so sweet and supportive of me. I went out and sang "Candy Kisses" and "Stand By Your Man" with the house band. As I glanced over at those guys I kept thinking how proud Dad would have been. I felt Dad's presence up on the *Opry* stage. I was home.

Well, my record label wasn't so happy about that. The next piece of bad advice was that I should hang out with "cool" new people. I won't mention any names here, but some of them had just arrived in Nashville, and had no respect for the *Opry* or traditional country music. Tony Brown also advised me to cut down on "the old crowd"—my friends who had been around the *Opry* for decades. In my proud brain, it sounded like somebody was telling me not to associate with Dad's friends, with my own family.

I was from the old school, and suddenly these people were being put down. I really respected Tony Brown as a record man, but I was not about to cut out my friends or my history. This did not help my record career. A few people around town thought I was a bitch, but the truth is I was shy. I wasn't good at schmoozing with people in those days. I waited until I got to know people before I said much. But I did have a few things to say about people who were giving me bad advice. They didn't like me, and to tell you the truth, I wasn't too crazy about them, either. After a while, I wasn't associated with MCA anymore.

For a while, I worked with my brother, Marty, who had moved to Akron and Birmingham and Dallas after college, but around 1984 he came home. I was sure some of his songs would sell, and he had some great ideas for promoting me. Plus, he drove the car on some of my road dates.

We had some epic adventures. One time he rented a Southwind Trailer, squeezed a bunch of musicians in it, and went down to Pensacola, Florida, where it must have been eighty degrees. On the way back through Alabama, we hit a snowstorm, and by the time Marty managed to get that trailer back to Nashville there must have been eleven inches.

Not long after that, I got a job at Acuff-Rose as a receptionist who did demos on the side. I had a great time, working hard by day, partying at night with Peggy Lamb and Roy Acuff Jr. and Ronnie Gant, who had produced my album on the Hickory label.

And that's where I was, when I heard that voice in the back studio.

Chapter Ten

My first few weeks with Keith were tempestuous, full of joy. He was the most sensitive man I had ever met, in tune with my feelings, in tune with my needs, and yes, I am also referring to bed. Not a day or a night went by that he did not tell me, in tones that were almost worshipful, that I was the most beautiful woman he had ever seen.

He seemed almost grateful for me. Most men will tell a woman anything the first time they meet, just to get her into bed, but Keith never lost his sense of delight, never stopped making me feel I was special.

Sometimes I almost got the feeling that Keith did not think he deserved me, that I was an unexpected blessing in his life. Whatever it was, he set off a fire in me that I had never felt before. I wanted to make love with him morning, afternoon, and night, every day.

But sometimes I had the feeling there was something I did not know about Keith. Most of the time, he absolutely refused to talk about his drinking. He was a guy, and guys don't talk about their problems. They deal with them, or so they say, but they don't talk about them.

He also would not talk much about his past. He would talk

about Nashville, about country music, about us; he would talk so optimistically about the future, about his plans for me, for himself, for Morgan, for his parents. But my woman's intuition told me there were blanks, or gaps, or blind spots.

I wondered about his marriage. I had seen him with his wife a few times. He had acted respectfully around her, and I remembered her as a dignified, attractive woman. I was curious what had gone wrong in the relationship. Although he never was very specific, it was my impression that his wife had divorced him, that she was fed up with the way they lived, that he was on the road too much, and maybe there had been other women. I couldn't be sure, but that's a fairly common scenario in our business.

If Keith was hurt or angry about the divorce, he did not show it. They had not had children, but he did get partial custody of his black cocker spaniel, Tate. Every other weekend, he looked forward to Tate's visits. Like all cockers, Tate had to be close to human beings, twenty-four hours a day. He would sleep right next to the bed, which led to complications because every time Keith and I started to make love, Tate would give a little yowl, like "Ohhh!," which could be disconcerting. Keith would have to pause and say, "Tate!" and the cocker would yowl a little lower, and Keith would say, "Tate!" and the dog would whimper again. Tate absolutely had to have the final word.

It was also my impression that Keith's family was disappointed at the breakup of his marriage. Kathi was from Grayson, she was from the mountains, and the Whitleys clearly loved her, which was only right. It is always hard when marriages break up.

There was also a huge gap between the mountains of Appalachia and the broad Cumberland River valley of middle Tennessee. The Whitley ancestors had reached the rugged and secluded hills of the Appalachians, had fallen in love with that region, and had chosen to stay. People in Nashville had pushed on, toward more open space. I would not say the gap was to the same degree as that of the Montagues and the Capulets, but it was there. We were of different people.

After that first trip with Keith to eastern Kentucky, I realized he was still trying to come to grips with his own background. He was a man with conflicts that he could not verbalize. It was the same way with his music. He was not sure what he wanted to be.

His voice was as distinctive as Patsy Cline's or Merle Haggard's. You knew it the first bar of any song he performed. But what would he do with those songs?

Keith talked about growing up listening to Lefty Frizzell, Hank Williams, George Jones, Merle Haggard, Lester Flatt, Marty Robbins. He once recorded a song called "Bring Back Buck," with all the hee-haw inflections that made Buck Owens so great. Keith loved the rural sound of country music. He also loved the intricate harmonies of bluegrass and the energy of honky-tonk. But he was having a hard time making it work in Nashville.

When I met Keith, Music City was working overtime to forge links with the East Coast and the West Coast. Nashville was not so much in love with the music from the remote villages of Appalachia, where the music had been transported from the hills of England, Ireland, Wales, and Scotland.

New singers like George Strait, Randy Travis, and Garth Brooks were a little softer on the ear. Keith was a musician's musician because he had all this great music running around inside him. He was a mountain boy trying to make it in the big city. He wasn't comfortable talking about himself as an adult, but he loved talking about his childhood, the roots of his music.

He had a normal childhood playing baseball and riding horses, and music was a way of life back in the hills. He was born in 1955, back when mountain people still had time to play instruments and sing, before people walked around with headsets, their heads bobbing in their own little musical worlds. Back then, bluegrass and country and old-fashioned folk tunes really were part of the culture.

"I remember standing up on the counter at the Lion's Den restaurant in my hometown and singing those songs," Keith once said. "I sang them in talent contests in school, too."

After winning a talent show at the local school, Keith made his radio debut with Buddy Starcher in West Virginia at the age of eight. He also played at some of the bluegrass and country festivals in the area.

At fifteen, Keith, his brother Dwight, and their band played at the local Opry in Ezel, Kentucky, not far from his house. There he ran into Hobert Skaggs and his son, Ricky, who was the same age as Keith. Ricky was already a child prodigy. He had performed with Bill Monroe at the age of six at a local bluegrass festival, and with Flatt & Scruggs a year later.

By now, most people know Ricky Skaggs as one of the most talented musicians in Nashville—Entertainer of the Year in 1985, the top award in my business. Back then, Ricky and Keith were just a couple of teenagers growing up twenty miles apart.

"There was a little dressing room downstairs," Ricky recently recalled. "Keith and I started talking about our favorite musicians, and we both discovered we liked the Stanley Brothers. We started playing different Stanley songs, and we must have played for thirty or forty-five minutes. If anybody came through that room, we never noticed. We were in our own world."

Ricky joined a little band that Keith and his brother Dwight had formed, the East Kentucky Mountain Boys.

"After that, we sang together constantly, night and day," Keith once told an interviewer. "Our voices just had a natural blend."

The two began hanging out together, more at Keith's than at Ricky's.

"I remember the first time I went over to Keith's house and his mother cooked supper," Ricky recalls. "I took one bite of the green beans and I said, 'Miz Whitley, you cook with lard.' I didn't mean anything by it, but my grandmother always cooked with lard, but my mother used Crisco, and I could tell the difference." I always think of that.

"Keith and I would even go hunting together. I remember one time we were playing music on the front porch of my house and my hunting dog treed a huge groundhog. We laid down our instruments and ran outside. We didn't have our rifles with us, so we picked up rocks until we knocked the groundhog to the ground, and the dog could kill him. It sounds gross now that I tell it, but that's how we grew up."

Later, they called themselves The Lonesome Mountain Boys, playing songs by Ralph and Carter Stanley, two of the great names in bluegrass, along with Bill Monroe, who is called The Father of Bluegrass. Carter Stanley passed away in late 1966, but Ralph Stanley continued to recruit great young musicians as he toured the mountains.

Keith and Ricky joined forces and played wherever they could. Keith used to tell how he sang in drive-in theaters, where the band stood on top of the concessions stand and people applauded by honking their car horns.

"I've swallowed many a bug," Keith would say, referring to playing in the bright spotlight in the lush summer evening.

That same year, when they were fifteen, they heard that Ralph Stanley and his Clinch Mountain Boys were booked at a club in Fort Gay, West Virginia, just across the Big Sandy River from Louisa, Kentucky. Ricky had actually met Stanley and played for him when he was eight years old, but he did not think Stanley would remember him.

"We got there early for the show, but Ralph's bus had broken down en route," Ricky recalls. "The club owner knew me and Keith and he asked, 'Did you boys happen to bring your instruments with you?' Obviously, we had. We never went anywhere without our instruments. We kept them in the car in case anybody asked us to play.

"The owner got up there and said, 'We've got some boys who sing pretty fine, and we'd like them to do a few numbers for you.' We started with 'Riding on the Midnight Train,' as I recall, and we must have sung only Stanley Brothers songs for thirty, forty minutes. Suddenly, our hearts sank because there was Ralph Stanley pulling up a bar stool, and listening to us playing his songs. I couldn't tell if he was digging it or hating it, but he applauded, and everybody else did, too, when we were done.

"We had left all our cases and stuff in the tiny dressing room, and when we were finished, there was Ralph and his band getting ready. I said, 'I'm sorry to be in your way,' and he said, 'That's quite all right, you boys did a great job. You brought back old memories of when I was coming along.'

"Then Ralph went out to play, but after fifteen minutes or so, he said, 'Those boys were awful good, and we'd like them to play during the break.' So of course we did. Afterward, I reminded Ralph that I had played for him at Olive Hill and Prestonsburg when I was younger, and he said, 'You have certainly grown up.' "

That was in April. In mid-summer, Stanley invited Keith and Ricky to travel with the Stanley group down to the big bluegrass festival in Reidsville, North Carolina.

The two kids became regulars with the Stanleys that summer. Ricky's father would drop him off at the Whitleys' house, and they would drive the two boys up to the Mountain Parkway in Campton, where they would wait for the Stanley bus to pick them up. Or sometimes Ralph would come to the Whitley house and visit with the family. It must have been quite a heady experience for Keith and Ricky to have Ralph Stanley come for them.

As soon as Ricky graduated from high school, he joined the

Stanley group. Keith joined after his own graduation a few months afterward.

The writer Hazel Smith once recalled the first time she heard Keith and Ricky, at Camp Spring, North Carolina: "It was awesome. I'll never forget the look on Ralph's face. He knew he'd come across a duo that was out of this world."

Starting in 1970, they stayed with the Stanleys for two years and were featured on seven albums. In 1971, the album *Crying from the Cross* was named the Bluegrass Album of the Year.

For a while, touring with the Stanleys was the dream come true for the two kids. Keith always talked about how he met the legendary Lester Flatt at one of the festivals.

"Ralph asked me, 'Would you mind going over to Lester Flatt's bus and booking him for my Labor Day festival?' I went over to the bus, and I think Josh Graves stuck his head out the door. I said, 'I'd like to see Mr. Flatt.' He shut the door and I figured, I ain't got very far, but they opened the door. Lester was sitting in his chair and I said, 'Mr. Flatt, Ralph would like to have you on his festival this Labor Day. He sent me over here.'

"Mr. Flatt said, 'Let me see now, what day does Labor Day come this year?'

"That threw me. I said, 'Doesn't it come on the same day every year?'

"And he said, 'I don't know, I can't keep up with all them days. Labor Day. Groundhog Day.' "

About that time, Keith began to realize that Ralph had set him up to be twitted by the great Lester Flatt, playing the role of the ignorant hillbilly picker. The kids in the band were fair game for all kinds of teasing.

"We got to be buddies," Keith would say later. "Lester Flatt gave me an old guitar in 1975 that he had played for years."

Keith gained something else—a perfect imitation of Lester's

side-of-the-mouth country drawl, which sounded like it escaped around a huge wad of chewing tobacco.

When they played shows together, Keith would perform both sides of a conversation with Lester Flatt:

"Lester, how long have you had this guitar?"

"Oh, about fifteen years."

Somehow, Keith would manage to get about six "sh" sounds in the word "fifteen." Lester's fans and family loved his imitation, which he continued after Mr. Flatt passed away.

At some point, the magic paled for Ricky and Keith. Ricky actually opted to work as a boiler operator rather than stay on the road.

"I was just fried," he once said. But he soon went back into music, joining Emmylou Harris, moving to Washington, D.C., and then on to Nashville.

Keith also left the Stanley group and played for other bands, closer to country, not bluegrass. In 1975, he went back for another tour with Ralph Stanley, but then he formed the New Tradition, later known as the Country Store. In 1978 he joined forces with J. D. Crowe and the New South, a progressive-bluegrass-country-rock band, based in the Richmond-Berea area, with Keith as front man and lead singer.

They did two albums for the Rounder label: "My Home Ain't in the Hall of Fame" and "Somewhere Between," in 1981, which had word-of-mouth success in Nashville.

Other musicians loved them. Mike Chamberlain recalls playing the same clubs with his band, The Migrant Pickers.

"The first time I heard him, we were both playing at North Park near Lexington, around 1983," Mike has said. "I was in awe, I couldn't believe the vocal aerobics he could perform, the control of his voice. I was raised on Merle Haggard, but Keith was equal to Merle, or better.

"I think Keith was bummed out on bluegrass," Mike has said. "He was such a traditionalist about country music. He relived the old days to an extreme. But I think Keith didn't have a lot of patience. He wasn't an overnight success, and he had a hard time coping."

Mike recalls Keith saying, "One of these days I'm going to have my own band, and I'm going to ask you guys to play with me."

Keith had been urged to move to Nashville years earlier by Don Light, a former drummer at the *Opry* who had gone into managing gospel and bluegrass acts and later managed Jimmy Buffett. Keith and Don had met at a bluegrass festival in Berryville, Virginia, when Keith was improvising with John Starling of the Seldom Scene and Mac Wiseman, two of the great musicians in bluegrass.

"When Keith started to sing, you could have heard a mouse peeing on cotton," Don says. "Everybody just stopped and listened to him, he had such a great voice. I told him, 'If you ever get serious, you should move to Nashville. Moving there is a commitment. It's letting go of your day job.' "

Keith was reluctant to move to Nashville, but a number of people encouraged him at that time, including an attorney named Bill Carter, a publicist named Bonnie Rasmussen and a songwriter and producer named Norro Wilson.

At the end of 1983, Keith walked into Don Light's office and said, "Well, here I am."

Don Light put Keith in the studio with Don Gant, which is when I first heard him making the demo of "Fort Worth." When they had four sides ready, they marched them over to the offices of Joe Galante, the head of RCA's Nashville operations.

Joe Galante was hot. He was from Queens, New York, with a BS degree in finance and marketing from Fordham University, a

Jesuit college not exactly known as a country-music stronghold. He had been only thirty-one years old when he took over RCA's country music in 1982, and he had promptly taken RCA to the top, with artists like The Judds, K. T. Oslin, Alabama, and later Clint Black. Some people in the music business regarded him as a risk taker but Joe has been quoted as saying, "I just regard it as decisions being guided by passions."

Joe's passions did not immediately extend themselves to Keith's music. Don Light felt he had to do a hard sell.

"Joe passed on Keith the first time," Don Light said recently. "But I went back to him and said, 'I cannot let you pass on him.' I told Joe that every other label has a great country performer, but that RCA didn't really have one. Joe agreed, and they recorded eight sides, only with Norro Wilson as the producer. Reba McEntire even sang backup on one of them, and Keith loved her because she spoke the same blunt language he did."

Keith was once quoted as saying, "I rode into town in a blaze of glory, so to speak. The day I cut my first session at RCA, everybody who is anybody in the industry was there. I mean, it was like a major star coming in to record."

He settled into Nashville. Kathi enrolled at Middle Tennessee State University and RCA began to put the first eight-side album together.

"That's when we discovered Keith had a problem," Don Light told me recently. "He was drinking beer at the pool at my house, and after a couple of beers, he was just drunk. Later, I discovered he had been pouring vodka into the beer cans, because my vodka bottle was half down. Vodka. That was his favorite drink.

"We got him in the backseat of the car. While I was driving I asked Kathi, 'What's going on?' and she said he had a drinking problem.

"Right after that, we were shooting the cover for that first album. He went into a back room at Jim McGuire's photo studio and never came out. We went in there and he was comatose."

Keith's first mini-album, *A Hard Act to Follow,* did not go over so well.

When Joe Galante would talk to managers of radio stations, they would say Keith was "too country." They were trying to capture urban markets, upscale Sun Belt regions where people professed to love country music but were embarrassed by an eastern Kentucky twang like Keith's.

Joe has said, "We were in the crossover time of Dolly Parton, Eddie Rabbit, Crystal Gayle, Ronnie Milsap. Keith was about heart and soul. Keith was in the country tradition of Waylon Jennings's 'Good-Hearted Women' or just about anything by George Jones."

Hazel Smith, a writer in Nashville, felt that Keith had not yet found his own style: "I was disillusioned. Oh, the music was there all right. If you liked Keith Whitley singing one line like George Jones and the next line like Lefty Frizzell."

While not a monster hit, the first album was successful enough for Don Light to encourage Keith to form a band with musicians from eastern Kentucky: Carson Chamberlain, the steel player and Mike's cousin; Randy Hayes, bass; Bruce Rutherford, drums; Joey Schmidt, keyboards. In December of 1986, he offered Mike Chamberlain a job as a sound guy, but on March 17, in rehearsal, Keith moved Mike to bass and put Randy on lead guitar.

The band did not have many bookings at first, and money was scarce. Keith used this lack of money to play a trick on one of his musicians, displaying a weird sense of humor very much like my father's.

According to Mike Chamberlain, Keith went out one day, trying to hustle up some bookings. Later he called back to the house where Randy Hayes was. Disguising his voice, Keith said he was a booking agent from Hawaii and had a job that paid $10,000 but would be even more if Keith had a band.

Randy said he thought something could be arranged, and the Hawaiian guy asked, "Are you his wife?" and Randy mumbled something like, "No, I'm his bass player."

A while later, Keith called Randy and asked "Coz, are there any messages?" and Randy went through this whole big deal about the $10,000 job in Hawaii, and Keith listened to it all, and said he'd take care of it. Just when he was getting ready to hang up, Keith asked, "Are you his wife?"

"You bastard," Randy said, knowing he had been set up. There was no $10,000 job. There was just Keith laughing at the other end of the phone.

It was slow going for Keith. I had heard that beautiful demo tape of "Does Fort Worth Ever Cross Your Mind?" but his first producer, Norro Wilson, just blew it. Norro is a talented man who once wrote "The Most Beautiful Girl in the World" for Charlie Rich, and he knew talent, but for some reason Norro did not want any Texas songs on Keith's album. The demo went over to George Strait, who promptly recorded it, with many of the same intricate warbles and phrasings as Keith's version. Naturally, it was terrific.

Faye Whitley called from Sandy Hook and was all excited about hearing her son's record on the radio.

"No, you didn't, Mom," Keith said. "You heard George Strait's."

Right after that, Joe Galante put him together with Blake Mevis, a new producer with a reputation for a nice, soft country sound.

"Keith's first album was very, very country," Blake said not too long ago. "My challenge was to cut something exciting and different—that the radio would play. I felt that 'Miami My Amy' would fit in with Keith's style."

Keith and Blake hit it off right away. Blake was a little older, had a solid marriage, was a bright guy, and Keith seemed to feel comfortable with him.

"Keith once told me, 'Blake, a lot of people don't know this, but every time I get on the stage, I get scared.' I think that's one of the reasons he drank the way he did. He was looking for a place where the world could not get him. He was the kind of guy who would make his driver stop the bus and he'd go into a store and buy a package of baloney because he'd seen a hungry dog. That really happened. He was such a sensitive guy. He could not afford to drink. A lot of it was genetic. He just couldn't handle it."

Keith was still right on the edge as they prepared his second album, and he did not help himself with his occasional binges.

Don Light had known several people who were alcoholics, and he recognized that Keith had a serious problem. He told Keith that he would have to seek treatment for his drinking. Keith was reluctant, but Don said he would lose his career, so Keith agreed.

"I went to Joe Galante and said, 'We've got a problem,' " Don recalled. "I told Joe, 'I don't even know if you're going to want to stay with Keith, but I need to tell you this.' I knew RCA had not made much money on him, and they might not want to pay for his treatment.

"Joe asked me how much it would cost, so I called Cumberland Heights, a place right here in Nashville, and they told me it would cost $3,500 for thirty days, and they could get him in by Saturday. This was a Tuesday. I called Joe Galante at ten in the morning and he had a check by three in the afternoon."

Keith stayed in treatment for thirty days and stayed sober

the whole time. Kathi and Lynn Simpkins from Don Light's office and Blake Mevis were among the people who went to visit him.

"Keith never said the words, 'I am an alcoholic,' " said Lynn, who was very close to Kathi and Keith. "He would say, 'I have a drinking problem' or 'The bottle and I don't get along very well.' But he was not convinced that he could not drink. He believed it was something he would outgrow, and six months later he could take a drink again."

"To be perfectly honest, it broke my heart to see him at the center," Blake Mevis has said. "I know that treatment centers are all about recovering potential, but I just found it very depressing to think about Keith's potential. It was the first time I saw a person who had that kind of potential, but who was battling a demon, and the demon was winning.

"One thing I've not told many people," Blake said recently, "is that one time when Keith was out of treatment, he had been drinking a little, and he started crying. He told me how much he missed his brother Randy, and then he said, 'You remind me a lot of Randy.'

"Keith was very sweet, very emotional. I've known other alcoholics. I had another friend who died at thirty-three, and one thing I noticed about Keith was that you could really care for him, but you could never get past this one gate, whatever gate that was."

They never got past the gate at the first treatment center, or any of the subsequent ones, either. Don Light went to the "graduation" ceremony, when the patients who have stayed sober for thirty days are congratulated.

"I believe in prayer," Don said recently, "because I've seen prayers answered in ways that could have no other explanation. I went to the ceremonies, and I remember saying that country music did not need another George Jones. I also said that prayer was not enough.

"I told the story about the farmer who took over a farm that had been neglected and was falling apart. The farmer worked hard for a year and restored the land, and one day he was out walking with a preacher who admired the land, and said, 'Isn't it wonderful what the Lord can do?' and the farmer said, 'Yes, sir, but you should have seen it last year when the Lord had it all to himself.' My point was that Keith had to work at staying sober." Keith would remain sober for six months; then he would slip. They put him back into treatment a second time, and then a third time.

"The only way treatment works is if you do it for yourself," Don Light said. "The first time Keith did it for his recording contract. The second time he did it for Kathi because they were separated and he wanted to save his marriage. The third time he did it for me."

Kathi divorced Keith in 1985. He never did talk much about it, but the closest I can figure out is that she had gone a long way with him, and was just worn down from covering up for him. It takes a lot of energy—a lot of lying, really—to back up an alcoholic, and she probably had had enough. I know Keith's mom and some friends of theirs had high regard for Kathi, and there are people who will say that Keith never stopped caring for her. I know I never heard him say a bad word about her. That was the caring side of him.

Working with Blake Mevis, Keith recorded "Miami My Amy," which soon was all over the radio, just as they all had hoped.

CHAPTER ELEVEN

By the time I met Keith, he had great memories of his childhood. To this day, his mother says Keith never had a drinking problem, or any problem, while he was around home.

In our first weeks together, I realized that the magic had long since vanished from his memory of his early days in the music business. He did not have nearly the same nostalgia for the road that he had for Sandy Hook. There was something on his mind.

We were uninhibited about sex—different times of day, different places, different ways—and in between we would talk about this beautiful, spontaneous passion between us.

One night, we were in bed talking, and somehow Keith mentioned that when he was younger—in some unspecified time and place—he had been taken somewhere to pay to watch a couple have sex. A man and a woman had gotten down on a mattress in some back room and gone at it, with a bunch of guys paying to cheer them on.

That sounded repugnant to me, and when I pressed Keith about it, he said it was something that happened once, a long time ago, and he did not want to discuss it. Later, when I asked him about it again, he said he must have been drunk and making stuff up, but I knew that was not the case.

Not long afterward, Keith came home drunk with a sackful of pornographic movies. He popped one in the VCR and sat down and started watching it. Trying to be a good wife, I sat and watched it with him for a few minutes, but, like most women, I find porno movies to be really pointless, to say nothing of being degrading to women.

"Come on, Keith, let's go to sleep," I said, but he insisted on sitting in front of that VCR for hours watching the porn.

I had heard Keith make vague references to pornographic magazines and videos, but it was always a reference to other people, with no names mentioned. I was sure he knew more than he let on.

Now when he turned up missing, I worried that he had gravitated to the ugly side of town—the strip of pornography shops on Dickerson Pike, not too far from where we lived.

Every town has an area like this—freedom of speech, First Amendment rights, and all that—even Nashville, with all its religious publishing and churches and gospel music. Every town has places where men duck down their heads and sneak into a corner and pick out some ugly magazine or book or video, stuff I cannot even imagine, that probably would make their wives or girlfriends, their mothers and their daughters, sick to their stomachs.

This man who was such an attentive lover, such a caring father, would start drinking, and want to wade through this filth.

This happened only a few other times, and only when he was drunk. But now my worries were out in the open.

I never had the slightest suspicion that Keith was indulging in sex with anybody else, but I did realize he had a curiosity about pornography that went back to his teenage years. The closest he would come to discussing it was to say it had nothing to do with us, that he loved me, there was nobody else, he never did anything—and he was telling the truth, as far as I could tell.

I think there were things, inner demons, that he was embarrassed to talk about. I don't know if they made Keith drink, but they were there—things that made him uncomfortable, things he could not forgive himself for, something, somewhere.

Was he introduced to pornography as a vulnerable teenager just going out on the road? There were rumors going around about a male musician having been caught with a man, and Keith casually said, "Well, I'd believe it," but he would never elaborate about it.

Was Keith attracted to men? I never saw any evidence of it. Was Keith abused by somebody close to him? I don't know. He would only say there were some things he wouldn't talk about.

My theory is that Keith was exposed to somebody else's bad habits, somebody else's bad patterns, at an early age, and even if he was just a bystander who knew something was going on, it bothered him.

As an adult, you can separate good things from bad, but a boy who'd never been out of eastern Kentucky might not have been able to make the distinction. Maybe he could have dealt with it when he was older, but as a young child, something scarred him.

I debate talking about this. I'm raising two children who loved Keith very much. But we live in a world where people are always making excuses, rationalizing. I'm all for healthy sex. But I have my doubts about the sex shops on the Dickerson Pikes in every town. They appeal to the baseness in all of us. So why do we allow them? Even if they have a legal right to exist, everybody has a right to resist them. I want my children to know that I do find this stuff ugly, that I feel sorry for people who need it.

I hope I can keep an eye on my children long enough to talk them through the temptations to drink excessively, to indulge other curiosities. I'm sorry that Keith was out unsupervised in his middle teens. I think he suffered for it, struggled with it, for the rest of his life.

I'm not telling these stories for the benefit of the tabloids. I'm telling them for the benefit of parents and children, me and my kids. Some things are just plain ugly. I'm sorry Keith was out there, exposed to them so young.

There were times we'd sit and talk about his frustrations with the business, and he'd say, "I'm so happy, I've never been so in love." It was almost as if he did not deserve it.

Raised as I was, in a big family, with priests and nuns teaching me, I had the feeling that love conquers all. You could be forgiven. You could overcome things. We were all brought up believing that. I kept telling myself, I'll love these demons right out of him. Drinking is not the answer. Life is all about having kids, loving someone, putting down roots, seeing the next day dawn.

Keith Whitley loved life as deeply as anybody I've ever seen. He was not some party animal who needed to be wearing a lampshade on his head and laughing at the top of his lungs.

Sometimes you're able to change those people. Keith had a serious addiction to alcohol and other substances, anything that would alter his mood, his consciousness.

What was the mood he wanted altered? What was behind his consciousness? I vowed I would love Keith Whitley until I found out.

CHAPTER TWELVE

I had promised myself that Morgan and I would find a place for the two of us to live and get out of Mom's hair. In June, Keith accompanied us to the Windsor Green in Goodlettsville and we inspected a cute little apartment.

"This would be a great place to live," he said. I had the feeling he was hinting at something.

"Do you think Morgan and I would be happy here?" I asked.

"Anybody would be happy here," Keith said.

"What about you?" I asked.

"I'd be the happiest of all," he said.

It seemed like the most natural thing in the world for me to say, "Why don't you think about moving in with us?" I envisioned a perfect little world, the three of us, starting life over. I never thought of rescuing Keith or changing his life. I just wanted the three of us to live under the same roof.

I started moving my belongings over during Fan Fair, the annual convention when performers meet with members of their fan clubs. I had asked Keith if he would sing to my fans, and he had agreed, and now we were trying to arrange it.

The phone rang and Don Light's assistant, Lynn Simpkins, said Keith had been drinking and was planning on driving out to my place. She said that would not be a good idea, considering the shape he was in.

I guess I did not take her advice very well, and I asked why she was taking such an interest in him. She did not take my comment very well, so now we had two cranky ladies going at each other on the phone.

I remember her saying things like: "You will never make Keith happy. Keith is an alcoholic. You will never be able to control him. You need to leave him alone and let him concentrate on his career."

Nobody had ever spoken to me that bluntly in my life, but I held my fire until Keith called me thirty minutes later.

"Who is this Lynn?" I asked, and I told him she had said some ugly things. He called Lynn at the office and said, "If you ever call Lorrie again, I can't predict what I will do. You work at my management office, but you have no right to talk like that."

Was Lynn jealous of me? Had there been something between them? I wondered then, although I realized later there was nothing like that.

Lynn Simpkins cared for Keith, she knew Kathi, and she had a history with worrying about his drinking. But I did not understand that then. Was it common wisdom that I would be bad for Keith's career? Or was everybody so worried about him that they feared any change in the structure, any potential loss of control? I felt there was a hostile tone in that woman's voice, but her words stayed with me.

Not too long afterward, Keith had another episode. I was performing at the General Jackson Showboat, called Keith, and discovered he had been drinking. By the time we reached him, his head was rolling back and forth. This time I could not get him out of the car, so I had to call an ambulance.

Once again, he lived to apologize, abjectly ashamed. By now, people were telling me that Keith was a binge drinker, who could go days or weeks without a drink, but then something would touch him off and he would have to drink until he was senseless.

I realized that I had walked into an ongoing problem, so I made a telephone call to Keith's counselor.

"Why are you attracted to Keith?" he asked me. "Have you ever thought about that?"

"He's charming, he's fun, got a great sense of humor, he's passionate, he's emotional, he's sensitive," I said.

"Many alcoholics are," the counselor said. "That's why it's so difficult to turn alcoholics away."

He continued: "Lorrie, what was your first husband like?"

"Passionate. Sensitive. Funny. And he tended to party," I replied.

He suggested there might be some kind of a pattern there, that I was attracted to the type of man who depended on me, that I felt I could make a difference in his life.

When we were finished with this brief conversation, I thought to myself, Hmmmph, this guy is crazy. He doesn't know us.

Now I can see that he had a point, but that is only with a great deal of hindsight. It's a pattern women can correct, if they recognize it. But I did not know that then. I was so enthralled with Keith that I just wanted to get him through the hard times.

Most of the time, things were fine. Keith would go weeks or months without drinking, and I would relax. But then something would touch him off again. He would start drinking, and I would try to stop him.

He would just wheedle, "Honey, please let me have a drink. Just let me have one drink."

I was afraid to take my eyes off him for a moment. If we were in bed at night, he would say to me, "Just let me go to the bathroom by myself," but I would refuse. There were a few times he was in the drinking mood that I insisted on staying with him in the bathroom even though he was sitting down—not a pretty thought, but that's the way it was. You never could trust him when drinking was on his mind.

Don Light was getting tired of the lies. Don tells the story of Fan Fair in June of 1986, just when Keith was riding high with "Miami My Amy" and Don took everybody out for dinner. He told Keith he detected signs of drinking, but Keith swore it was not true.

Keith even pulled out a little plastic container and made a big show of swallowing one of his Antabuse pills, which he knew would guarantee his being sick if he drank any alcohol in the next few days.

But right after allegedly swallowing the Antabuse, Keith went off and got drunk. Just passed out with half a vodka bottle in his car.

"You can get anything analyzed, even drinking water, if you pay for it," Don said. "We got that plastic container and sent the pills out for analysis. It cost us fifty dollars to find out that they were vitamin pills. Vitamin C or D, I forget. Keith was deliberately lying to us. I can tolerate mistakes, but he had been preparing to get drunk, and that really ticked me off.

"I tried to do things by the book," Don added, "but now I was having to redo bookings, and I just didn't want to do that."

Don did not want to harm Keith. He had another manager in mind. Don had already introduced Keith to Jack McFadden, a crusty old-timer who has been managing Buck Owens for over thirty years. Jack also had managed Ray Price, Merle Haggard, and Freddie Hart, and had eventually moved from Bakersfield, California, to Nashville.

Jack liked to say that the first time he had ever heard Keith was six-thirty one morning when Ralph Emery introduced him on television and said Keith was "gonna blaze a trail." Jack wasn't impressed with "the scrawny new kid" until he heard Keith sing "Does Fort Worth Ever Cross Your Mind?"

At that point, Jack liked to say, "I hollered at my wife, who was still asleep, 'Hey, Jo, wake up and listen to this.' "

That same day, Jack added, he had been sitting at the Pancake Pantry where a lot of the country music people start their working day, and he had told a bunch of people—including, he thought, Eddy Arnold—about this great kid he had seen that morning on Ralph's show.

"I wonder who manages him," Jack said.

"I do," Don Light had replied.

Keith was up for the new artist award at the Academy of County Music affair in Los Angeles, and Don asked Jack to accompany Keith. The two of them got along well on the trip, and a week or two later, Don Light finally packed it in.

"I had a meeting to discuss the settlement," Don said. "Keith told me, 'I'm sorry.' He seemed scared. He told me that the last time he overdosed, the doctors had told him, 'You came very close to dying.' Keith said, 'I don't want to die.' To this day, I believe he did not plan to die."

Keith's career was at the crossroads that summer of 1986. Joe Galante, the strong-willed head of the RCA records division in Nashville, was a believer in Keith's talent, but Keith was not making any money for RCA or himself.

"Keith was still a kid in many ways," Joe said recently. "He had this smile, this glow, that he was just happy doing these things. You always felt he was totally sincere. You could see he loved it."

Mary Lou Turner got to listen to Keith a lot, and she thought he was terrific. But she felt he never came to grips with how much talent he had.

"I heard him on the radio from the *Opry*," Mary Lou recalled recently. "The next time I talked to him, I asked, 'Who played guitar on that one?' and Keith said he had. I told him he was a great guitar player and he said, 'Do you really think so?' Keith did not know how good he was. He lacked self-esteem."

Maybe this was part of the problem of being Keith Whitley. He just did not fit in. Was he bluegrass? Was he country? Joe Galante, trying to sell records all over the country, all over the world, had to worry about where Keith fit in.

"Over time, Keith built friendships with radio people, with song writers," Joe Galante said. "You could see somebody growing. But meanwhile, we were struggling. I was thinking, Man, am I the only person who believes in this guy?"

Joe still talks about going to a rock 'n' roll business conference at a resort just above New York City, and bringing Keith up to play for all the different musical tastes in the company.

"When Keith was finished," Joe recalls, "I asked Gene Simmons from the rock group, Kiss, what he thought, and he said, 'I like anything that's done well, but this isn't done well, this is done *great.*' I mean, Keith had the ability to communicate. These great blue eyes that said 'I love you, I'm going to do everything for you.' "

Most of the time, Keith was a solid citizen who tried to stay sober. Joe remembers having lunch at Mario's and seeing a panicked look on Keith's face after the first bite of salad.

"Is there any wine in this dressing?" Keith asked.

The waiter said the dressing did indeed have a wine base.

"I can't have this, I'm on Antabuse, and this is going to make me sick," Keith said.

Joe and Keith had to take a break from lunch while Keith went outside and walked around until he felt better.

Joe said he never saw Keith drinking. Yet we were constantly reacting to problems Keith had caused. His drinking was dominating our lives. We were going to have to do something.

We just didn't know what.

CHAPTER THIRTEEN

None of us were prepared to deal with whatever was troubling Keith. He could not stop his binges, and no amount of talking either by me or other people who loved him could get through to him.

Joe Galante was getting nervous about rescuing Keith again.

"I'm an executive, I don't know about alcoholism," he said with a helpless shrug of his shoulders.

Blake Mevis, who had seen Keith go through three treatment centers, recalls a meeting at which he feared Joe was going to cut Keith from the label.

"I said, 'If you take away the drinking and the drugs, we wouldn't have any legends at all,' " Blake said, perhaps exaggerating slightly, to make the point that Keith had a rare talent, and that he was worth another effort.

RCA had already bankrolled three expensive sessions; you could understand Joe Galante being a little reticent about spending any more company money on a man who did not seem able to help himself.

Some large companies, I have learned, have addiction counselors on staff, while others have programs for automatic referrals.

This was not the case for Keith, but Joe Galante, Jack McFadden, and Don Cook did the right thing by him.

Joe and Jack spoke to the therapist who knew Keith best, and he advised them to confront Keith, to threaten that unless he got help, Joe would suspend him.

"You're going to lose your record deal with Joe Galante," Jack warned him. I could see that bothered Keith, and he would immediately promise to stop drinking. Which he did—until the next binge.

Joe tried to threaten him, too.

"I'd say, 'You're on suspension,' " Joe has said, "but I had a fake bat, so to speak. The reality is, none of these things was really effective."

I offered to go to meetings of Alcoholics Anonymous with Keith, but that was out of the question. In Keith's view of the world, I was not supposed to go to Al-Anon, either. He was afraid I would come back from an Al-Anon meeting and have a new, hardened attitude toward him.

I think now that he was afraid I would leave him, but I know at that stage in my life, I was so much in love with him that I could never have practiced any form of "tough love."

Maybe he was more right than he knew, but it never came close to that. He blustered and cajoled and pleaded and begged, and so I stayed home and tried to love him into not drinking. Which did not work.

The next step was to recommend that Keith go to a treatment center out of town, where he would be treated as a patient rather than somebody stopping in for a visit.

This is a frightening thing for anybody to hear. Treatment centers are for "other people"—drunks and dope addicts, people with serious problems. Keith could not admit that he could not handle alcohol, and he resisted going to a center. Finally, Jack warned him that his life and his career were in jeopardy, and that he would have to go to another clinic.

Jack checked around and chose the Hazelden Foundation in Center City, Minnesota, about fifty miles outside the Twin Cities—one of the most reputable treatment centers in the country. No center claims to have a high recovery rate. The fact is, addicts slip over and over again. But the experts recommended Hazelden, and we were eager to see what they could do.

RCA did not have a company policy, and the money would come directly from their operating funds.

"We did what we could to support him," Galante recalls. "We weren't making money on Keith. We weren't selling that many records. He hadn't gone gold yet, he was still struggling; but you have to support the artist, he's family. You do everything you possibly can."

I have never felt so helpless in my life. Keith had a terrible sickness, and my love meant nothing. He was not a social drunk, a social alcoholic. He had some private disease, one that struck him when he was alone.

There were plenty of examples of people who had gone to treatment centers: Betty Ford, Elizabeth Taylor, Billy Carter (the president's brother), plenty of athletes with drug and alcohol problems, everybody knew public examples of people who had learned to live sober lives.

Keith did not have one company or one team that could threaten him with unemployment. He was an entertainer, a man in the spotlight. He was used to being alone, and he treated alcoholism as he would treat a case of stage fright. He'd take care of it himself. He was isolated, trapped in the glare. Only he could handle it.

But we all tried. In the summer of 1986, Joe and Jack told Keith he had to fly to the Twin Cities and enter Hazelden. I was not part of the confrontation, but Keith and I talked about it when he came home that day.

He agreed to go, but you could see it was unwillingly.

"I don't really give a damn about this. I'm just going to breeze through this so I can come back. I don't want to lose my record deal."

He said he was doing it to make me happy, and I figured that anything that got him to the center was fine, as long as he got help.

On the night before Keith was due to go to Minnesota, I came home from doing a Statler Brothers video and I saw two dozen roses. Keith stood up and hugged me and kissed me as if it was the first time. Then he said, "Sit down, I've got another present for you. I wrote you a song today."

He took out his guitar and sang a melancholy love song:

"Tell Lorrie I love her,
"Tell Lorrie I need her,
"And if I leave this old world,
"Tell her she's the only girl for me."

It was so sad, and so sweet, that I started crying. Keith had barely begun to tap his own emotions as a songwriter, but here was a song wrenched deep from his soul, words of loneliness, maybe even desperation, of a man who loved me deeply. It was a beautiful song, but it was more than a song. It was a confession of love, of need, of sadness, that Keith could never make in front of other people.

"It's beautiful," I said, when I could find my voice.

The next day I drove him to the airport. He kept insisting that he was doing this under duress. I tried to tell him that I would come up and be with him, that this was important for all of us, but he took the attitude that we were setting him up, that he was only doing this to humor us. I hoped the people at Hazelden could reach him.

Jack McFadden flew with him to the Twin Cities and

escorted him to the center, to make sure he was checked in, but then Jack had to leave. Keith had to go through the early process himself.

The way I understand it, all addicts checking into a center must go through early medical and psychological evaluation. Then they take individual and group therapy, with trained counselors and other addicts prodding each other to discuss why they drink. Most centers try to understand the emotional feelings that lead somebody like Keith to drink, as well as the chemical imbalances that make drink so dangerous to some people. Would they get at Keith's demons?

I also knew that most clinics have a family week, when people close to the patient come up and confront the patient about the drinking. These sessions get pretty emotional, as people bring up their feelings about how the drinking affected them. I knew this was necessary to purge the demons from Keith.

"Keith, I'll come up whenever it's time," I said, but he was dead-set against my coming.

We talked every night on the phone, and he sent me postcards or letters every day, very sweet letters. In one letter he said, "I just finished talking to you early this morning and I came back to my room and sat down and thought about how much I love you. Honey, I have never felt this way about anybody or anything before."

In another letter, he wrote, "I can't believe how complete you make me and how complete this relationship is. The only thing left is our getting married, and that won't be too long."

However, in all his letters, Keith never discussed what they were doing at Hazelden, or talked about any changes in him, or insights into his problem. It was as if he was serving his time, and couldn't wait to get out. Also, he absolutely refused to have anybody go up there. On that, he could not be budged.

On the day of Keith's return, toward the end of August, Jack and I went to the airport. Jack was bringing a box of Goo Goo candy bars, which were Keith's favorite. Most alcoholics love chocolate, I found out later.

Jack and I went out to the gate to meet the flight. I was so anxious to see Keith, hoping that our life together was going to be all right now.

There he was, weaving from side to side, a big goofy smile on his face. Loaded, just loaded.

Keith spotted us and his smile got even broader and goofier.

"Well, if it isn't my two old buddies," he chortled.

"That son of a bitch," Jack muttered.

Keith was trying to pretend he was sober. I felt a pang of fear and sadness, but at the same time I could not help but smile, it was so ridiculous. I felt, Here we go again.

"Keith, when did you have your last drink?" Jack asked, as we hustled him toward the baggage claim.

"Why, I haven't had a drop to drink," Keith insisted, but you could smell it a yard away.

Jack was extremely upset. Entertainers often think their managers and agents are just in it for the money, and we had our share of complaints about Jack, but I know for a fact that this man loved Keith the way a father loves a son. It had to hurt to see all our hopes vanish the moment Keith staggered off the plane.

"What the hell were you thinking about?" Jack snapped. "They just spent $15,000 on you and you're getting off the airplane half snookered?"

When Keith was drunk, he was a different person—flippant, disinterested, unreachable. You could not reason with him. He was too far gone.

"It's just a good thing Galante's not here," Jack muttered.

Keith insisted on driving home, but we would not let him. When we got there, I took his toiletries bag into the bathroom and I found ten little bottles of Jack Daniel's, all empty.

"Keith, what about these?" I asked.

"Oh, those guys," he said with a laugh, as if the other patients at Hazelden had put them there as a trick on him. He was too looped to have a conversation, too looped to do anything.

After the long absence, I had been looking forward to making love with Keith, had imagined what it would be like to be alone with him, laughing and talking, knowing things were all right now.

I did not want a new or different Keith Whitley. I loved the sweet and passionate man I knew. But I had envisioned Keith coming home and saying, "I'm better now. I learned some things. I don't have to drink." Now he was cockeyed drunk, and love was out of the question.

I was back on guard again, protecting him from himself. I knew how he got when he was drunk. On our first night together again, I was worried that if I fell asleep, he would go out looking for alcohol, looking for whatever he needed on those terrible benders, so I hid his keys, locked up the apartment, and guided him to our bed.

I knew I could not sleep soundly unless I was confident he was not roaming around, so I took the belt from my terry cloth robe, tied his leg to my leg and made a secure knot. Then I fell asleep, by this time more weary than sad or angry.

At two in the morning I felt a tug on my leg.

"Keith, what are you doing?" I asked.

"I've got to go to the bathroom," he said.

There was no way I was letting him in there by himself. I suspected he would even drink any toiletry with a trace of alcohol. That's how bad it was.

"I've got to go," he said, urgently. He was too drunk to untie the belt around our legs.

"I'm going with you," I said, hobbling alongside him, our ankles tied together, and I stood next to him at the toilet while he peed. Then we went back to bed and fell asleep.

The next morning, knowing he had not had any alcohol in over twelve hours, I gave him his Antabuse pill. It was as if he had never gone to the treatment center. Everything had failed—him, the center, me, us, the process.

After that, whenever I would bring up Hazelden or Cumberland Heights, Keith would say, "Man, you don't know what I'm going through." I'm sure he felt terrible pressure, but beyond that there was some stubbornness about opening up. He refused to do it. Keith was afraid to reveal himself. Even at Hazelden, he had managed to get through those weeks without opening up.

People say it doesn't have to be that way. A friend of mine tells about the addiction treatment center he attended, which was run totally by recovering addicts. (They never say "recovered," it's always "recovering," meaning that the process is never finished.)

"At the place I went, if you tried to cover up, the head counselor, an addict himself, was like a bulldog. He would put his face into yours and say, 'Don't bullshit me!' You either walked out or you said, 'Whoa, this guy knows something about me.'

"Hazelden is a good place," my friend told me, years later. "But somehow Keith slipped through."

That was exactly how I felt when Keith came back. I tried to ask him what had happened there, what they'd talked about, but his response was, "Oh, nothing. They tried to get me to make up stuff." More likely, they had tried to get him to talk about himself, to tell the truth, and he had resisted.

He had refused to let any members of his family come up. I can't speak for his mom or other members of the family, but I'm sure they had to know something about his drinking, about the reasons behind it. At the very least, they would have reacted to seeing him in a treatment center, and some emotions would have come through. I know I would have discussed some of the things I had seen—the overdosing, the binges, the lack of control. The sad thing is that Keith's family and I never did get together and confront this. Keith divided us, and he divides us to this day.

He did bring home some things he had written at Hazelden. In those writings he said it used to bother him that his dad drank. But other than that, Keith revealed almost nothing of himself.

He was home and I had the panicky feeling that something was terribly wrong, something had failed. Now we would have to deal with the failure ourselves.

We never did give him the Goo Goos.

CHAPTER FOURTEEN

Keith soon discovered a kindred soul in my family—Lane Palmer, Beth's husband, the rogue of the family. Although Lane was terrible to Beth, he quickly became Keith's buddy.

They met one Sunday night before Keith and I were married, when we visited their house. Nobody knew the extent of Keith's problems back then.

"We even offered him a drink," Beth recalled not long ago. "We didn't know. He drank one C&C and seemed fine. He did say, 'I'll just have a little one,' but I didn't see anything in that. He also drank a lot of coffee, but that didn't mean anything, either. Mom was out there, too."

I remember just being in ecstasy, telling them about my new boyfriend, and trying to explain, "Oh, he's the guy who sings 'Miami My Amy,' " and everybody went "Oh." Then I explained that he came out of the bluegrass bands in eastern Kentucky, and that didn't do much for them. But they saw how crazy I was about him.

Keith and Lane hit it off right away, bonded by motorcycles. Keith had built his own back in Kentucky but had sold it to finance his move to Nashville.

"Keith loved Harleys," Lane recalled recently. "He wanted a

new one and wanted it bad, but he wasn't making a whole lot of money yet. I got a real nice new one and I didn't tell him because he might want one, and here I am hogging the Harley market."

Today, Lane has been sober for a while. Every so often, he will talk about his wild days, as a way of reminding himself what he does not want to be anymore. He's a body-shop man and has never been an entertainer, but he's got a big, deep voice and is a born storyteller.

"One day Keith called me and said he managed to get himself a new one," Lane added. "I came and found out, independent of me, he had gotten one just like mine. I didn't much care for the windscreen he put on, but aside from that, it was cosmic."

Every so often, Keith and Lane would take off on their Harleys.

"There wasn't a whole lot of people I'd rather go riding with," Lane said. "Have somebody ahead of me or on my tail." Lane said he could always trust Keith not to do anything stupid on his Harley.

They occasionally played guitars together, and Keith once gave Lane the black Gibson he used in "I'm No Stranger to the Rain," but their friendship was based on Lane's not being fascinated by Keith's being a performer.

"I'm not too crazy about the circus atmosphere," Lane has said. "I liked it better when we were just all hanging around, without the hoopla. I've known a lot of performers. Even wrestlers, when they're working, they're not your buddy, they're somebody else. They're getting ready to perform.

"But Keith was just as sweet a son of a bitch as came down the pike. A crazy son of a bitch, but sweet. He always wanted to know more about things. But give him a drink and he didn't know he had a wife, a home, a career, anything that mattered.

"Keith was up for anything when he was drinking. I never

started drinking with him but if he was drinking, hell, I'd drink with him. I was the adult. If things got out of hand, I'd be the designated driver. He had a lot to lose by drinking. Galante was going to ditch him, so was McFadden, so the best I could do at that time was try to keep him out of trouble, out of the public eye. And I wanted to maintain a low profile myself.

"That sweet part of Keith, I really liked," Lane concluded. "That wild side that came out when he was drinking, I was accustomed to that. Want to pitch a bitch? That's all right, too."

The fact is, Keith and Lane did not see each other that often, but they were the kind of buddies who got together when there was mischief to be done. They did some drugs together, too, although Keith had little interest in drugs. His chemical of choice was alcohol. Lane, as he has since explained, had more universal tastes.

The amazing thing is that Beth was married to him for so many years. For a long time, he was using dope and she didn't know a thing about it. He could afford dope, but she could not afford groceries.

Keith really liked Lane, but he hated the way Lane treated Beth. At his worst, Keith was never abusive to me, never yelled, never touched me, just came home messed up, slinking into bed like a whipped puppy.

Lane, on the other hand, when he was ingesting the chemicals or injecting cocaine into his arm, had some pit bull in him.

"What is there about the Morgan girls?" Lane recently mused. "They seem to attract drunks and dope fiends."

There is some truth to that. Our track record has not been so great. All four girls plus Marty have each been divorced at least once.

Sometimes I wonder what it means that all of us have had broken marriages, with the Lanes and the Keiths in our lives. Mom and Dad were married over twenty years before he died so young. We had this *Ozzie and Harriet* or *Leave It to Beaver*–like existence. The kids were around for meals. We'd pray first. Never a drinking family. I never saw Dad take a drink.

We thought all men were going to be like Dad. We wanted all that Mom and Dad had, and we searched for it. As soon as we felt good about somebody, we said, "This is it. The other one was the mistake."

We were all hungry for that kind of relationship, but it just didn't pan out that way for us. Some days Beth and I talk about it. Dad spoiled us, Beth will say. Why did Dad have to be so good?

On the other hand, I can see the attraction we had to these charismatic guys riding in on their Harleys. Dad was a grown-up in a suit, driving a Lincoln. Dad was the fifties. We were not rebelling against him, not that I can see, but now it was the eighties, and Beth and I had our motorcycle men.

Lane was trouble. He'll be the first to tell you, now that he's lived to tell the tale. But there was also an air of competence to him. I saw that the day he disarmed the kid with the pistol. Lane could take care of himself. I generally felt good when Keith was in Lane's company. Poor Keith needed people watching over him.

My hope at the time was that Lane could keep Keith's wheels on the road.

CHAPTER FIFTEEN

Most of the time, Keith was not drinking and our life together was wonderful. Keith was raised Protestant, but he came to love the mysteries of the Catholic religion. At night we would kneel down and hold hands, silently saying whatever prayers we knew. He loved the rosary, and sometimes we would lie in bed and I would explain the sorrow, the agony in the garden, the scourging, the crucifixion and the death, all the Hail Marys, and he would be in tears from the Catholic vision of the sadness of the cross.

Keith felt things very deeply. I don't tell this story to try to preach my religion to anybody, but merely to show how Keith would feel the pain as we talked about Jesus being literally nailed to a cross.

There were also many hours of great joy. Months after we met, I still found Keith to be a wonderful lover, so considerate and sensitive. We could not get enough of each other, each night better than the last. He was no sodden drunk; he was hardly ever too far gone to make love. Except for the rare times when he would go on a binge, Keith was incredibly aware of me, kind, and funny. We would just look at each other sometimes and wait for the first opportunity. Unbelievable. Hours at a time.

One night in early September, we were in bed, making love, and Keith whispered to me, "I want you to be my wife; I want you to have our child," in such a beautiful romantic way, not just something you say to turn on your partner, but deep from his heart.

We were both crying as we finished, and then something happened that I had never felt before. I knew—just absolutely knew—I had conceived right then and there. I felt this magical lifting moment, and I knew. Lying there in bed, I told Keith, and he said again, "I never thought I'd ever say this, but I want you to be the mother of my child."

Two weeks later, sure enough, my period was late and I came down with morning sickness. Keith rushed out to get the pregnancy test kit, and I tested positive. Keith was so thrilled, as if having a baby with me was a blessing beyond any dream.

Every morning as we got up, he would talk to my stomach, even before I began showing. He said the baby was going to be a boy, and he named him Jesse. I don't know how he knew, he just knew. We went over middle names—eventually selecting Keith—and he was so proud. He would put his head right against me and talk to Jesse, and sing to him.

Before people knew our plans, they could sense that Keith and I were getting serious. Keith wanted me to keep singing, and sometimes I would travel with him and perform on his shows.

He asked me to be in the video of his song "Homecoming '63," so we went up to Franklin, Tennessee and shot it at the high school.

I was still working with Ralph Emery on *Nashville Now*. One day Keith was on the show to promote his latest record, and a lady from the audience asked if it was true we were "courtin'."

More than that, Keith said. We were going to get married. The audience cheered.

Well, not quite everybody.

I went down to Florida to play a date for a friend of ours named Bobby Lord, who used to have a show in Nashville during my father's era.

While I was visiting, Bobby said to me, "I don't know you real well, but I feel I should tell you this as a friend of your dad. I hope you're getting ready to marry your best friend, because over the years, the sex appeal goes down, and you've got to be sure you're ready to spend the rest of your life with someone. If it's your best friend, you can handle anything."

I reassured him that Keith was surely my best friend, but his words stayed with me. He was talking about qualities that would bind people together for a lifetime. These are not things every young couple thinks about.

We began making plans. Keith called me from the road and said he wanted us to have a house before we got married, so I called a friend of my sister's and we found a three-bedroom house with a pool, very homey, in a nice neighborhood. I knew Keith would love it. Of course, it was more than we could afford. Houses are always more than you can afford.

But my friend Mary Lou Turner had already come over and had decided what color we were going to paint each room, and which room was going to be the baby's. She had everything planned.

Keith called me and said Jack McFadden was coming out to look at it. Jack is a great guy, but he was somewhere between a realist and a pessimist, so I was not surprised when Jack said, "It's a great little house for you, but I don't know how you're going to get the money."

Nevertheless, Jack was delegated to arrange a mortgage from a Nashville bank, which proved impossible. Keith and I were very disappointed, but then I remembered that my friend Ruth had married a banker in West Palm Beach, Florida, who hated country music but knew I was Ruth's best friend.

It was embarrassing, but I told Ruth, "I understand if you can't do it, but could you see if Jay will give us a down payment for the house?" Jay called us back within an hour and said, "How much do you need? Consider it done." It turned out to be $40,000, and with that generous loan from a friend, Keith and I were able to buy our first house.

Keith came back off the road, went out to look at the house, and was delighted.

"Oh, I can make love to you in this room, and I can make love to you in that room, and I can make love to you over there. . . ." Well, you get the picture.

Eventually, he also noticed other features like the pool and the outdoor grill, and he promised to make me the best hamburgers and steaks. He was elated. He was also getting a lot of bookings, his career starting to take off. He would call me five times a day, six times. I would say, "Hello," and he would say, "I love you more than anything in this world."

He wanted to do everything for me, and he also wanted me to go back to work after I had the baby, so he wanted to hire a nanny to help with Morgan and the baby. We hired a woman named Margaret, from Guyana, who said she was a healer, a midwife, and a cook with a knowledge of healthy diets. We had two stipulations: that Margaret be able to swim and to drive.

After we hired her, she admitted, "I am taking driving lessons but I do not know how to swim." By that time, Keith loved her so much that she was here for a while. Margaret always had a Bible with her and she would talk with us about the importance of marriage.

It did not take long to realize that she did not know how to cook—at least not for American palates. Most things she cooked were unidentifiable. But Margaret was part of the family—more than she might have imagined.

One day, I was outside and Keith called on the phone; Margaret picked it up and said, "Hello?"

Keith promptly gave his normal greeting: "I love you more than anything in the world."

"Oh, Mr. Wheetley, this is Margaret," she said with a giggle.

Keith was so embarrassed that from then on, whenever he called, he would say, "Margaret?" unless he absolutely knew it was me.

Mary Lou and I painted the house, stripped the carpet, papered the bedrooms. Her favorite color was lavender, which she promptly used to paint Morgan's bedroom, where we installed a small white bed.

We didn't have much. One of our prize possessions was a green crushed-velvet chair that rocked, and that cost one hundred dollars, a lot of money for us.

Having borrowed money for the down payment, we were in over our heads financially, so Jack put us under the watchful eye of Keith's accountant, Kirke Martin, whom I could not stand.

Everything I bought, even a lightbulb, I had to clear through Kirke. If I needed a new brassiere, I would call Kirke and say I needed twenty dollars, and he would ask why, and I would have to say, "To get a new bra, that's why!" Because I was the one staying home and doing the decorating, I had to deal with Kirke regularly, yet he felt he was responsible mostly to Keith.

We would go around in circles. I would call Keith and say, "Kirke won't give me any money," and Keith would call Kirke, who would say, "Keith, you don't have any money," which usually did not satisfy Keith, who would instruct Kirke, "Well, you take care of it." (Kirke was so conscientious that he works with me to this day.)

Keith and I were short on money, but we were having a great time. A bunch of our friends helped us move our belongings from the apartment into the house. People were around all the time. And Keith did not mind going out to the bus stop every day to pick up Margaret.

There was another danger sign before the wedding. My doctor, William Wadlington, who was my pediatrician and still treats me for migraines and allergies, told me that he had never met Keith, but that he had heard he was an alcoholic. He said my life would not be good married to somebody like that. I remember being annoyed at him for volunteering that, although I like and respect him and never stopped going to him. I remembered the words, even though I disregarded the advice.

About two weeks before the wedding, Keith and I got antsy with each other, just couldn't look at each other. It wasn't that we were mad at each other, we just were not ourselves. We felt different, weird.

Jack McFadden called out to the house and asked how things were, and I said, "Jack, I don't even know if we should get married."

"I'll be right out there," Jack said.

Jack sat us down in our bedroom like we were children. I was crying and Keith was crying, and Jack asked, "What is going on here? Keith, do you love Lorrie?" and Keith said, "With all my heart," and Jack asked, "Lorrie, do you love Keith?" and I said, "More than anything in this world."

Jack thought about this for a moment, then he said, "This is normal. Jo and I went through it. It's prewedding jitters. I'm glad I was here to point this out. You guys are the picture of love." He made us hug each other and he got us laughing and then he told us to go out to dinner and forget about it, which we promptly did.

We went out to the Chinese Moon over in the Rivergate Mall and we ordered virgin bloody marys, and Keith said, "I'd like to make a toast." I was expecting something sweet and romantic now that we had gotten over our prewedding jitters, and Keith raised his glass and said, "Here's mud in your eye." Beautiful. Very romantic. I started bawling all over again, and I told Keith I did not appreciate his sense of humor, but after that we were back to where we had been.

We set the wedding date for November 22. Because I had been married before, we could not get married at a Catholic church, so we went scouting around for churches, but none of them seemed—how can I put this?—quite godly enough. Finally, we went to the Calvary United Methodist Church at Green Hill, a very pretty church. Both of us felt at peace there, so we made arrangements to have the wedding there.

We thought it would be corny for us to sing at our own wedding, so we asked our old friend, Curtis (Mister Harmony) Young, who used to sing backup on all my dad's records, and now was singing backup for Keith.

One of the songs we wanted Curtis to sing was "Tell Lorrie I Love Her," that sad song Keith had played to me the night before he went to Hazelden. Keith had never played the song in public, and hardly anybody knew it existed.

One evening, while Morgan was inside watching television, Keith turned on our rudimentary tape recorder and strummed his guitar and in his hoarse, sad voice, he recorded the song.

The tape was not so great. In fact, you could hear the television squawking in the next room. But it would be fine for Mister Harmony to learn Keith's song.

The night before the wedding, we were having a rehearsal dinner at the Stockyard Restaurant downtown, and I found out from Keith's sister, Mary, that his mother wasn't coming.

I could understand Mr. Whitley's not coming because he was ill. I thought that maybe Mrs. Whitley felt guilty about leaving him for a few days. But I also knew it would devastate Keith if his mother did not come, so Mary and I went to a pay phone and I said, I hope politely, "Your son will never forgive you if you're not here." I wasn't trying to be mean, but I needed to get my point across. I must have, because she was there by the next morning.

I don't remember where Keith stayed that night, but it was with one of his friends, just to keep up the tradition of the bride and groom not seeing each other on the day of the wedding. Whoever he stayed with, he behaved himself. He was so thrilled, so happy, that he never touched a drop that whole time.

I wore a white dress, and gave no signs of carrying the baby, although most people already knew.

I remember being nervous, the way I am before concerts. Mary Lou remembers it a little stronger than that.

"A few minutes before the wedding," Mary Lou said recently, "Lorrie came up to me and said, 'Lucy, I can't do this.' Even though *she's* really Lucy, that's what she calls me. I told her it would be all right, and she went ahead. But she was very nervous."

I don't remember telling Mary Lou I couldn't go through with it, although maybe I did say something like that out of sheer nerves. I knew I wanted to get married to Keith. I was so happy, so fulfilled. And the ceremony was beautiful.

My brother, Marty, gave me away, just as he had at the first wedding, with Morgan, my nephew Aaron, and my sisters taking part in it. Keith had six attendants in gray tuxes, including his best man, his producer, Blake Mevis. Mom was there with Paul, and Keith's mom made it and seemed to have a great time, chatting with Ralph Emery and all our friends.

Curtis Young's rendition of "Tell Lorrie I Love Her," made everybody stop breathing, it was so beautiful.

The reception was at the Conservatory, downstairs at the Opryland Hotel, and we had a harpist named Lloyd Lindreth, along with a guitar and bass. It was magnificent, something out of a fairy tale.

We took a short honeymoon down to Destin, on the Gulf Coast of Florida, where we walked on the beach, talking about Morgan, and Jesse to come, ate a lot of seafood, and celebrated this marriage, which seemed so right to us. And then we came home to reality.

We were a couple now, a unit, which was great for us, but apparently threatening to other people.

Every so often I would travel with Keith and his band, and I would sing a few songs. One night in San Diego, before a show on an aircraft carrier, I was sitting on Keith's bus and I heard one of the musicians, Mike Chamberlain, saying, "Boys, I think we ought to get more money for backing up another artist." And everybody else was going, "Yeah-yeah." Mike added, "I mean, after all, what are we, Keith Whitley and Everybody Else's Band?"

Needless to say, I got teed off, and I said, "Well, gee, Mike, I am only his wife."

Today, Mike works with me and is like part of the family. Every time we mention it, we laugh. I say, "Mike, if I had remembered that, I wouldn't have hired you."

The musicians I could handle, because I was one of them. You just speak your mind, and that's it. I could tell that Carson Chamberlain, Mike's cousin, hated my guts, but we would have to get along. Carson and Mike were responsible for Keith taking his Antabuse, and they were successful, most of the time. Mike was always kind to my face, and that's all that mattered.

The wives and the girlfriends were a different matter. They had been hanging around together for months and years, going back to the band's origins in eastern Kentucky. They knew each other and were real tight. I was a threat to all of them because I was from Nashville. Because of Dad, I was part of the history and the structure of the music industry. Not only that, I had paid my dues coming up in all the clubs and lounges. I was a performer, I was not a hanger-on, *and* I was also Keith's wife. This was a recipe for conflict.

I'd walk into a room and know they had been talking about me. Rita Chamberlain, Carson's wife, annoyed me with everything she said. Even when we were pretending to be friendly, she had a way of saying things that just ticked me off. She liked to talk about clothes, and she would say, "Well, you and I are the same size," which was a joke because basically I was a Volkswagen and she was a semi. I know I shouldn't say this, but that is one woman I truly cannot stand.

Mike's wife at the time, Pam, was pretty nice. One time the band was on the road and I was playing at the General Jackson and did not have anybody to go with; Keith suggested I give Pam a call. She agreed to go with me. We were sitting around the dressing room talking about the band and the women, and she said, "The truth is, they talk ugly about you." Then she added, "But please don't say I told you."

That night Keith called when the bus made a stop on the way to Branson, Missouri. He could tell something was bothering me, but I didn't want to talk about it while he was away.

"Lorrie, tell me what's wrong," he persisted, so I told him what Pam had said.

"That does it," he said. "I'm going into that bus and I'm going to fire the whole bunch of them."

"Now, Keith, that's exactly why I didn't want to tell you. You can't fire the whole band when you have shows to perform. Plus, no matter what Carson may think of me, he loves you, and he'd do anything for you, and that's important when you're out on the road. So just forget about it."

However, Keith went directly to the bus and called Mike out of his bunk—and that man loves to sleep.

"Get out here, right now!" Keith screamed, and Mike came stumbling out. Keith started yelling at him, saying he should fire every last one of them right now.

A couple of times Keith headed toward the front to tell the driver to stop and let everybody out. Mike's a big guy with a dark beard and a deep voice, and he relies on reason rather than force and emotion. At that moment, he needed to calm Keith down.

Mike had visions of all the band members standing on the highway out in the Ozarks somewhere, trying to hitch back to Nashville.

"Keith, this isn't the way to go," Mike said. "Let's talk about this and if you still feel this way when we get to Branson, at least we can catch a plane."

Keith fumed all the way to Branson. Finally he said that wives and girlfriends were no longer allowed to travel with the band, nor were they allowed backstage or in the dressing room.

"From now on, they are just like any other guest," Keith said. "They get good seats and they sit out front and they wait for you outside."

Randy Hayes quit over it, saying, "If my wife isn't welcome, then neither am I."

After that blowup, a couple of the women called me and said they wanted to get along. They sounded as if they meant it, which was fine with me.

When they got back into town, Keith brought Carson and Rita into the office and he asked them if they had a problem with me. Rita said, "Yes, I think she's a bitch." And she walked out. But I didn't want Keith to fire Carson just because Rita and I didn't get along.

Right after that, Keith pulled one of his major-league drunks. The stress would set him off, would get him feeling ugly, and he would head straight for the alcohol. And he wouldn't stop. He couldn't handle the bad feelings inside. Mike still has the tapes of Keith onstage, slurring his words, thinking he was cool, but out of control.

They were out west somewhere, and Mike and Carson cleaned out Keith's hotel room because by that time they understood that he would drink anything with alcohol—after-shave lotion, cough medicine, you name it. This went way beyond merely protecting the talent, the-show-must-go-on kind of thing. This was love for one of their buddies. Then they sat outside his room and would not let him out.

"I mean it, Mike, you'd better move, you big son of a bitch," Keith shouted.

Mike just laughed at him.

"I'm gonna fire you," Keith said.

"You can fire me but I ain't moving," Mike said.

"Get these SOBs away from my room," Keith would scream.

"Keith, you know you can't drink," Mike said.

"I'm not gonna drink," Keith said.

They knew he would say anything, just to get out the door and vanish into the night. Keith was around five feet nine inches tall, and Mike is about six feet three and a half inches, two-forty, so Mike leaned against the door and would not let Keith out. They sat outside his door and kept Keith Whitley alive for another night.

CHAPTER SIXTEEN

We had a little unfinished business. Keith had been going around calling the baby "Jesse" and "my son," but we had no evidence to support it.

I was praying, "Dear God, please let it be a boy," because I wanted Keith to be happy. This was not exactly like China or India, where your whole life, your whole future, is wrapped up in having a boy instead of a girl. As far as Keith was concerned, he already had a daughter he loved, and that was Morgan. Now it was time for a son. I had no problem with that. We're long past the days when a man felt a son was more important than a daughter.

I was fairly confident it was a boy because I felt different than I had with Morgan. If anybody wants to come up with the scientific evidence that boys and girls feel exactly the same, I'll believe them. But I knew I had a boy. I just needed the proof.

We went to get the ultrasound done, and the doctor asked, "Do you really want to know what the baby is before I look?"

I could see the look on Keith's face. He was never one to hide his emotions. He was all wrapped up in this being a boy.

"Yes," I said, "we want to know."

The technician had some device placed against my stomach,

and the image was projected onto a screen. A human form flashed on the screen.

"Well, he's a boy," the doctor said, pointing at the proof.

Keith was thrilled. They gave us a copy of the ultrasound image, and Keith took to carrying it around with him, pointing to the baby and saying, "Look, there's my boy, there's Jesse, there's his penis." And all of Keith's buddies would stand around and say, "Yeah, that's a boy, sure enough." It's a guy thing.

No man could ever be happier about becoming a father than Keith Whitley. All the kindness, all the love, all the tenderness, all the hope, came pouring out of him. His emotions were strong and pure, none of the tension and fear that set him to drinking.

Just the sight of me would touch off Keith's smile, or his tears. If he was home in the evening, he would take out his guitar and sing to me and Morgan—and Jesse.

He would put his face right up against my stomach, now protruding quite visibly against my loose clothes, and he would sing to the baby.

"You have the most beautiful mommy in the world, and your daddy loves you. You'll never want for anything," Keith would say, touching my stomach and feeling Jesse kick.

After Morgan fell asleep, we would put her in her own room and Keith would continue to sing to the baby. I had been told that women should phase out lovemaking the longer they are pregnant, just as I had always heard that men were turned off by pregnant women, but Keith would say, "You are more sexy pregnant than you ever were." We made love regularly, right up until a few weeks before the baby was born. We made love. That's the right way to say it.

I was due to have the baby on June 17, with a C-section, the same way I had had Morgan. My doctor, Joe Allison, said that the scar tissue from the first birth would make natural childbirth a little too difficult. I started having contractions a week ahead of time.

Keith was leaving on a short trip up to Pennsylvania, two dates and then back. He knew I was getting close, and he offered to cancel his show, but Jack McFadden said, "You're only seven hours out; do the shows and come back." So Keith went out on the road.

The next day he tried to call, but couldn't reach me. I was out by the pool, using the time to try to teach Margaret, our housekeeper, how to swim. I would be leaving two children in her care once I went back to work, and I wanted her to know how to get somebody out of a pool. (She still hadn't learned to drive, either.)

Margaret and I were the funniest thing you've ever seen. She had never been in the water before she came to work for us. We had bought ear plugs and a bathing suit for her, and she would watch each day as my sisters and their families came over for a swim.

I was the pool attendant, having promised Keith I would take full responsibility for the pool. All through my pregnancy, I had poured in all the chemicals, swept the pool clean of leaves, then worked out each day in the water. As a result, I was in great shape, only twelve pounds above my normal weight—all of it belly, this huge baby just bulging out in front of my well-toned pool attendant's body.

After a considerable amount of coaxing, I had persuaded Margaret to get into the pool at the shallow end, with her ear plugs inserted, and I would try to teach her to hold her breath.

"I can hold my breath," she would insist, but each time I tried to teach her to put her face into the water and take the right strokes, she would turn rigid and pop straight up, her feet touching bottom. She could not even tread water. Just couldn't go anywhere.

This day, Candy and Beth were over at the house, watching

the swimming lesson. They were laughing so hard they were hysterical. We all loved Margaret, who was a bright and accomplished adult, just somewhat out of her element in a pool in suburban Tennessee.

I was not taking no for an answer.

"I know how to do it," I announced. "I'm swimming down to the deep end, and I'm going to make her swim back."

I was treading water as we went to the deep end, and I had my arm around Margaret's waist, and she was holding on to the side of the pool. Suddenly, she panicked, grabbing onto me and flailing and saying, "I'm going under," and I was reassuring her, "No, it's all right, you're pulling me under, stop, just let go of me."

She almost drowned me, but I was laughing so hard that if I had drowned, I would have drowned happy. I finally towed her back into the shallow end and told her we'd get back to the swimming lessons—as soon as I was not carrying around this baby.

I stayed out by the pool for a few hours, and when I went indoors I heard the phone ringing, but Margaret was not picking it up. I grabbed the phone, and it was Keith. He was anxious.

"I love you more than anybody in the world—but where have you been?" he blurted.

"Right here," I said.

"Lorrie, I've been trying to call for the last hour, but nobody answered."

I called Margaret's name. No answer. Then Margaret walked into the room. She hadn't heard me. She hadn't heard the phone ring, either.

I pointed my index finger at my ears. Margaret popped out her ear plugs. Now she could hear again.

The night of June 14, Keith called at midnight after his show and said, "I'm on my way home, is everything okay?"

The day I became Mrs. Keith Whitley.

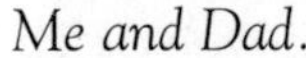

Me and Dad.

My father, George Morgan.

The whole family in 1975: Marty, Beth, Dad, Mom, Candy, Liana, and me.

The big day. Keith and I were the two happiest people on earth.

Our wedding party.

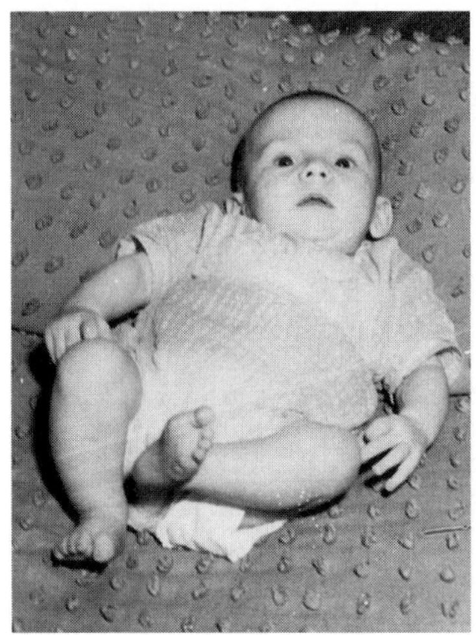

Keith at 3 weeks old.

A special day in Sandy Hook.

Keith and Morgan at a 1988 Fan Club Breakfast.

Keith and I sing "That's the Way Love Goes" at the same breakfast.

The two of us with Buck Owens.

On Keith's beloved Harley on a perfect day.

Morgan with her Granny Faye Whitley.

Jessie at his father's grave.

Morgan and Jessie.

With my director and friend, Kenny Ortega.

"Sure, I'm feeling great, take your time, have some dinner at the truck stop, I'll see you in the morning."

I no sooner hung up the phone than I started getting contractions, strong and clear.

"This is it," I told Margaret.

Margaret could not cook, or drive, or swim. But we had hired her because she was a nice person and because she had helped deliver many babies back in Guyana.

"I am a midwife," Margaret told me. "I know it is not time."

But I was the one with the contractions.

My niece, Rachel, who is a few years older than Morgan, was staying with me, and I asked her to call my mom, who came out to the house.

When my contractions got down to every ten minutes, Mom said it was time to call Dr. Allison. Margaret was still insisting it was false labor.

"Margaret," I said, "pack my suitcase or I'm going to kill you."

Meanwhile, we had state police from Kentucky and Ohio trying to locate Keith's white bus out on the interstate. Mom took me to the hospital around three-thirty or four in the morning. They took me to the delivery room and started putting that epidural in my back.

Around five, Dr. Allison started poking my stomach so I could tell when it was deadened. He also allowed my sister, Candy, to stay in the room because she was a professional nurse. I was still asking if Keith had arrived, but nobody had reached him.

I had another concern. I begged them not to tie my hands because I panic at that, but the anesthetist said, "I have never let a patient not have her hands tied down because if you feel something, you're going to grab at it, and you could make something go wrong."

I said, "I promise to Daddy, I won't do anything, just don't tie my hands down."

Finally, they agreed to let Candy hold one hand and the anesthetist hold the other one. The surgeon went to work. I felt nothing more than a tug at my stomach and then I heard a nurse say, "Oh, he's so beautiful."

They held him up for me to see, and I had to agree that he was gorgeous.

I was so happy that Jesse Keith Whitley had arrived, safe and sound, June 15, 1987, but I was sorry for Keith that he had not arrived in time. The troopers had never been able to flag down the bus and reroute him to the hospital.

Around seven, the bus pulled up in front of our house. When Keith saw Jack McFadden standing in front of the house, he panicked, thinking the worst. Then he noticed Jack was holding a box of cigars.

Keith started waving at the other band members and shouting, "It's a boy! It's a boy!" Then he got in Jack's car and they sped off to the hospital.

When he saw me, he fell to his knees and started kissing me. The nurse brought Jesse in and laid Jesse in Keith's arms. Keith cradled him instinctively, tenderly.

"Jesse, your daddy loves you so much," Keith said.

At that moment, Jesse pooped all over him. The first poop of his life. And Keith said, "That's the sweetest thing I've ever seen." The nurse took Jesse while Keith cleaned himself off, then he sat in the chair and fed Jesse his bottle because, by that time, I was out of it.

Keith stayed overnight, feeding Jesse and holding him. They brought Morgan into the hospital and people took photos of the four of us.

When we were making plans to go home, we heard that TNN and the other channels wanted to take some footage.

Most couples who have a baby do not have to worry about how they look, but this is one of the mixed joys of being an entertainer—you always want to look presentable.

Keith found Ramon, who did our hair, and he came to the hospital and fixed us up. The attendants brought the wheelchair and sat me down in it. Keith walked alongside me to the camera crews outside. I was holding Jesse in my arms as they rolled me out; then Keith picked up Jesse in front of the cameras and said, "Hi, Grandma," in case his mom was watching back in eastern Kentucky.

We went home, and my mom helped me for the first few days while I mended from the C-section. We put Jesse in the bassinet by the bed so we could reach him more easily. Keith was amazingly helpful making the formula, feeding Jesse, and cleaning up.

We would take turns feeding our new son, but every time I fed him, Keith got up to sit in that green crushed-velvet chair, and he would get the formula, and would sit near me and talk and keep me company. We always got hungry ourselves when we fed Jesse, so Keith would feed me chips. Then we would lay him back in the bassinet and go back to sleep. And when we both were awake, and things were smooth, Keith was taking pictures of us.

Keith also helped get Morgan out to school in the morning. She might have been a little insecure about sleeping by herself, with all this activity centered around her brother, and sometimes she would walk down the hall into our room, afraid of the dark. Keith made sure she was part of everything.

After we got into a routine, Keith had to do something that was very unpleasant for all of us. He sat down with Margaret and said, "Margaret, you know we love you, but we're going to have to let you go. You can't drive, you can't swim, and we can't keep driving you to the bus depot."

The real thing that bothered Keith was that she was a midwife back home, but she had not recognized that I was going into labor.

Soon there was another painful crossroads. It was time to go back on the road again. I could see Keith was torn, but Jack had set up the tour, and this was how Keith supported us, so he got his clothes together and prepared to leave.

The bus usually left around midnight. Keith was very emotional as the hour approached. I had a tape of children's lullabies, one side with lyrics, the other side with just music, so parents could sing along to their children. Keith had already started singing to Jesse, fixing his bright eyes on him, letting his son know that his father loved him.

That night Keith was meticulous about making sure that everything was in place around the house. He must have gone in a hundred times to make sure the lullaby tape was in place, to make sure the diapers were right, that Jesse's bed was secure. Everything had to be perfect. He got on the white bus at midnight, a very emotional parting for all of us, and he said, "I'll call you first thing in the morning."

But I was reminded of him all night. When I got into bed, I found a beautiful note placed on the pillow: "Angel"—that's what he called me all the time—"It's killing me to leave you tonight. You know I love you and miss you. I'm forever yours, faithfully."

I was so reassured that I fell asleep calmly, and was awakened at two by Jesse crying for a bottle. I went to the refrigerator and found a note taped on the front bottle of formula: "Take care of our son. Say hello to Morgan in the morning. I love you, Keith."

He was so precious. In the morning, I woke up, went to brush my teeth, opened the drawer, and saw another note: "I love you more than anything in this world. I'll call you." Even though he was gone on the road, he had found a way to reassure me.

When Keith came back from this short trip, we recognized that we would need somebody else helping at home, particularly if I was going to resume working. We found a woman named Barbara Powers through some in-laws, and she was more practical than Margaret. Every working parent knows how important that is.

Jesse began sleeping more regularly, and life got back to normal. The doctors had suggested that I wait two months before making love, to give my body time to heal, but our attraction was so strong that we could not wait that long.

Sometimes I go back over these moments in my mind. They remind me that Keith was not simply playing at being a husband and a father. He loved life deeply and was proud of himself and his family.

All of us have had to deal with the stigma of the man who drank himself to death, but at my worst moments I think back to Keith Whitley, talking to Morgan, singing to Jesse, making me comfortable, and I know that no man could have seemed more fulfilled.

Then the demons returned. The band members were diligent about making him take the Antabuse, but one day Keith managed to trick them, and he went for whatever he could find.

He was intent on getting alcohol, and he got it. He drank so much, made himself so sick, and became so dehydrated that the band members had to take him to a doctor for an injection to get some fluids back in him.

When they put him back on the bus, Keith tried to close the door to his private room in the back. But Mike and the other musicians kept opening the door so they could keep an eye on him, which only made him mad. He clearly had something in mind.

Mike went back to investigate and found Keith getting

ready to drink 409 cleaning solution. Mike lunged and grabbed it out of his hands. Keith's need for alcohol was so great that he was willing to drink anything—mouthwash, cologne, cleansers, cough medicine.

We checked with doctors and discovered that Keith's system was so chemically dependent that it craved alcohol. There was some kind of imbalance that just made him crave the stuff, beyond all rhyme or reason.

We started having to be careful around the house. I couldn't keep cleaning solutions or beauty-care products around if I knew they had alcohol in them. I could not keep screw-off tops on any kind of medicine unless it was alcohol-free.

Not long after that, Keith was booked for a tour to England and the Netherlands, and I went along. On the flight over, Keith and I were flipping through the duty-free magazine, and he pointed to one of the advertisements.

"I've got to buy Joey a bottle of Polo," he said, meaning he owed one of his band members some of the Ralph Lauren cologne.

"Why do you owe Joey some Polo?" I asked.

"I drank his last bottle."

I looked to see if Keith was joking. He was not.

Only a few months after she started working for us, Barbara quit. Keith was drinking more frequently and starting to act up around the house. Barbara did not want to have to worry about his sobriety and the kids, too.

I was already working again, and I was desperate. We heard about a nineteen-year-old girl—I'll call her Trudy, but that's not her name. She arrived at our house with a Bible in her hand. Now, I respect religion, but who goes to a job interview with a Bible in her hand? When I asked about her references, Keith said, "Oh, she's such a sweet girl, we don't need references."

His impulsive, trusting side won out, and we hired her. But I had a creepy feeling about her, and I was not happy with the way she handled the kids, either. I was very particular about the kids taking a bath in the morning. I loved them smelling good. What parent doesn't? But I began coming home after being downtown and Jesse would be lying on the floor in the kitchen, sleeping in dirty clothes. I would question Trudy about it, and she would say, "He just fell asleep and I didn't feel like waking him."

I was not getting good vibrations. Jesse was just an infant, but I noticed that he reacted badly whenever Trudy came near him.

One time I came home in the middle of the day and found her in the house, naked, fast asleep on Morgan's bed. She had no explanation. Keith wasn't around, so it wasn't a matter of her trying to snag him. She was just a homely, weird girl who took off her clothes in the middle of the day. And we needed a babysitter. So we warned her, and muddled onward.

The next time Keith went on the road, I got a call from his sister over in Ashland, and she said he had been drinking. I asked her to put him on the phone, but she said, "I think I need to let him sleep this one off."

I got ticked off at that, because I was the one living with the problem. I said, "Fine, I'm heading for Ashland," and I drove over there and brought him right home. When we arrived, Jesse was downright filthy, in the same clothes he had been wearing twenty-four hours earlier. I also discovered that Trudy had left Morgan with somebody else, while she had taken one of our cars the night before and gone for a ride with Jesse in the car.

I got settled in our room. Then I grabbed Trudy by the hair and dragged her into a back room.

"You need to leave my house this moment!" I snarled.

She wanted to know why.

"I think you're a pervert," I growled. "My child cries every time you come near him."

I picked up the cord to the vacuum cleaner and I waved it in her surly face, and said, "If I ever see you again, I promise you I will wrap this around your neck, you little bitch."

She picked up her clothes and got out of my house. I did not pay her for the previous two weeks, and she never asked, which told me she was guilty of something.

I took Jesse to the pediatrician and he could find no evidence of Jesse's being mistreated, although he added, "On a baby this small, it's hard to tell." I can only hope the worst of it was just my imagination, but the filthiness and the creepiness were real.

CHAPTER SEVENTEEN

I was ready to go back to work, but my aspirations were modest.

There was one star in the family, and that was Keith. It hadn't happened for me up to that point; maybe it never would, and that was all right.

I had two great children, and I could be home part of the time, cleaning, driving them around, cooking, just raising them, being supportive to Keith.

In my spare time, I'd work at the *Opry*, play some dates with Keith. Whatever. I'd already had four record contracts, more managers than that. It hadn't happened.

The one thing I lacked was a manager, a mentor, a guru, a kindred spirit, somebody who thought I was great. It turned out, I had married him. Keith had always loved my music, from the first time he said hello in the studio, years earlier.

"I wasn't just trying to put a move on you," he told me later. "I was married. I sincerely meant it. You have a great voice."

Other people had told me that, too. But I had come along after the originals—the Lorettas, the Dollys, the Tammys—had blazed the trail. Country music was looking to go mainstream.

Nashville's new poster-girl-next-door could come from a

subdivision, not the headwaters of an Appalachian creek. I fit that model. I was Nashville, not Los Angeles, but I was parochial-school Nashville, establishment Nashville. I was George Morgan's daughter. I was a trouper. I'd been there forever. I'd be there forever. Let's find somebody new. I couldn't blame them. I had listened to so many managers and producers that I didn't know who I was, either.

But Keith would listen to me at the *Opry*, or on tour with him, or maybe just singing around the house, and he would encourage me. He even began talking me up to the people representing him. He was taking a risk promoting a female singer moving along in her twenties, who'd never had a really big record.

Keith asked his producer, Blake Mevis, to see what he could do. Blake was a terrific producer who had worked with George Strait. He and his wife, Janice, would come over to our house. Maybe he was acting out of friendship, or maybe he was just trying to pacify a talented client, but Blake spoke up for me.

One of the people he approached was Joe Galante, the top man at RCA.

"I knew about Lorrie Morgan, and obviously I knew about her dad," Joe said recently. "After Keith's marriage broke up, nobody could find him, but soon we noticed that Keith was with Lorrie. I started calling Lorrie to get ahold of Keith. But a lot of people didn't know Keith was with Lorrie.

"I remember being at a show one day with Keith, and Lorrie was performing," Joe continued. "Guys were saying, 'Wow, listen to her—and what a looker.' And Keith said, 'I ain't worrying about anything. I'm going home with her right after the show.'

"After a while, Keith would say, 'We're going to get married,' " Joe recalled. He was there, and he knows how happy Keith was at the wedding, what a beautiful day that was.

"One day Keith brought in a tape," Joe Galante added. "He

said, 'This is my favorite singer. Help her be a star.' Coming from a great country singer, you pay attention."

Maybe so, but it took months and months for me to get a deal at RCA. I did not want Keith to weaken his own position by pushing me, but everybody needs a friend to put the right tape on the right table. He enlisted his manager, Jack McFadden, to speak up for me, too.

"Keith had 'Miami' out already," Jack said recently. "He was becoming a superstar. He was one of the finest gentlemen I ever met. A caring person. He'd call me from the road and ask me a question or two and I'd wonder what he really wanted, and he'd just say, 'I just want to say I love you guys.'

"Keith wanted me to represent Lorrie, too," Jack added. "I saw her on the Ralph Emery show and I told her, 'You sound great.' I told Galante, 'This girl can sell records,' but it took me eleven months to get Galante to go for it."

I had never lacked for encouragement from my family and friends and management, but now I was being encouraged by an artist who was better than I was. This wasn't people saying, "Nice job, Lorrie," because they loved me and were loyal. This was a great musician who saw into my soul and dared me to be better. I wanted to sing for Keith, wanted to please him, not as some servant performing but because I knew his talent, and I knew he understood talent.

If Keith was around me, he would say, "Oh boy, that's the best you've ever done that song," and if he wasn't around, I would think to myself, Man, I want Keith to be proud of me. He called me all the time. If I was singing around Nashville somewhere, I'd get home, and there would be Keith, back in his hotel room, or at a pay phone, with the bus waiting for him, and he would ask, "How did it go?" Then he would ask me about certain songs. Did I get that little inflection right this time? Did I slow it down? He knew. And because he knew, I wanted to sing for him.

Keith pestered everybody, including his own label. Whether it was because Keith was bugging him all the time, or Blake Mevis was bugging him, or a combination, Joe Galante found it in his heart to sign me up for a couple of singles.

I remember the first meeting with Joe. I said, "Look, I know I'm going to make a lot of mistakes, but none of them are going to be intentional. If there's anything I've done wrong, I'll correct it. Please, don't assume I've been a bitch on purpose or slighted someone on purpose."

From that day on, Joe Galante and I have always had a good relationship.

But there was some pain involved with my new contract. The label did not want Blake Mevis to produce my first album. I said, "Oh, great. I get a deal, and Blake gets canned."

Joe arranged a meeting with a producer named Barry Beckett. Jack played some of my tapes, and this new guy said, "I don't believe a word you sang." Terrific. And the rest of the meeting didn't go any better.

I went back to Galante and McFadden and I said, "I can't stand the guy, get rid of him," but cooler heads prevailed. We scheduled another meeting, and I brought in some tapes of my appearances on the *Opry* and with Ralph Emery, where I was more comfortable. I talked a little more about my feeling for traditional country, and Barry said, "I got it. I can do that."

Later, I realized Barry had been right. Everybody was operating on a formula. I just hadn't found mine yet. Barry Beckett turned out to be the right producer for me. You know the old story about the overnight sensation? This one took almost a decade.

Early on, I mentioned to Barry that I had an old demo tape I wanted him to hear.

When I was working as a receptionist for Acuff-Rose and making demo tapes at night, two songwriters named Carson Whitsett and Scott Mateer had asked me to record their song,

"Dear Me," about a woman writing a letter to herself about a failed love affair.

We had recorded it in the studio with just a piano in the background, a sweet, sad song about a woman taking stock of herself. They hustled my demo around town but nobody wanted it—the song or me.

I hung on to it for nine years. The companies kept saying, "Nah, I don't think it's you." Or sometimes they would say, "It ain't country enough."

Finally, my time came. I pitched the tape to Barry Beckett, and he listened, and he said, "Please, God, tell me that's you singing the demo." I said it was, and he said, "We'll do it."

That became my first top-ten song. Went all the way up to nine.

Joe Galante liked it so much, it evolved into an album, *Leave the Light On.*

"There was something really vibrant about her," Joe Galante said recently. "She was elegant, sexy, soulful. Her voice was smoky, crisp, a pure country singer with versatility I had not heard in many other women.

"They made a great couple," Joe said. "They had so much in common."

Maybe that was it. Joe knows as well as anybody that I had been around Nashville a long time, but maybe there was something different about me now. I was in love with a talented, vibrant man. I felt sparks whenever I was around Keith, and maybe that carried over into my singing. I had not been complete before, but now I was. I learned from his voice, I learned from his love, I learned just from being around him.

I'm very proud of being an independent woman, proud of all that women have done in country music, but it is also true that my career took off at this point because I was in love with Keith Whitley, and he was in love with me. I cannot deny the rush of pure sensual love I felt when I saw him. It made me want to open up, give everything I had. Maybe the music industry people knew it. Maybe the fans knew it. I certainly knew it.

Keith was extending a great amount of his time and energy promoting me. He should have been thinking about himself. His records still had not taken off, and he had a bit of a reputation because of his occasional binges. Still, Joe Galante was not about to give up on him.

Keith had gone back into the studio with Blake for a third album, but when it was completed, Joe told him, "Look, this is good but it's not great, and it's not what I would expect."

Keith agreed.

Blake had been responsible for the lush, mellow sound on "Miami My Amy." Musically, Blake had been in favor of the urban country sound—horns here, violins there—which, though not originally Keith's style, had produced a major success for him. RCA was now talking about looking for a producer who might bring out the rural country roots in Keith.

Keith felt terrible. Blake had been Keith's best man at our wedding. He's a genuinely nice man, and I really loved him for standing up for me. I felt badly that the friendship with Blake and Janice might be jeopardized if RCA made any change, but it is a cold fact of life in the record business that very few working relationships last a long time.

You say to yourself, "I am the artist, I should have the power," but in fact you are under the control of the record company. They can force decisions on you that break your heart. Did Keith agree with the move? Yes, but he felt terrible about doing it.

To give you an idea of what a fine man Blake Mevis is, this is what he said recently about the turn of events:

"Joe Galante called me into a meeting and said they were

making a change," Blake said. "Country music is so close, so personal, and there are changes going on all the time. Joe remained my friend, and so did Keith. We never missed a beat. I'm not saying I felt good about the change, but I did not take it personally."

Joe suggested Keith work with Garth Fundis, who had worked with Don Williams. They looked over some material, and they went into the studio.

"Normally we allot six weeks to make a record," Joe said recently, "but Garth called me after a week and said, 'If you want to come by, we're done.'

"I said, 'What do you mean, you're done?' And he said, 'I'm telling you, this guy is an amazing musician.' "

The result was Keith's breakthrough album, *Don't Close Your Eyes*. Released in the spring of 1988, it would send three separate singles—"Don't Close Your Eyes," "When You Say Nothing at All," and "I'm No Stranger to the Rain"—to the top of the charts.

Keith was there during the shoot for my first video, "Dear Me." They did it in one of those old loft buildings on Second Avenue, which has now been restored with all the restaurants and clubs, near the new arena. There is a big open area upstairs. Keith drove his Harley right into the freight elevator, and he was standing up there with the cameramen as they shot down on me. I was a nervous wreck, but then I looked up and saw Keith, half-smiling, half-crying, looking down at me, waving, so proud of me.

Jack had some dates for me, which meant I would need a band. There would be no more of those little pickup bands every trip, and I would not have to rely on Keith Whitley's and Everybody Else's Band, as Mike Chamberlain had called it.

Now I could have my own group, which I named the Slam

Band. I auditioned them, it was *my* band, and Keith loved them. He had nicknames for all of them. Noel was the Noble Roman. Eventually, we did a couple of shows together, my band and his.

One thing I really envied about Keith. Whatever inner anxieties he had, he did not seem nervous about performing. I was the other way around. I've always had stage fright, and I would get it real bad at times. I'd be sitting around backstage, wondering if people would accept me. What if they booed me? It kind of freaked me at first. I wouldn't get sick to my stomach the way some performers or athletes do, but I would become very quiet. Once I got on the stage I was all right. It was before that was the problem.

Maybe Keith was nervous about performing, but he didn't ever show it. It was the rest of life that made him nervous.

One consequence of being around Keith so much was that I started smoking again. I had quit for four years, never touched one while I was pregnant. He was addicted to them, needing nicotine so badly that he would actually have his bus driver wake him up in the middle of the night just so he could have a smoke. It doesn't make sense, but that's what he did.

One day, he lit up a cigarette and I said, "Hey, gimme one of them. I haven't had a cigarette in years." And bam. I was back on them.

Keith respected my opinion as well as my voice. He loved any song by Whitey Shafer, but he was having a hard time making up his mind about one of Whitey's songs called "I Wonder Do You Think of Me?"

I urged him to do it, especially using that little tremor in his throat. He went into the studio with Garth Fundis, didn't say much about it, but one day we were driving together and he said, "I want you to hear the final mix on 'I Wonder Do You Think of Me?' " It got to the final part, he did that swirly thing with his voice, and I said, "Yesssss!" It was so good, they named his next album after that song.

Sometimes we had to be apart. My old friend Ruth was still in Florida, running a club with her husband, and she booked me into their club. It was a great chance for the two of us to hang out, talk about the old days. Keith, meanwhile, was back in Nashville. He said he didn't object to sharing the load, watching the kids, but it was quite obvious that he missed me badly. He must have called a hundred times that weekend. It was as if I were his rock, and he couldn't get along without me.

Keith knew I was taking off, and I think it scared him. He was torn between wanting me there at home—to be the doting wife, to make the meals, to take care of the kids—and wanting me to be a great performer. He loved me either way, but it couldn't be both ways.

I'm told that one of the trademarks of the addict is that he uses the alcohol, the drugs, to cover up his feelings. Keith was hiding his feelings as long as I knew him. I did not drive Keith Whitley to drink by going out on the road. He already had that pattern. When he was feeling rotten, when something would eat at him, he could not deal with it, could not discuss it. Instead, he would perform, joke around, be super sweet and loving—or he would get wrecked.

I think he was scared. It was like the doctor creating the monster. At the same time, he was proud of his creation, proud of what I created by myself. He loved me deeply. He was so proud to introduce me onstage. If we were at the same show, he would say, "I want to introduce somebody I love more than anybody else. She's a great singer. She's my wife. Lorrie Morgan!" He would beam. Just beam. And I would get out on the stage and just kick butt.

Keith asked Jack and Joe if they could book us together, let us record together, but Joe didn't think it was a good idea at that stage.

"She was just taking off, and really, so was Keith," Joe said recently. "I told them I did not think it was a good idea to record them together. Of course, now I could kick myself."

How was Joe Galante to know that Keith's star was moving too fast? Back then, so much was happening. We could only assume it would go on forever.

CHAPTER EIGHTEEN

I walked into the bedroom and saw Keith sitting in his underwear on the green chair with his briefcase on his lap.

Then I noticed the gun.

I knew he had the .38, and I had no problem with a gun around the house for protection.

This did not look like protection to me. This looked like a man fiddling with a .38, about to do something terrible.

"Keith, give me the gun," I said quietly.

I waited to see if he was going to pick it up and cock it. I had no idea what was going through him at that moment. I just knew I had to stay in control.

"I'm not going to do anything." His voice was eerie, distant.

I remembered Lane Palmer coldcocking the guy outside our house, not waiting to ask questions. I did not want this to develop into a test of wills. I walked straight up to Keith, reached out, picked up the gun, and walked away from him.

Then I started shaking. I handle emergencies well, but as soon as they're over, my nerves kick in; I start thinking about what could have happened. I did not want to show it, but inside I was flipping out. This man, going through one of his dreadful hangovers, had been sitting with a loaded gun, contemplating who knows what.

"Keith, you have got to take your Antabuse," I said, trying to count up the hours since his last drink.

"All right," Keith replied, "that's how much I love you. I'll take it. But I don't think it's been that long."

I was finally getting wise to the ways of an alcoholic. I knew he would appear to give in, to set up a personal debt from me to him. That way I would feel sorry for him and relax long enough for him to slip away and find a drink.

I brought over a glass of water, watched him pop the pill in his mouth and take a sip.

"Let me see," I demanded.

He opened his mouth and I inspected. There was no trace of the pill in any corner of his mouth. Then he went into the bathroom and started taking a shower.

I was not totally convinced. I walked over to the chair and found the pill stuffed behind the pillow.

I marched into the bathroom, angry.

"You didn't take your pill."

"Yes, I did."

"No, you didn't." I extended my hand and showed it to him.

"Now, how did that Antabuse get in the corner of the chair?" he asked.

I almost broke out laughing. I hadn't told him where I'd found the pill—he could not even lie convincingly.

It was almost like a mother catching her little boy drawing on the wall, but the drawing is an affectionate portrait of Mommy. You say, "This is bad," but somehow you are touched and you cannot stay mad. Keith was like a little boy. The deeper I got into dealing with his problem, the more I loved him.

I would get mad at him, of course, but the only time I remember any physical confrontation was when he insisted on driving the Corvette home—and he'd been drinking.

"You're too drunk to drive," I told him.

"Damn it, Lorrie, let me be a man!" he insisted.

That just made me furious, so I slammed the keys into his hand and sat back to see what he would do as a man—a *drunken* man at that moment.

He defiantly drove the Corvette down Dickerson Pike. When we got to a school zone, plainly marked, speed limit fifteen miles per hour, he just floored that sucker. I mean, he went through that school zone at ninety miles an hour. My seat belt didn't work, and he never used his, and I just flew backward as he accelerated. I could see the crossing lady frantically waving her hands and blowing her whistle.

"Keith! Slow down!" I screamed.

I looked at his eyes and saw the vacant stare of a man out of control. He was gone. Incoherent. Eyes a thousand miles on the horizon.

"Slow this damn thing down!" I shouted.

He would show me. He whipped a one-eighty right in the middle of Dickerson Pike and started roaring back to the school zone again, going even faster, if that was possible.

I was afraid for my life, but I was more afraid for the lives of some innocent kids in the neighborhood. I turned sideways and started kicking at him with both feet, trying to make him slow down while he had to fend me off. But he just kept flooring it. I could see the terrified crossing lady ducking for cover as we barreled through there again.

I grabbed for the gearshift of the automatic transmission and tried to pull it into a lower gear. We wrestled for control; I could feel gears grinding, that transmission just rattling around. Keith finally slowed the car down as he turned into our subdivision. I was pounding him and cursing, trying to get him to focus and trying to unleash my fury.

Then I noticed the blue lights, in front of us, behind us. The crossing lady had called the cops. We were surrounded, and Keith slowed to a halt.

From an incoherent madman, there now emerged the crafty drunk.

"Lorrie, you're gonna have to cover for me," Keith said.

What he meant was obvious. I was sober. I was a local. I was a woman. I was going to have to charm these boys into not asking Keith to walk the line or take the breath test. And the horrible thing was, I was willing to do it.

"You son of a bitch," I muttered.

I got out and walked over to the Goodlettsville police, most of whom I recognized.

"What's going on?" I asked, as innocently as I could muster.

They told me there was a complaint that we had been speeding through a school zone.

"I am so incredibly sorry," I said. "It was totally my fault. You know we're musicians, and I had this tape on, and we were so into it that we just didn't notice."

Keith leaned out his window. His eyes were focused again. His smile was sincere.

"It will never happen again, I promise," Keith said in a steady voice.

The police did not get close enough to Keith to smell the alcohol.

Five feet would have been close enough.

They warned us to be careful and they let us go. Apparently, they were responding to Keith's first foray through the school zone. The lady had not gotten back to them to tell them about the second pass.

Keith pulled the car into our driveway.

"You conniving son of a bitch," I said.

I could not believe he had pulled it off. I was half-disgusted and half-admiring of his gall.

"Lorrie, I'm sorry," he said. Again, the sincerity was overwhelming. "I swear, it will never happen again. I'll take my Antabuse as soon as this wears off."

Keith knew he had a problem, and he could talk about it. In July of 1988, he gave an interview to Robert K. Oermann of the *Nashville Tennessean*, in conjunction with "Don't Close Your Eyes" reaching the top of the charts.

"I have no doubts in my mind that I would not be sittin' here today had it not been for 'Miami My Amy,' " Keith said. "That song saved my life.

"It gave me confidence; it gave me work; it started me; it made me a working act; it took me from being a two-hundred and fifty dollar a week songwriter to being booked for real money," he told the reporter.

And then he got into his drinking habits:

"They say that once you start drinking heavily and it becomes a part of your everyday life that you don't mature from that point on," Keith said. "If that's true, I'm about fifteen or sixteen years old, 'cause that's about the time I started drinkin' heavy."

He talked about the favorable reaction when he first came to Nashville: "I don't think I ever believed any of it. I wanted a career worse than anything in the world. But I was scared to have it. I was really all twisted around. Somehow or other I told myself that if I don't do it, it won't be as bad as doin' it and failing.

"Every time I'd get close to something happening, I'd get drunk."

He said our marriage had changed him:

"After fifteen years on the road I was just reduced to this

quivering mass," he said. "I went through the worst bout of stage fright you have ever seen. I was without that crutch. I had to learn to do everything all over again.

"Lorrie came along, which is the best thing personally that's ever happened to me. I straightened up my life."

He could talk like that, and I believe at the time he meant it.

The benders started getting worse, with an uglier side to them.

One day Keith took off for a business meeting in his black Jeep Cherokee. Normally, he would call me four or five times a day, and when I didn't hear from him for hours, I became suspicious. He only disappeared when he was drinking. Jekyll and Hyde.

I called Jack McFadden and said, "I've got a bad vibe. I haven't heard from Keith in hours and nobody knows where he is. He left the house around ten."

We all waited for a sighting, and finally it came from a neighboring state. That afternoon, I received a call from the Kentucky State Highway Patrol. They said Keith had flipped the Jeep up in Elizabethtown, which is one hundred and thirty-five miles away. Some passersby had seen the Jeep going eighty miles per hour before it flipped over. The amazing thing was that Keith had escaped unhurt.

"Just keep him there," I told the troopers. "Don't let him leave, and we'll be there."

Jack and I drove up to E-Town and walked into the emergency room. Keith would not even look at us, he was so embarrassed. He reached out his hand to me and said, "I love you." It was heartbreaking.

Jack took care of the details. Somehow Keith was being released.

"Please," he said, the helpless little-boy side of him emerging. "Just take me out of here."

He threw up in the backseat most of the way home.

The next day I force-fed Keith his Antabuse and, one more time, he promised never to do it again. Because the Jeep was totaled, he had to agree to do three shows for an automaker, just to get another car for us to drive around.

Right before Thanksgiving in 1987, we were preparing for our annual trek to Doylestown, Ohio, where my mom has nine brothers and sisters. My cousin was getting married there. I bought a new dress, bought Keith a new suit, new clothes for Morgan and Jesse, and all of our households prepared for the trip north, by the carloads. We are talking Beverly Hillbillies.

On Monday afternoon, I did not hear from Keith. Around suppertime he called me and said, "I love you; I've had a few drinks and I'm over at Ireland's. I'll be home in ten minutes."

Ireland's was a bar in a mall close to our house. I waited an hour and a half and he never showed up. I called Jack and said, "He's disappeared again. But I have this strange feeling I know where he is."

It was times like this when I had to reveal some of the truths that no one knew about Keith.

"Well, where is he?" Jack asked.

"I want you to go over to Dickerson Pike to some of the adult book shops and see if he's there."

"Come on," Jack said. "That's the last place Keith would be. He loves you."

"I'm telling you, just go there," I said.

An hour later, Jack called me from the car phone and said, "You were right. I found him."

Jack found Keith, drunk and immobile, just where I said he'd be. He loaded Keith's inert body into his car and hauled him home.

Keith was unconscious but breathing, so I let him sleep it off.

The next morning, I could not wake him, so in a panic I called the paramedics, remembering the couple of other times I had seen him this way. They were there in a few minutes, and they hooked him up to the machines, which started waking him up. The paramedics were accompanied by a few police officers from Goodlettsville, a necessary measure any time there is an overdose, because you could be dealing with illegal drugs or an intent to hurt somebody or even a death.

Keith woke up and saw the police officers. Now I was seeing the fighting side of Keith Whitley.

"Get the fuck out of my bedroom," he snarled.

"Mr. Whitley, we just want to check you out," one officer said.

"You ain't checking nothing," Keith snarled.

One of the officers was familiar to us, a veteran who patrolled the neighborhood on his motorcycle. He was standing between the door and the bed, trying to keep Keith out of further trouble.

"Now, Keith, I'm telling you," the officer said. "Sit right down and calm yourself."

Instead, Keith hauled back and coldcocked him. That cop went flying. I knew they *had* to arrest Keith.

They cuffed him while he was still in his underwear, and Keith was just flipping out. This sweet elf was a raging madman. He never said a word to me, just glared as if I were part of the problem. As if *I* were the one hauling him off to jail. Some kind of inner anger had broken loose, the kind of rage that makes a man want to take on the world.

"Miz Whitley," one of the officers said, "this was a simple domestic case, but now your husband is going to be charged with an assault on an officer."

I couldn't argue with that. I know police officers well enough. When they are threatened, when their minds are made up, you just go with it.

They let him get dressed, and they took him to jail. We were due to leave for Ohio.

Candy called and said, "Y'all ready?" I explained what had happened and, while she was sympathetic, she wouldn't let me feel sorry for myself. "You're going to Ohio," she said. "The kids are going, we're *all* going."

I called Jack and said, "When Keith is released from jail, you bail him out. I'm tired of this." And I went to the wedding and to celebrate Thanksgiving in Ohio.

Jack got the dirty end of the deal. He went down to the station house and tried to talk them into letting Keith go. He recalls that just about half of Davidson County had been arrested that day, and they were being processed by the dozens. Around seven in the evening, Jack posted bond.

"He went too far," one of the officers said, and Jack couldn't disagree.

Then Jack started thinking that maybe it would be a good idea for Keith to spend the night in jail, just to get a sense of how things worked.

"The clerk was ticked off when I got my bail money back," Jack recalls. "But he did it. Then I got ten dollars worth of quarters and candy bars to give to Keith. There was a short, fat little lieutenant, a woman, and she said, 'Don't you worry. I'll keep an eye on him. You're doing the right thing to leave him overnight.' "

Jack went back the next day and got Keith released. He didn't have any clean clothes for him because the rest of us were all in Ohio, so Carson Chamberlain had to go to our house to find Keith some clean clothes. Keith was remorseful as Jack took him home. It was the day before Thanksgiving.

"My wife adored Keith, and she was talking to him in the car," Jack told me. "When we got to our house, I took him outside to our little orchard, three or four acres, and tried to reason with him.

"I said, 'Keith, you're going to kill yourself.'

"Keith was crying. He said, 'Man, I don't want to die.' "

Jack did not have to remind Keith that he had so much to live for. Keith expressed that all the time. But Jack tried to hammer home that getting drunk on the ugly side of town and fighting with the police was not a healthy thing for any human being. It was not great publicity for a singer, either. Of course, Keith agreed. Keith always agreed.

When Keith got home, he called me in Ohio and blustered, "How could you let them send me to jail?" All I could tell him was, "I didn't hit the policeman, you did."

We came home from Ohio a day early. I went to a friend of mine who had some connections on the police force and asked for help in getting the charges dropped, since Keith had never had any problems with the police before then.

My friend set up a meeting between Keith and the officer who, like everyone else, liked the sober side of Keith Whitley. They became instant friends, Keith apologized, and the charges were dropped.

They became such good friends that Keith wound up going out for a night in the patrol car with the officer. The poor man would, tragically, be killed in the line of duty a few years later.

But he would outlive Keith.

CHAPTER NINETEEN

I went through my photograph and letter collection not long ago, opening up the images of my three short years with Keith.

Spilled a few tears on a few photos and letters, but mostly found myself smiling at the memories of Keith's antics.

I'll never get all the memories into this book.

I'm afraid people are going to get the wrong idea, reading this book, thinking our marriage was one big binge and one big hangover.

Let me describe a few of these souvenirs, in no particular order, just as I pulled them out of the boxes. By now, I can't even remember the dates or the sequences. But, for the moment, I want to remember the good times.

This one was taken in the car on a trip back from Sandy Hook, the first time we took Morgan along, just before we got married. I took the photo from the front passenger seat, with Morgan sitting in between.

She had a great time, seeing Keith's old haunts and meeting his family. On the way home, Keith was driving and I was taking a nap when Morgan put her arms around Keith's shoulders and said, "Can I call you Daddy? Would you adopt me?"

I guess I wasn't sleeping too soundly because I heard those words and my eyes jolted open. Keith broke down and started crying, great big tears rolling down his cheeks. I thought he was going to lose control of the car on that twisty country road, but he got a grip on the wheel and he said, "Why, of course I'll adopt you."

Keith and I had already talked about this, but Morgan and I had never discussed it. It was totally her idea. He was so sweet to her all the time.

At the time, her dad owed me thousands of dollars in child support, but we never made an issue of it around Morgan. Keith was friendly with Ron and encouraged him to come over whenever he wanted to see Morgan.

My attorney, Jim Harris, arranged for Ron to agree to the legal adoption in return for my waiving the back child support. It worked out for all of us. Ron still sees Morgan every couple of months. To this day, he has only good things to say about Keith.

There's Keith diving in the pool. One-legged. He didn't know how to dive when we met, but I taught him.

I once bought him these red silk pajamas, very glamorous, very romantic, and he loved them—at least until he brought them on the road and the guys on the bus made fun of him. After that, he only wore them at home.

One morning we were having breakfast out by the pool and he was wearing those pajamas. Suddenly, he winked at me and got up and jumped in the pool—still wearing his red silk pajamas. Morgan laughed. She thought it was the funniest thing she'd ever seen. We all jumped in the pool in our pajamas.

That's Jesse in his little Superman outfit. Keith is flying him around the room.

Look at Jesse in his little ball cap and blue overalls and red sneakers. Keith loved him in this outfit. This was taken at the Frosty Freeze back in Sandy Hook.

That's Jesse at the pinball machine, and that's Keith in the black leather jacket and jeans. Keith was so proud to take his son back to his hometown and show him around.

They had Keith Whitley Day the year before he died. They named a street after him, Keith Whitley Boulevard. We went up there, they had a little parade before the unveiling of the street sign.

This next photo is Keith, riding his Harley through Sandy Hook. That's his brother Dwight with him.

We were always laughing around Keith. He'd say, "Lorrie, help me with my hair," and we'd see what we could create.

In this one, Morgan and I were doing his hair, and we put it up in pigtails with those little rubber bands, just for a laugh.

And this one is when I cut his hair, permed it, then frosted it. He's got the frosting cap on his head.

Here's Keith, grilling hot dogs at our first little house. When we moved in he promised he would do the grilling, and he did.

There's that green crushed-velvet chair I mentioned before. We spent a hundred dollars for it at Haverty's. We were just piecing together our collection of furniture, and we were so proud of the chair that we actually took a photo of it.

See how he's looking at me. He hung on my every word.

This is Keith, doing Elvis, sticking out his stomach on the bus. That's Keith with the J. D. Crowe band, before I ever met him. He was heavier then. There's Keith and Morgan at my fan club breakfast, the last one we had.

I also found some letters from Keith that show different sides of our marriage.

Here's a note that Keith had left on the seat of the car just before he went on a trip: "My Precious Baby: Buckle up and be careful, 'cause I couldn't make it without you. I love you. Keith."

One time I was traveling with him in Salt Lake City and we renewed our marriage vows in writing on stationery from the Salt Lake Airport Hilton. Keith wrote: "Dear God: Lorrie and I come before You to renew our vows of holy matrimony. Not because we need to but because we want to. We bring two halves of a medallion that we each shall wear as a symbol that neither of us is whole without the other. It is our prayer that You will bless this ceremony and continue to bless our marriage, as long as we both shall live, and throughout eternity."

He never put dates on his notes, but I found a letter that seems to have come after we had an argument, maybe about his being away too much. I don't remember.

"Dear Lorrie: I love you more than anything. You're all I think about and all I care about. . . . It kills me when you say you don't think I feel about you like I used to. We both have to make sacrifices to support our family, and when you start back working you're going to be making more. But the only reason I do it is for you. Without you and the kids, I wouldn't even try. Please, I pray to God, that when I'm not with you, I'm thinking about you. When you're not in my arms, you're in my heart. When I'm not touching you, I'm wanting to. I love you with all my heart. Please know that. Love, Keith."

This is our ski trip to Steamboat Springs. Look at him, flirting with Tanya Tucker. No, I remember what he was doing. He was imitating Bill Snowden, a Nashville musician everybody knows: "I've been in this business thirty damn years." Keith was such a great mimic. He also was very athletic, very graceful, loved to play softball and basketball, but he must have fallen twenty-five times skiing that day. I never fell once.

This is me on the beach in Florida. Mary Lou Turner and I went down there and I was working. I was so in love with Keith. She was up in the balcony of the motel and I was on the beach and I spelled his name in great big letters in the sand. When I got home, I noticed I had spelled his last name W-H-I-T-E-L-Y. Nothing I could do about it then.

Here's Keith in his reading glasses. He was so cute in them. So perfect. So beautiful.

Keith playing the guitar and singing to Jesse. He was very involved with his family. The kids never saw much of the bad stuff. When things got rough, I'd have the nanny or my mom take them.

Morgan and Jesse were just the beginning. We were going to have five or six kids.

That's Keith mowing the grass as a boy.

And that's Keith when he was little, at his grandma's house. Look at how his cowboy boots are on the wrong feet. He often put his boots on the wrong feet when he was little. I'll be doggoned if Jesse doesn't do the same thing.

Keith with Faron Young and Teddy Wilburn. Faron committed suicide in 1996.

Keith setting up our stereo so that the music could be heard out by the pool. He was very handy with tools. Here's Keith putting together a high chair for Jesse.

Here we are in Holland. Keith is in the hotel room, trying to figure out the European plugs and adapters. I had burned out two curling irons already, and he was not amused.

Jesse with a wig on. Jesse with Roy Acuff.

That's a friend of Keith's. I'll call him "Sammy." He used to come around once in a while when he and Keith were looking to drink—or worse. We are just introducing him to our favorite hot chicken, and he is sweating heavily, reaching for a glass of milk to douse the fire.

Christmas. Mom bought red flannel shirts for Marty and all the sons-in-law. They all put them on and posed.

Keith swimming in the pool with Tate, his black cocker. Cockers are great swimmers. We liked Tate so much, we got another one and named him Lefty.

Big benefit in Sandy Hook for one fund or another.

Softball game in Centennial Park. Debbie Schwartz. Dianne Sherrill. Everybody came to our house afterward for a cookout and pool party.

Keith on the Academy of Country Music awards show. Rodney Crowell won it that year.

That's Keith's sister, Mary, and her second husband, Farrell, when they got married in Nashville. We set them up with General Sessions Judge Barbara Norman Haynes, who married them at a private ceremony. Keith and I were the best man and maid of honor. I bought her the corsage and the garter; then we came back to our house for cake and stuff.

Keith and Morgan coming back from a ride on Keith's Harley. Look how beautiful his legs are.

Within a year after we were married, Keith was finally able to afford another Harley. He said he wanted to take me for a ride, but I was afraid. I was never allowed to ride a motorcycle when I was young. My dad said, "No way, period, I won't allow you kids on a motorcycle," so I had never been on one.

I'm not sure what I was afraid of more—falling off the

motorcycle, or Dad looking down at me and saying, "Hey, I told you, no motorcycles!" Either way, I was frightened.

Keith said, "Please, I promise you, just sit on the back behind me. If you're the least bit scared, we'll put it by the side of the road and we'll walk back." So I agreed.

He went and bought me a helmet, goggles and black gloves and put me on the back of that bike; then he eased that thing onto the main highway and out into the countryside. I remember it as a warm and sunny day.

It was like holding on to a cloud and knowing you're really high up but knowing the angels are not going to let you fall.

He drove so smoothly, nice and slow, over some long bridges until we got to a lake near Joelton, and we stopped at a country store and bought sandwiches and soda. We sat near the bike and ate our lunch and kissed; then we got back on the bike. He said, "You're not scared anymore, are you?" And I wasn't. After that, we'd ride our bike all over the valleys and into the sweet little hills around Nashville. It was our haven.

Keith used to take Jesse for a ride on his motorcycle, just down to the end of the street and back.

Now that same motorcycle is on display at the Country Music Hall of Fame. Not too long ago, I took Jesse down there and they let him sit on Keith's Harley.

CHAPTER TWENTY

Keith was going downhill. You can see it in the clips of the last shows he did with Ralph Emery. He always had an amazing smile when he sang—he would look in the camera and sparkle—but in the last months he was just grayish, wrinkled, washed-out looking.

We tried every possible approach to save him. Jack, who really loved him, would threaten him with doses of reality: "All right, if you drink, the label's going to drop you." Keith would never argue or fight back, but he did not like to be threatened. Deep in his eyes you could see defiance, as if he were saying, "Fuck you all, I'm gonna drink anyway."

They say alcoholism is a progressive disease, that it keeps getting worse. Even if you don't drink for awhile and then you start in drinking again, you'll be further down the road. Keith clearly could handle alcohol less well at thirty-three than he could at thirty, or twenty. It was eating him alive.

You could not predict what would set him off. In 1988 we got word that his father was fading fast back in Kentucky. Keith was working over in Paducah, at the opposite end of the state, so we got in the car and rushed across to Sandy Hook.

All the way over, Keith was just devastated, thinking he was going to lose his dad. I kept thinking, Oh, man, this is going to push Keith over the edge.

When we got to the hospital, his mother, sister, and brother were already there. Keith held his father's hand, but Mr. Whitley was too far gone to know Keith was by his side. Then Mr. Whitley took one last breath and died.

Mary was shaken up, but Keith kept his composure. He hugged his mother and talked to everybody, so sweet and kind. It reminded me of watching my own dad die, thirteen years earlier. I had so much respect for Keith, right up through the funeral and beyond. When his mother needed him, he was strong for her. He kept calling her every day, reassuring her that she would be all right—and eventually she was. But as soon as the crisis was over, Keith began to slip again.

He began missing more dates on the road. He could not be depended upon to get out on the stage, which put a tremendous burden on his band members. They were his friends, his colleagues, and their hearts were in the right place, but they were not trained in dealing with an alcoholic.

Mike Chamberlain acted as an unofficial bodyguard, standing around while Keith signed autographs. Ostensibly, Mike was there to protect Keith from possible danger from the crowds. In reality, Mike was there to protect Keith from himself.

"The first time I saw Keith drunk was in Pennsylvania," Mike recalls. "Keith said, 'I've got the best band in the world, and just to prove it, I'm going to let them perform by themselves.' He came back after one song and said, 'They're so good, I'm gonna let 'em do another one,' and when he came back onstage he was so drunk he couldn't pronounce the lyrics. The band just played loud, finished the song, and that was it."

One clue about Keith's state was if he was dancing. Sober, Keith never danced, but if he downed a six-pack in a matter of minutes, he thought he was Elvis, dancing around, slurring his words.

"I asked him once, 'Keith, I've had my share of liquor and hangovers, but how can you *stand* being so drunk?' " Mike once told me. Keith's response, according to Mike, is chilling. He said, "The best thing in the world is to pass out with the bottle, and when you wake up the bottle is right there and you take another swig and you just pass out again."

Mike remembers a trip to Bakersfield, when Keith passed out, scaring the band members.

"We took him to the hospital, his eyes open but not looking at you," Mike recalls. "Almost in a coma, really. They pumped him with sugar water and revived him. We asked if he could go back on the bus, so the orderly in his white uniform wheeled Keith to the front lobby and lifted him onto the bus, into the front lounge.

"Keith went into his bathroom in the back," Mike continued. "This was right in the hospital parking lot. I could hear him. He had Windex in a plastic container and he was about to chug it down. I just smacked it out of his hand and said, 'That's it, buddy,' and told him to lay down.

"We sat there in Bakersfield and canceled three shows. He could be really mean when he was drunk, but when he was sober he'd hug you and was very appreciative. I had an uncle who once said, 'There's two things I hate more than anything in the world—a drunk man when I'm sober and a sober man when I'm drunk.' And that was Keith."

One time, Keith opened for Reba McEntire somewhere in Virginia. Mike swears that Keith was sober when they drove the bus onto the grounds. However, they could not maneuver the bus to the stage entrance itself, so they transferred Keith into a van that would take him the rest of the way. Between the bus and the stage door, Keith managed to cajole a beer out of somebody, and by the time he got onstage, he was slurring.

There's a song with the words "corner table" and Keith kept getting it wrong. He kept saying, "torner table." That tape still exists, a hideous testimony to what alcohol did to that man's brain.

At the same concert in Virginia, there was a high stage, maybe twenty-five feet above the ground. Keith was so bombed he could not read the song list. The band was afraid he was going to lurch right off the stage and break his neck, so they played "Going Home," his encore song, signalling that the show was over. He got furious at them, but their part of the show was done. By the time they got him into the bus, he had already passed out.

If he did not take his Antabuse, that's what happened. But if the band got his Antabuse in him, without his conning them, he would stay sober for days or even weeks at a time.

"One night my brother had a birthday, and everybody wanted to party," Mike says. "I didn't know if it was a good idea because of Keith, but that night Keith wanted no part of it. If you had poured beer on his head, he would not have stuck out his tongue."

Alcohol was the chemical of choice for Keith, but he was not totally unfamiliar with cocaine. I never saw him use the stuff because he knew how I felt about it, but as a close friend of ours put it, "If it was on the table, he'd take some."

I know that people would shake his hand at a show and slip him a little bag of coke for free, out of friendship, because he was Keith Whitley. And if Carson or Mike didn't catch it, he would try to pocket it. If they spotted it, Keith would say, "Oh, yeah, I was just gonna hand it over to you."

He would ingest anything, if the time was right.

His old pal Sammy would show up every so often, a face from the past, bearing gifts, sometimes in little clear packages. As far as I know, Keith did not have a regular habit or a regular supplier. He could get what he wanted by slipping off to the convenience store for a six-pack when nobody was keeping an eye on him.

People don't want to hear that alcohol, which is legal, is just as dangerous as illegal drugs for somebody like Keith.

In September of 1988, the rest of the band was already up in Hazard for the big Black Gold festival, celebrating coal mining. Keith and Carson Chamberlain were arriving by commuter plane into Knoxville, and we were waiting to drive them up to join the band.

The plane landed, and the other passengers disembarked. After a while, Carson came out, but no Keith. Right on the runway, Carson went to the attendant, asked for a wheelchair, and the two of them headed back to the plane. We all knew what was coming next.

"Mike, I am so tired of baby-sitting," I said. And I *was* tired. I was exhausted.

When they started to wheel Keith across the tarmac, he jumped off the wheelchair and started weaving around the runway.

When he saw me, he said, "Well, look who's here." He gave me a hug, which just annoyed me more. It turned out that he had gotten his hands on those little whiskey bottles they pass out like candy on planes and he kept ducking into the bathroom to drink them. All the way up into the hills to Hazard, he was pretty much out of it, just looking at us with a blank stare. He was supposed to perform with Jeannie Seely and Glen Campbell, but they went on first. We needed extra time to pour black coffee into Keith before sending him out.

In between drinking bouts, he was still so sweet. One time, right after the Thanksgiving episode, he came home from the road sober and took his Antabuse. After the kids were in bed, he lay down in bed and started crying. He asked, "Would you sing to me?" I asked what he wanted, and he said, "I want you to sing me the lullabye you sing to Jesse all the time."

It's the one where you spell out the words "I L-O-V-E Y-O-U."

I sang it to him until he fell asleep.

He never mentioned it again. Never asked me to sing it again.

I felt he was a lost little boy, seeking peace, needing sweet maternal sounds. I tried to give that to him. But sometimes that was not enough.

Keith was like a naughty child who gets overly excited in the week leading up to Christmas Day. He behaves himself in anticipation of something wonderful, but once that moment is over, he goes back to his old ways.

The time right after Christmas is the most depressing time for people. The best way to explain Keith is that he was in a constant state of either December 24 or December 26. If he was preparing for something, going in for a new album, he was great. When it was over, that depression would set in; the demons would come back.

He was such a little boy at times, full of life and love and passion, and you'd think, What is the deal here? Why can't this moment last?

How is it possible for somebody to be so perfect and yet so flawed?

I often wonder. You hear about people married thirty, forty years, people like my parents. Is that just old-school people? Did wives from that era really communicate like we are taught to communicate? Did they really talk about all their problems with their mate? I don't know. I don't know how you can hang in there, through good and bad, rich and poor, better or worse. I've never gotten that far. At least not yet.

The sixties changed so much. Suddenly, people had options, people were overstimulated, people went for a divorce the way you'd take a couple of aspirins.

It's different in the music business, period. You're dealing with creative minds, artists. In order to be good, you have to be constantly changing, revising, in your own world. It's hard to be normal. Fortunately, during this terrible time in my life, I had my solid family all around me.

Mom was great. When things got bad, I'd call her up and say, "I'm bringing Morgan and Jesse for a visit," and she would take care of them as long as was necessary.

I suppose I should have confided more in Mom as things got worse with Keith, but I figured it was my burden, my responsibility.

She and Paul knew that Keith drank; they knew we had problems, and I could see she was concerned, frightened, for me. She had been around it a little, but it wasn't something we discussed too much.

Paul did talk about it a little. As an ex-priest, he had counseled people with the problem. He would say, "Keith needs treatment. You have got to get him into another treatment center." I would say, "It's not that easy. You just don't tell Keith Whitley to check into a center. We've tried that before and it didn't work."

Even in a close family there are bound to be differences. What I'm about to say is nothing I have not said to my sisters, but I began to feel that Candy and Beth were a little envious of me because Keith and I were so close. Their marriages were not going so well, and as far as anybody could see, on the surface ours was fine. Whatever our problems, we were madly in love.

In 1986, right after our honeymoon, Keith and I had gone over to Mom's for Thanksgiving, and I had felt the jealousy in the air. I don't think they meant to make me feel that way, but I came home and had a migraine that lasted for days. I'm sure that's one of the reasons Keith pulled his disappearing act at Thanksgiving of 1987.

In 1988 he flat-out said he wanted to stay home and simply have a quiet Thanksgiving with me and Morgan and Jesse. So I cooked dinner and we watched television, but it was like a chunk of me was missing. Those big family gatherings were such a big part of the Morgan family. I didn't feel complete away from my family, and yet I felt the strain when I was with them. I guess most families are like that. The one who is going good at the moment has to feel the sadness of somebody else.

If Keith would fly me to one of his shows out of town, I could hear the tone in their voices: "Oh, it must be nice to be able to fly all over the country." Keith would call home and he would hear the guilty tone in my voice. He would say, "Lorrie, don't you deserve to be happy? I'm your husband. Don't you deserve to enjoy yourself?"

That Thanksgiving was a statement, mostly by Keith, that he was pulling back a little. So I can't say that any members of my family did know, or should have known, about Keith's problems. The fact is, we thought we were keeping them hidden from everybody.

I don't make excuses, but Keith didn't live in a vacuum. There was more going on in his world than in our love affair and his alcoholic binges. He was under extreme pressure, worried about record labels, worried about shows. Now that we were a two-career family, I think he was partly afraid he would not be able to handle it, that his career would go down while mine was going up.

I always compare it to the movie *A Star Is Born*, with Kris Kristofferson and Barbra Streisand. It wasn't as if Keith's career was over, not by a long shot, but maybe he knew in his heart that he could not control himself, and that lack of control was going to ruin him and his career.

People say it is hard for a man when his wife is more successful than he is, particularly if they are in the same field. I can see that. This has been a man's world from the start, and men have become accustomed to success. They're expected to do well. If their wives start having good careers, maybe it is a blow to their egos. But I know, and I hear about, plenty of men who are comfortable with their wives' success. They know that's just the way it is in today's world.

I think that Keith was afraid I would leave him, that I would get tired of baby-sitting him, making sure he took his Antabuse. To be honest, that was the only way life would ever be with him. And we both knew it.

I don't think he wanted to die, but I do believe he did not want to continue on as he was—whatever that meant. To straighten up meant to deal with his problems. He chose to hide his problems behind a veil of alcohol.

I've been told that alcoholism is a disease of feelings, that you drink to hide the feelings. That's exactly what he was doing. The only way I could have gotten through to him was to have given him the kind of tough love that says, "You have to choose. Either you do something or I'm walking." It sounds easy enough, but I loved him so much. The thought of leaving him was unbearable to me; it was not a viable choice. Yet, even so, we had that conversation many times. Each time, it would end the same way: Keith would say, "I'll never drink again. I'll never put you through this." And he wouldn't. Until the next time.

I've often wondered what would have happened if I had gotten a piece of paper on him, a legal separation, something short of divorce. One of my fears was that, if I was his life, if I was his rock, and I walked out, if he died it would be on my shoulders. And how could I deal with that? In a way, he had control over me. Alcoholics are very manipulative. They know what the other person is feeling. I was committed to Keith, and he knew it. And he used that to his advantage.

Keith begged Jack and Joe to arrange our schedules so we'd tour together and record together. One time Jack said, "Look, boys and girls, you've both got careers. By the time you got to Memphis, one of you would be on the way home. Familiarity breeds contempt."

Joe Galante felt that I had to stick to my own schedule, no matter what Keith did. He didn't want another George and Tammy.

However, Jack did say, "We can direct traffic," and he tried to arrange our schedules so that neither of us would be on the road for more than five or six days. After that, we would have time home together.

At times, I would offer to give up my career if that would help Keith, but Jack told us, "You'd end up hating each other. Lorrie's career is important, too."

And Keith would always agree.

On March 20, 1989, Keith appeared with Ralph Emery to plug his new song, "I'm No Stranger to the Rain."

On the air, he told Ralph how his records had made their debut on Ralph's show, then gone into the top ten.

"Keep debuting 'em here, son," Ralph said.

Whenever we play back that tape, I can't help but notice

how Keith's eyes are so sad and drawn. It would be the last time he would ever perform with Ralph.

Joe Galante was running out of patience. He scheduled a big meeting with Keith on Wednesday, May 10, to discuss the missed shows, the bad reputation Keith was getting. Keith knew he was in trouble, that his career was threatened. Joe told him he would have to go into treatment again.

Keith pleaded with Joe not to drop him. RCA is a historical place. He was proud to be on a label that had so many *Opry* members, so many Hall of Fame members. Joe told me he could hear the fear in Keith's voice. Joe told me recently, "He was scared. He didn't want it to happen. I guess I believed he wouldn't let it happen. You can't threaten him. It's a Band-Aid on an aorta about to break. That was a terrible experience. You want to be tough, but you can't be tough with a man who's never made you mad."

In retrospect, we all know that Keith did make us mad, or that he should have made us mad, mad enough to seriously threaten him with the loss of things that were important to him—recordings, shows, wife, children. But we never got that far.

Maybe things were worse between Keith and me than I ever saw, ever understood. Jack McFadden, who was as close to Keith as anybody, was talking about Keith recently:

"I've had eight years to think about this," Jack said. "I think Keith was jealous. Lorrie's first single, 'Train Wreck of Emotion,' jumped on the charts right away, whereas his first hadn't broken the top twenty. They were putting her out on a promotion tour. She went on the road without him. I think it bothered him more than it showed.

"Keith confided in me. He couldn't bear the thought of Lorrie being on the road. He was an insecure guy. He was jealous."

Right around the end of April, Keith pulled one of his vanishing acts. This one would hurt me more than the others.

About nine o'clock at night, I realized I had not heard from him, so I called Jack, who said he had not had any contact with Keith since three-thirty. Jack knew a few aliases that Keith used when he was out drinking, and he called around to some of the local bars and hospitals, but there was no sign of him. At eleven that night, Jack got a call from a hospital in Louisville, three hours north of us, saying that Keith had been taken to the emergency room after an auto accident, but that he did not have a scratch on him.

Witnesses had seen his car make a sudden turn at ninety miles an hour, and the car had rolled end over end six times. The top of the car was flattened from the impact, and Keith had been thrown through the windshield, leaving shattered glass in his hair.

Jack and I drove up to Louisville to bring him home.

"Son, somebody's sending you a message," Jack said sadly. "It's getting out of hand. Get a hold of yourself."

Later, I found out there was more to the story. Keith had been driving to meet a woman in Lexington. Just south of Louisville he realized he had taken the wrong turn on the interstate, and tried to swerve off of it, turning his new Cherokee, a typical reaction of a man out of control.

Up to now, there had never been any indication that Keith was cheating on me. We had both said that if either one of us cheated, the relationship was gone, and I know I kept my end of the deal. I also believed Keith did. There was no sign that he was looking for women when he was not out on the road because he was either at home with me, sober, or passed out somewhere else.

If he cheated on the road, I had never received any clues. I knew we were bonded. I knew he was not lying when he called me six times a day to say hello. If he was cheating in between, he surely covered his tracks.

But I also know what the road is like—and I know what men are like. If he took a quickie here and there, well, I've seen 'em all standing around outside the men's buses, and I know he wouldn't have had to work very hard to find 'em. All I can say is, I think I would have seen the signs. And this was the first.

Jack told somebody recently, "When he totaled his Jeep, he was despondent. I said, 'Man, you've got a great thing going.' But his attitude was, "I'm gonna go home and bicker with the old lady some more."

Keith knew I was scheduled to go out on the road soon.

RCA was hot at the time. They had made money from the Judds and K. T. Oslin, money from Ronnie Milsap and Dolly, and they had money to spend. They had invested a lot of money on my *Leave the Light On* album. They wanted to promote it. And so did I.

Galante and his people were sending me to some army bases in Washington State and Alaska because military people buy a lot of albums.

Just before that, Keith had a trip out to Texas for a few shows, and then he was coming back. We would overlap for a few hours.

I called Joe on the phone and expressed my concerns about leaving.

"You've got to go now," Joe told me. "Keith wants you to go; he's just not in a state to support it."

What state was Keith in?

His sister, Mary, says that on his last trip home to Sandy Hook, about three or four weeks before he died, he made a rather sad request:

"Keith asked me, 'Will you swear?'" Mary has said. "You have to understand, that with the Whitleys, if you swear to do something, you will keep your word. I said, 'Of course I would swear.' Keith said, 'Please swear that you will bring Jesse and Morgan to your house so they will know how the Whitleys live.' I said, 'Honey, you know we would do that.'"

It was an eerie thing to be asking, a man not quite thirty-four, asking his sister to take an active interest in his two children. The Whitleys might see this as Keith feeling that the kids did not know his family as well as he wanted them to. But the main thrust of that request was that he might not be around to bring them home to Sandy Hook himself.

I never heard this until recently. It makes me realize that as close as we were, I might never have known what he was really feeling.

By then, I had realized that things were not going to get better by themselves. I did not want to bring my kids up in the environment in which we now found ourselves, one of constant tension and fear. But I did not know what to do. And I never got a chance to act on these concerns.

Chapter Twenty-One

Keith's concert in Brazoria County, just south of Houston, was memorable for something that happened off the stage. Mike Chamberlain was driving the bus on the getaway, and when he tried to swing it around, he got the rear end caught in the sand and needed a tractor to pull him out.

Some stars might have pulled a temper tantrum, but Keith was just one of the boys. They all had nicknames for each other. Keith's was The Whit-Bomb, shortened to The Bomb.

"He just laughed at me," Mike said, about the bus incident. "Then we went out for Mexican food. Keith was fine. He shook my hand, gave me a hug, and said, 'Love you, brother.' "

They dropped Keith off at the Houston airport while the rest of the band stayed on the bus for the long haul back to Nashville. Keith was flying home because he had a hot date on Sunday morning—me.

We had only a few hours of overlap because now it was my turn to go on the road. I had a lot of worries about leaving, but once again Joe and Jack reassured me that I had to get on with my life.

He called me from Houston that night and said, "We'll have a great day Sunday before you leave."

But Keith was drunk when he got off the plane on Sunday morning.

When we drove home, I called Jack and told him Keith had done it again. "I can't go," I said. Jack was livid.

"You've got to go," he told me. "This is your career."

My career. Part of me was very ambitious and part of me wasn't at all. I'd been doing this a long time, since Dad introduced me on the stage of the Ryman. Here I was, almost thirty years old, a late bloomer. I loved Keith Whitley, but at the moment my love was not uppermost in my mind. I was too worried. And mad.

"I'll think about it," I told Jack.

Then I talked to Joe Galante on the phone. He said, "Look, Lorrie, this album is really important to you. We've got to do it. If you don't go, Keith will know that every time you're scheduled to go out of town, he can just drink and you'll stay home."

Joe was much too cool to ever remind me that RCA had laid out many thousands of dollars on my album, and that now it was up to me to go out and promote it. We talked in terms of career and living up to my potential and being professional.

I started packing. By now, Keith was a little more sober. I was in the pantry getting something to eat, when he took my face in his hands and said, "I just want you to know, you are the best singer I ever heard in my life." Then he kissed me.

Looking back, it was almost as if he was giving me a final praise, a final blessing. I did think it was strange at the time, but I was happy to be kissing him, and hearing nice words from him, so I didn't dwell on it. The kids were out, so we locked the doors and made passionate love. I had no time for premonitions or gloomy thoughts.

Still, I was worried about Keith, knowing that I'd be gone for a while. It was a breaking point. I would be thousands of miles away. I would be the one with the airplane itinerary and the motel phone numbers and the distant time zones. Keith would be the one staying home, the one left behind. I felt guilty.

I also had very real fears that something terrible would happen. I knew he had not taken his Antabuse at least since early Saturday because he arrived home drunk on Sunday, and he could not possibly have been walking around if the Antabuse were in his system. I knew there were other Antabuse pills around the house. It was too soon to take one, but I reminded him to take them while I was away, and as always, he promised. Keith always promised.

Call it premonition or logic, I was afraid for Keith's safety while I was gone for those three days, so I reached out for somebody to keep an eye on him. I called Lane, who was still married to Beth after all those tumultuous years.

In some weird way, I trusted Lane. He was bad to my sister, but he was brotherly toward me, and I knew he loved and protected Keith. Lane did indeed say he would get on the case, so I called Beth and told her he was going to help me out. I felt greatly relieved.

Keith drove me to the airport, parked the car, and walked me out to the Delta flight at gate B-3.

When it was time to board, Keith handed me an envelope with a card inside. He said, "Don't open this until you get on the plane." I remember him wearing his tortoise-shell sunglasses; so cute.

Then we both said, "I love you." And this time I was the one who got on the plane and left.

My road manager, Dave Fowler, was accompanying me on this trip. As soon as we were in the air, I opened Keith's envelope and saw a beautiful greeting card.

Keith had chosen a card with a printed message that said he hoped my "troubles, worries, and problems" would not linger, and that I would find "success in my path."

Troubles? Worries? Problems? Success? Path? What was Keith trying to tell me? At thirty-thousand feet, I felt a sharp pang of panic.

"I've got to go home," I told Dave. If I could have, I would have parachuted out of the plane.

"Lorrie, you can't," he said, but when we changed planes in Atlanta, I called Jack and Joe at their homes and told them something was wrong. They reassured me that everything would be fine. I calmed down somewhat and agreed to continue on.

When we got to Seattle, it was five-thirty in the evening. I called home and did not get an answer. Then I called Beth's house and said I was trying to get in touch with Keith. Beth told me he was right there, at her house, sleeping on the couch.

"Tell him I'm here," I said, but she replied, "No, we'd better let him sleep." And then she said, "Lane's got his keys to the 'Vette."

As soon as I hung up, I wondered why Lane would need to take the keys to the Corvette Keith loved so much, unless Keith was already messed up? I was just shaking. I knew something was not right. I tried calling Beth's house again, but nobody picked up. Then I called my house, but the kids were out. I got no answer anywhere.

On Monday morning, I tried my house again. Still no answer. I called Beth and she said Keith had left a little while ago. She told me he was fine.

I did not necessarily accept that.

I have not told too many people about this, but at that point, I called my attorney, Jim Harris, and I said, "I can't live like this anymore." It wasn't as if I was filing for divorce, but I needed to talk to somebody. I needed to know what my options were. Things were reeling out of control. No Keith. No answers. No peace.

I made my appearances on Monday, chatting and singing and autographing, a smile plastered on my face. In between shows, I tried to contact Keith, but he was nowhere to be found. It was over twenty-four hours, the longest time I had ever gone without talking to him. Something was wrong. Very wrong.

On Tuesday morning, there was still no word. I went out to an army base to sign autographs. Security was tight. I was surrounded by fences and guns, too many people, with airplanes roaring overhead, and I began feeling claustrophobic, the panic attack of impending doom.

"I need to get out of here," I told Dave Fowler, so we took a break for lunch.

Suddenly, there was an announcement, a phone call for Dave.

I thought that was strange, and suddenly I could not eat another bite. I was just waiting for some kind of bad news.

When Dave came back, his face was white.

"Jack needs to talk to you," he said quietly.

"Keith's dead, isn't he?"

"Lorrie, Jack needs to talk to you."

"I know Keith is dead."

"Lorrie, talk to Jack."

I staggered to the phone and heard Jack say, "Lorrie, Keith is gone."

"What do you mean? *Gone* gone?"

His next words sounded so unreal, as if they had to be about somebody else, not the man I loved.

"They found him in bed with an alcohol overdose."

All I could think—and pardon my language—was: "Those stupid fuckers. They made me go. He'd still be alive if I hadn't gone."

I was furious at Jack and Joe. I wanted to blame them for Keith's death. I may even have expressed those sentiments to Jack. I don't remember. I was furious at everyone. At the world.

Jack said there was a limousine waiting for me, that all the arrangements had been made.

I started putting one foot in front of the other, and somehow I made it to the limousine and out to the airport. I felt I was dead, but I was still walking around. There was a hole in me that nothing could ever fill.

The rest of the trip is a blur of sadness. The Delta people were very nice, giving me privacy. I remember a flight attendant telling me to rest.

Dave Fowler sat next to me, trying his best to comfort me, leaning over every five minutes and saying, "Are you okay?"

I remember thinking to myself, "How am I ever going to face Jesse and Morgan?"

I remember being mad at Keith. How could he have put us all in this position?

I was mad at Beth and Lane for doing this to me. In reality, Keith was not their obligation, he was mine. But in a way, I needed to be angry. My anger kept me tethered to the world. Kept me from breaking down totally.

I could not help but imagine how Keith had looked, lying on our bed, but I was not dwelling on how he had died, what he had taken, whether anybody was around. That would come later. Right now I just knew he was gone.

After the long flight to Atlanta and the shorter flight to Nashville, we landed around midnight. Dave escorted me off the plane. The airport people had thoughtfully set aside a special room for us, in case emotions got too high, or the press was too intrusive, but nobody bothered us.

I saw the whole family, Mom and Paul, the four kids, some of their spouses, friends, Jack McFadden. They all surrounded me and hugged me and told me we would get through it.

I wasn't convinced.

They took me to Mom's house, and we all stayed up talking, keeping busy. I know that at some point I was on the phone with Kathi, Keith's former wife. I don't remember if I called her or she called me, but I told her, "Kathi, I know you may not be happy about the way things worked out, but I just want you to know you are welcome at the funeral parlor and the funeral. We want you to be there."

Ever since that awful Tuesday in 1989, it has been seared into all our memories just where we were when we heard the news. People in my circle remember it the way other people remember where they were when President Kennedy was killed, or when the first man walked on the moon.

My mom said somebody had called her, and she urged Paul to rush over to school. She did not want Morgan to hear about it from a friend who might hear it on the radio. Mom said Morgan was surprisingly calm when she heard. Maybe she, too, had been aware of Keith's free-fall.

Joe Galante was having lunch with Eddy Arnold when somebody from the company called and gave him the news. Joe tried to finish the lunch with his friend but quickly realized he could not sit there.

"I went over to Jack's office," Joe said later. "I had the roughs to Keith's 'I Wonder Do You Think of Me.' We had just finished it, and I was driving around with it in my car. I was just driving around asking, Why, why, why?"

"I got a call from Dave Wheeler," Blake Mevis said. "He told me Keith was dead and I said, 'My God, what happened?' But I knew. I knew. You know, Keith called me the week before, and he said, 'Hey, man, I want to spend a whole day, the two of us, just driving around, talking.' But I knew I'd get that call, and I knew it would not be long."

Ricky Skaggs happened to be back home in a neighboring county, attending the funeral of a young male cousin who had also died much too young. As soon as Ricky heard the news on the car radio, while driving through Lexington, he turned the car around and rushed over to Sandy Hook to be with Mrs. Whitley, who had fed him so many meals back in the old days.

Mrs. Whitley was telling people how she had spoken to Keith that morning but had a premonition that something was wrong and had tried to call him again.

His sister Mary told people she had glanced at a photo of Keith that morning, and that it had seemed to fade away and then reappear.

Mike Chamberlain remembers unpacking his car on Tuesday back in Berea, and getting a call from Carson, who broke the news with typically morbid musicians' humor.

"No need to come back to Nashville," Carson said.

Mike asked why.

"You know how The Bomb drinks enough to pass out? Well, this time he drank enough to pass away."

It sounds cold, but I totally understand. Those guys loved Keith as much as I did. If they didn't talk like that, they couldn't get through it.

Bill Anderson heard the news in Nashville, and right away he thought about my friend Mary Lou Turner out in Branson. He knew how much she loved Keith, so he called out to Boxcar Willie's show and said he needed to talk to her, immediately. He had no way of knowing this, but they were right in the middle of the noon show. Mary Lou was just at the edge of the stage, waiting for her cue.

They said the call was an emergency, and she got on with Bill, who told her what had happened. Mary Lou took the news like a punch in the midsection, but trouper that she is, she walked out onstage and performed as if nothing had happened.

"And all the time, I was thinking to myself, I didn't do enough," Mary Lou said later.

Somebody in the press noted that Keith had once recorded the song "I've Done Everything Hank Did But Die."

The next day, I had to face reality. Keith had died at thirty-three without a will or life insurance. As his wife, I would inherit his estate, which was estimated at only $50,000. What that meant was, I had no idea how I was going to hold on to the house, much less pay for the funeral. Joe Galante made the wonderful gesture of paying for the casket, and the next day we picked out a beautiful silver one.

We did not have enough money for anything but a little stand-up tombstone in Spring Hill Cemetery in Madison. We chose a spot in the Crestview section, fairly high up, so the mountain boy would feel comfortable.

I wanted my name on the tombstone, too, so they put both our names right under the name Whitley. J Keith and Lorrie M.

In the office, I was asked what inscription I wanted. I remember looking at Ruthie and it just came to me: "Forever Yours, Faithfully," right from the song "Faithfully," which had been our song. And underneath I had them inscribe: "His Being Was My Reason."

Then I had to face it. I had to go out to the house, where Keith had died barely twenty-four hours earlier. I had heard that Lane had been in there, trying to save his life, and I knew the police had been in there, too. Everything else was still a mystery.

Gilly drove us over. I took a deep breath and walked inside. Mom had asked Bernice, one of our housekeepers, and Barbara Powers, who was still helping us, to clean up the house, so it looked pretty good, pretty ordinary, no trace of the gruesome event that had taken place the morning before.

At first, I could not confront the details of what had happened. I just had to get through this. I had to select clothes for Keith to wear in the casket. I remember going into that bedroom, trying not to think about him pouring all that vile stuff down his throat, lying there on that bed.

I could not help but glance over at the water bed where Keith had died. The Goodlettsville police had taken the lime green sheets with the white floral pattern down to the laboratory to test them, and for some reason the housekeepers had not made the bed. It just sat there, showing no sign of the last horrible hours of my husband's life.

I shuddered and turned away, toward Keith's clothing.

"I remember when he bought this," I would say, touching a favorite shirt. Or, "He loved this sweater."

For Keith's last appearance on this earth, I wanted him to look good. I picked out the green stage coat that he had had made for himself, with small sparkles on it, his best pair of blue jeans, and Giorgio cologne, his favorite.

As the hours passed, I began to ask what had happened. It was clear that Keith had not been sleeping on the couch at Beth's house on Sunday night. It was clear that Lane had made Beth lie, that Beth had never seen Keith. It was not clear where Keith had been for the next two days.

Lane said he had been hanging out with Keith on Sunday and that Keith was drinking. He said he had grabbed the car keys away from Keith, but that Keith had taken a cab home, gotten the other set of keys, and reclaimed the car. Bernice said Keith had come home Sunday night, apologized for bothering her, picked up his keys, and got back in the cab.

Lane said he saw Keith again Monday out at Lane's shop, and that Keith was still functioning.

Then Lane had gone to the house Tuesday morning. Keith appeared sober. They drank a cup of coffee together and Keith seemed fine. Three hours later, Lane returned to find Keith dying or dead. Lane had tried to give Keith CPR, but it did not work.

Lane was giving me the short form. The real short form. But I did not realize that until later.

The police did not seem to regard anybody as a suspect. Keith drank too much and Keith died. End of story.

Lane was pretty shaken up. I could not find it in my heart to blame him.

Other people had tried to contact Keith in those two days. Mom had gone out there Tuesday morning after getting Morgan to school. Jesse was in the back with Barbara, in the apartment we had set up in the garage. Mom knocked on the front door, but nobody answered. She assumed Keith wasn't there, or wasn't answering, so she went home. She never realized anything was wrong. She also thinks she talked to Keith on the phone early that morning.

Keith's mother had talked to him around eight-thirty Nashville time and said he sounded great. But when she had her premonition and tried him again, she couldn't reach him, so she began calling Jack's office.

Jack had also gone out to our house on Tuesday, around ten-thirty, with Carson Chamberlain, looking for Keith. They heard the television on in the bedroom, but they could not get in. The bedroom door was locked.

Jack said he heard "grumbling" from inside and shouted "Keith, open the damn door," but there was no response.

"We have a meeting with Galante," Jack yelled, but still there was no response.

Jack said he then wrote a note that said something like, "If you want a career, you better be ready for Galante at 1 PM tomorrow." Jack put it on the bar in the kitchen and went home.

Jack promptly called Lane, who reassured them he "just had coffee with him at eight o'clock." When they asked where Keith had been over those two days, Lane said Keith had been "out at one of those joints" and had not come home until Monday.

At eleven-thirty on Tuesday, Lane returned to the house. The bedroom door was now open, and Keith was lying in bed. At first, Lane said, he thought Keith was watching television, and that Keith said something to him. Lane talked to Jack on the phone and said Keith was there.

"Are you sure he's okay?"

Lane said he was, but as soon as he got off the phone, he went back to Keith, discovered that he was lying facedown and was already turning cold. Lane tried to revive him but to no avail.

Fifteen minutes later, Lane called back and said, "Jack, I think he's dead."

The report from the Davidson County medical examiner, Charles Harlan, said Keith's blood level was 0.47, far above the lethal level of 0.30 and nearly five times above the level of legal intoxication, which is 0.10. The report said Keith had the equivalent of twenty one-ounce shots of 100-proof whiskey in his system.

Traces of cocaine and a tranquilizer were also found in his body, but the direct cause was an accidental alcohol overdose. The time of death was eleven-thirty on Tuesday morning.

Lane must have walked in just as Keith was dying.

What had Keith been drinking? There had been no alcohol in the house when I left, but he had had plenty of time to get into trouble on his own. Lane said Keith had seemed sober at eight in the morning, but Keith was known to drink a huge amount of alcohol in a very short time. He had come close to dying before. All of us were shocked—yet none of us were surprised. The only mystery was that we heard there were reports of a greenish tint to the fluids in Keith's system.

The police later said that there was no suggestion of foul play. Nevertheless, I should have asked many more questions of Beth and Lane at the time, just to know all the details, but I was too numb, too stricken, to make any sense. I let the mystery sit there for days and weeks and months and years before I got answers. I still don't have *all* the answers.

But I do have some.

I will admit, I was terribly upset with Beth and Lane, and stayed mad at them for a long, long time. I hadn't asked many favors of my family, but I had asked them to keep an eye on Keith. He had probably lied to both of them, Lane had certainly lied to Beth, and both of them had lied to me. I wasn't blaming them for Keith's death, but I was angry with them for not telling me right away that he was off on a binge.

Our love affair had lasted barely three years. Now I had to prepare myself to be a widow, to raise two children who loved Keith very much, by myself. Poor Jesse, poor Morgan, I thought to myself.

I felt as if my own life had been drained away.

I had a few minutes alone with Keith at the funeral parlor, before the visitors came. He looked so beautiful in his stage jacket and jeans, a great look of peace on his face, the haunted appearance of the past months was gone. His beard and hair were combed nicely—and he smelled so good. Every woman who bent over to kiss him said the same thing: "Keith smells just like he always did."

So many people came to the funeral parlor that I could never thank all of them—or even remember them.

I felt terrible seeing Mrs. Whitley. In the space of five years she had lost Randy, her husband, and now Keith.

Mrs. Whitley says that she said a prayer to help her keep her composure. It obviously worked, because she was so gracious and so poised, she was a model for everybody else.

Jack McFadden was standing by the open casket, rocking back and forth on his feels, wailing like a baby. Jack had loved Keith like a father, had taken him for a walk that Thanksgiving when he got Keith out of jail and warned him he was killing himself. And now Keith was gone. Jack's sobs filled the room, until Mrs. Whitley comforted him.

"Jack, you know the old song, 'I Hate to See a Grown Man Cry'?" she asked.

Jack shuddered and pulled himself together. "You're right," he said.

Somebody came up to me and said, "Ralph's here." Ralph Emery had been there for us when Dad died; now he was there for us again. I met him in a private room off to the side. He gave me a big hug and said he was sorry, and then he said, "Lorrie, this is a time when you need to be strong, and I know you can do it."

Just feeling Ralph's hand holding mine gave me the strength to keep going. I walked him out to the casket thinking of the times he had plugged Keith's new records, how many times he had begged Keith to do his goofy Lester Flatt imitation, how many times he had cared about us.

I spotted Don Light and Lynn Simpkins and could remember how many times they, too, had tried to help Keith. I also remembered the testy conversation I had had with Lynn the time she called and told me that Keith was an alcoholic. At the time, I had been angry and resentful, but now it was time to mend fences.

"I know you thought the world of Keith," I said. "You tried to tell me something. I'm sorry it took this for me to give you a hug."

I also saw a few wives from the band. Some things just never change. They had not softened toward me, and I had not softened toward them.

Mary Lou Turner came up from Branson, Missouri, and she remembers my telling her, "I was always afraid to die, but I'm not afraid to die anymore." I think I meant that Keith looked so peaceful that it put a different perspective on death.

When things got overwhelmingly sad for me in the funeral home, I went out and took a walk with my brother, Marty. I don't remember what we talked about, but I remember his being there for me, comforting me.

At the end of the viewing, Mrs. Whitley and I had to do one of the most painful things either of us had ever done—we had to observe while the funeral parlor people covered Keith up for the last time.

Mrs. Whitley went first. She leaned over her son and put her cheek next to his. I would not have blamed her if she had tried to stay there, but she was remarkably composed.

Then it was my turn. He looked so sweet and peaceful lying there. I put my lips on his lips, closed my eyes, and thought of all the kisses we had shared, from the first time in Centennial Park, to the last time at the Nashville airport. I pressed my lips harder against his and did not want to let go, but somehow I found the courage to stand up and turn away from my beautiful husband.

I'd like to tell you I remember a lot of the funeral, but I don't. Some of my friends say I looked serene; others say I looked sedated. It was probably both—but I don't remember that, either.

I've seen photographs of myself wearing a black dress, cut above the knees, with a gold chain, and Morgan wearing a white dress. So I know we were there.

They say that St. Joseph Church was packed with five hundred mourners on Friday, May 12. I've had to rely on the memory of others to reconstruct the funeral.

"The saddest part for me was when Keith's band all came in together," Candy recalls. "It brought it home to all of us how sad they must be that he wouldn't be with them anymore."

One of Keith's best friends, Blake Mevis, would mentally write a new song while he was sitting in that church.

"Keith was such a tender and nice person," Blake has said. "I was sitting there and I remembered the song 'Blue Kentucky Girl,' and I thought about a song called 'Blue Kentucky Boy' because I truly believe Keith had some kind of sadness underneath. The words came to me right away:

He was a gentle soul, with a heart of gold,
The kind the world destroys,
He was a blue Kentucky boy.

Among the other performers and friends in attendance were: Duane Allen of the Oak Ridge Boys, John Hartford, Paul Overstreet, David Frizzell, Jack Greene, Billy Walker, and Vic Willis.

I do remember Ricky Skaggs singing a medley of country

hymns. The papers listed them as "White Dove" and "The Fields Have Turned Brown" and "Drifting Too Far from Shore."

Ricky also said a few words, including the message: "If any of you have a drinking problem, or a drug problem, or an emotional problem, please go get help. There's one person who can help: Jesus. Keith would say the same thing."

Then Ricky looked down at the closed casket and said, "I've lost so many friends."

There was another poetic touch in the eulogy by Father Pat Kibby, who was then attached to St. Joseph's but is now at the Cathedral in Nashville. Father Kibby did not know Keith very well, but with very short notice he called some members of the family to ask about him, and he produced a very personal and touching eulogy. He told about hearing stories about Keith all over town, and from Keith's loved ones, and realizing how many people loved and enjoyed him.

Father Kibby incorporated the gospel of Mark, telling how Jesus had calmly taken a nap while a terrible storm pelted the fishermen on the sea of Galilee.

"And I bet you thought Keith Whitley was the first to sing 'I'm No Stranger to the Rain,' " Father Kibby said.

> Yes, from the very beginning, Christians have never been strangers to the rain. At one time or another, all of us could describe our lives as terrible storms. At one time or another we have all known what it is like to have our lives pushed and shoved and knocked about by powers we cannot control. We all have our fears, and we have had those moments when our boats began to take on water.

He added that Keith was at peace, and that it was up to all of us to find our own peace.

Let us put this cloud behind us because that's how God designed us, to ride the wind and dance in a hurricane. The story of Jesus and the story of Keith remind us that indeed we are no strangers to the rain. We are called to be its conquerors.

I think Keith would ask us to look into our lives, into the storms of our lives, and search for stillness by awakening the presence of the God, who is with us. I think he would ask us to beg, steal or borrow, do whatever we must do, to come into the sunshine, to get the clouds behind us, to bring our lives out of darkness and into the light.

After the funeral, we all got back in the three stretch limousines. Keith's body was in a white hearse up front. Before the cortege departed, our friend Curtis (Mister Harmony) Young knocked on the window and handed me a tape.

"I thought you might want this," he said.

It was the tape of "Tell Lorrie I Love Her" that Keith had played for me just before his failed trip to Hazelden, the one he had recorded just before our marriage.

The limousine had a tape recorder in the back, and I popped the tape in. There was Keith's voice, husky and reflective:

"And if I leave this old world,
"Tell her she's the only girl for me."

Needless to say, we all started sobbing all over again. We played the tape repeatedly on the way to the cemetery. It was imperfect—you could even hear the television from the next room—but it gave us something very special of Keith's to remember.

I have one other memory of the procession to the cemetery:

Looking back at the long string of Harley riders, Keith's friends and fans, guys who knew that Keith was a Harley man. At the front of the line was Keith's Harley. Lane was riding it, performing the vigil for the friend he loved so much.

There were crowds outside Spring Hill Cemetery on Gallatin Pike, and a large crowd at graveside. I know Liana and some of my cousins were upset at the fans and the reporters who jostled around me, but I did not complain. Everybody was trying to be nice to me, and I felt I had an obligation to be nice back.

Joe Edwards of the Associated Press spoke to me and reported these words: "I don't know that I'm bitter. You know that old saying, 'God never puts anything on you that you and he can't handle.' There's a reason for all this. I'll probably never know the reason until I go up to heaven and ask."

After the funeral, Mrs. Whitley and her two surviving children, Mary and Dwight, came to the house. I gave them some items that had belonged to Keith, including his .38 pistol, some of his stage outfits, and some of his clothes. I told them I was going to donate his Harley to the Country Music Hall of Fame.

I know they were sad at his being buried in Nashville. People in the mountains always have the most beautiful cemeteries up on the hill. Every year on Decoration Day (Memorial Day) people come home to their local villages to pay their respects at their family cemeteries. It must have seemed like a terrible distance to them, but I hoped they understood. We had such a short time together, and I wanted Keith near me.

Forever.

Chapter Twenty-Two

It got worse. Keith's death was more unsavory than I had been hearing.

I found the first clue under the front seat of the car.

On Wednesday night, after making the arrangements at the funeral home, I had gone back to Mom's house. Keith's Corvette had been blocking somebody in the driveway, so I started moving it out of the way.

I felt something sliding out from underneath the passenger seat, reached down, and came up with a L'Oreal lipstick.

That's strange, I thought to myself. I don't use that brand.

I stuck the lipstick in my pocketbook. I had other things on my mind.

The next day I went outside and again felt under the seat. There was a small plastic container for contact lenses and a little makeup kit with a few other L'Oreal products.

I knew Keith didn't use them. I wanted to get my hands on whoever did, but I had a funeral to attend—the funeral of my husband.

A few days after the funeral, I was out at the pool with Ruth when a detective arrived. He was wearing a business suit and tinted glasses, very professional. He introduced himself as Lieutenant Harry Bell of the Goodlettsville Police Department and said he had a few questions.

Lieutenant Bell asked if Ruth could leave for a few minutes, but I said Ruth was one of my best friends and could hear anything I could hear.

He seemed a little uncomfortable about that, but he shrugged, as if to say, "It's your choice."

The detective repeated that Keith's death was apparently self-inflicted, but he said that obviously the police still had to investigate everything. I knew the police had been working on the case, but this was the first time I had spoken to them. Lieutenant Bell had intentionally left me alone until a few days after the funeral, which I appreciated.

On my own, I had learned a few things, but I still had many questions. Why had the house been relatively clean when Barbara and Bernice got there? Why would a man on a binge clean up like that? Was anybody else in there with Keith? How did he overdose on alcohol? Where did he get all this alcohol?

Before I could ever get to my questions, the detective looked at Ruth again, took a deep breath, and then did what he had to do.

"Do you know that Keith was seen with a woman on those last two nights?"

That explained the L'Oreal in the Corvette.

Lieutenant Bell said the police were investigating a report that Keith had been seen at the Starlite Club, a seedy joint on Dickerson Pike, on Sunday night. He also said that Keith and Lane had picked up a woman in Tootsie's Orchid Lounge, the famous bar just below the Ryman on Broadway.

The description of the woman was an aging blonde, with big

boobs, a tourist from California. Well, there are a few of those on Broadway. She and Keith supposedly had been seen having an argument outside a market. Later, Keith had taken a cab home and gotten the other set of keys to the Corvette. Then he had spent the night in a motel out by I-24 and Old Hickory Boulevard.

As the detective told me these details, I kept thinking, You've got the wrong man. This is not Keith Whitley. Here was a man so passionate, who made love to me two or three times a day, who loved Morgan and Jesse so much. The detective did not know what had gone on inside the motel, but he had enough to convince me. Keith had been cheating on me.

The thought ran through my mind: Was this woman in my house? Was this woman in my *bed*?

The police also had to continue their investigation inside the house. I told Lieutenant Bell that we never kept alcoholic beverages, that Keith was adamant about that. He wanted to preserve the facade of not drinking around me.

We went into the bathroom, where I inspected my medicine and makeup cabinet. I had tried to buy hair products and cough medicines with no alcohol in them, but there were as many as four bottles with some alcoholic content, including one bottle of hair spray. All four had been full when I left. They were now half-empty.

I pictured my beloved husband roaming around the house taking a swig out of a hair-spray bottle and I shuddered with disgust and sadness. I could not begin to imagine. None of us can, unless we have the sickness.

I was too sad, too angry, to ask any questions of my own.

After the lieutenant left, I had to confront the facts.

This was the first time I had ever been faced with evidence that Keith was fooling around. How could he do that to our marriage?

I began to wonder what would have happened if Keith had

not died. Would I ever have had to confront what he did on his ugly rampage? Given that Nashville is a small town, and our industry is a small family, I probably would have heard some gossip here or there.

I probably would have heard that Keith and Lane were seen with a woman at Tootsie's and the Starlite Club. But Keith would have told me, "Oh, man, Lane and I got rid of her," and Lane would have told Beth, "Oh, man, Keith and I got rid of her," and both sisters would have believed our men. (Or, as Richard Pryor once said in a similar situation: "Who you gonna believe—me or your lyin' eyes?")

Now there was no Keith Whitley to shine his eyes on me and make me believe something. Now I had to think about what he had done. The *truth* about what he had done.

I know Keith loved me. I know he probably did ugly things when he was drunk. But this was different. This was the first betrayal in our own town. Maybe even in our own bed.

I honestly believe Keith could not face what he had done. This was a man who went on binges when he was feeling bad. This was a man who could not face himself about some unknown things in his past.

I started to believe Keith Whitley drank himself to death on purpose.

I went into a shell, brooding about this act of betrayal.

I heard other theories about Keith's death. Mike Chamberlain had a thought about the autopsy and the report of the greenish tinge in his system.

"This is just my theory," he has said, "but they had a garage where they kept old cans and stuff, and I had cleaned out the garage but left some cans of anti-freeze back there figuring they could use them for the cars. I can see where Keith would go out there and drink that stuff."

There was no evidence that Keith had done that, but Mike had seen him at his most desperate for alcohol, and believed Keith was capable of anything.

I also heard that some people at Carrie's Corner Market near our house had definitely seen Keith jump out of a white pickup truck and buy a six-pack of beer. They said it was either Monday or early Tuesday, but since Keith was gone by eleven-thirty on Tuesday morning, let's say it was Monday.

The only person I know with a white pickup truck was that old friend of Keith's, the one I'm calling Sammy, who used to supply Keith with a little bit of dope once in a while. Sammy never came to the funeral, never sent a condolence card. I have never heard from him since.

After brooding about Lieutenant Bell's information for a few days, I called Lane and Beth for some answers.

Lane was pretty much wrecked, and he did not volunteer much. He was mourning a dear friend of his, was feeling dreadful about not being able to hang on to Keith during this final rampage.

He confirmed some of the basics. The bars. The motel. The Corvette keys. The coffee at eight-thirty. The trollop from California, including her name. I'll call her "Carmen" and leave it at that. But he was pretty vague on details, and maybe I did not want to know.

There was one thing more on my mind.

"That bitch has Keith's lighter," I snarled, referring to the Zippo lighter with Keith's initials on it. She had called Jack and said she had taken it as a souvenir of her fling.

Lane allowed that he just might be able to find a phone number for Carmen, who had hauled her fat ass out of Tennessee as soon as she heard Keith was dead. I rang her number in California, and to my amazement, I got her on the phone.

I started out politely, identifying myself to her. I did not want to blow her off the phone too soon. I said that Keith's lighter was missing, and I wanted it back.

Then I launched into a higher gear.

"You were here feeding alcohol and cocaine to my husband—and now he's dead," I said rationally. "I ought to have you charged with murder. I want you to come here and explain to my two kids why their father is gone."

I got the feeling Carmen was not coming back from California any time soon.

Then I lost it.

I called her every ugly name I had heard backstage, or in the bars in Printer's Alley, or from musicians punching each other out, or from two women fighting over a man, every foul word, every vile description, anything disgusting you have ever heard, I called this pig from California. And she took it for a long time, which tells me she knew I was right. And then one of us hung up, or maybe the phone line just burned out from my anger.

She couldn't do much about sending my husband back, but a few days later, the bitch sent back the lighter.

CHAPTER TWENTY-THREE

Right after the funeral, Jack called and said he assumed I was not going to play the *Opry* the next night.

"I think I want to," I said.

Jack told me there was not a person in the world who expected me to perform. In fact, he said, a lot of people would think it was in bad taste for me to perform the day after my husband's funeral.

But I was on my own now. I had to start making decisions for myself.

In the first few hours at home, I was having anxiety attacks just sitting around the house. I could feel the walls coming in on me. I had never experienced anything that overwhelming in my life, even when Dad died. It was a terrible mixture of sadness and anger, leading to emptiness, wanting to lie down and die. I needed to be in a familiar place, doing what I do best.

"Jack, as long as they're asking me if I'm going to perform, the answer is yes."

So I went down to the *Opry* the next night and went onstage. I can vaguely recall the familiar faces, the old *Opry* hands, the real Nashville, forming a wall of support around me.

I'd like to tell you who said what, but the truth is, I don't remember a bit of it. However, I know I was there. I've got the negative press clippings and the critical letters to prove it.

I guess I did not realize how strongly people would take it, but there was a huge flap over the next few days. I kept reading in the papers and hearing on the television, people asking, "How could she go out and work right after burying her husband?"

They made it sound as if I had no feelings, but it was quite the opposite. My feelings were so strong that if I did not get out and do something, I thought I would explode.

People did not say anything to my face, but if they had, I would have said, "You deal with your grief your way, I deal with my grief my way."

I also think it was my way of being close to Keith. If there was anybody in the world who would have understood, it was Keith Whitley. When he was right, he loved being up onstage performing, and now that's how I felt, too. He was very supportive of me, and this was my way of repaying him. Just keep going.

My family was also a huge source of support. All the normal tensions in a big family seemed to vanish when there was real trouble. My mom, my sisters, Marty, all the others, let me know there would be better days ahead.

Nevertheless, I felt alone. In three short years, I had gotten used to the two of us functioning as a unit. I looked out for Keith, and he looked out for me. If a decision needed to be made, I might ask Keith's opinion, or he might give it anyway. I could tell people, "Keith and I think . . ." Everything was "we."

Now it was all up to me, a single person, having to make decisions affecting my two kids. I know millions of other women do this all the time. They make the meals and plan the money and drive the kids and read the stories and do the disciplining. But this was all so sudden.

The emotions kept coming in, like one storm after another. Things would hit me at different times, from different angles. Sometimes it was really bad, just devastating.

I probably could have dealt with it better if I had not been so terribly sad for Jesse. He kept asking me, "Where's Daddy? Where's his bus? Daddy coming home?" And I had to make up stories, try to explain, in words he did not yet understand.

Keith had given me a two-carat diamond ring for Christmas, and had been paying his sister for it in installments. We came up with a few hundred dollars to complete the purchase, and I put the ring in my safe deposit box for Jesse when he gets married. I could not wear it anymore.

I could not eat. I got down to ninety-eight pounds, seventeen pounds below my recent weight, and was just big sad eyes and a bunch of bones.

And all the time, wracked with guilt. If only I'd stayed back. If only I hadn't gone. Then I'd find myself mad at Jack and Joe again for persuading me to go out on the road.

I felt so damn cheated. I started getting these morbid thoughts about "Morgan luck"—losing my dad so young, and now losing the other important man in my life. What was I, bad karma?

I felt deprived, rejected, full of self-pity, mad at the world.

Then I got furious at Keith.

Like, Damn, how dare he leave me with all this shit?

With no explanation.

He promised me that he would take care of Morgan and Jesse and me.

I began to think he had taken the easy way out.

If he had died in an airplane crash, it would have been different, but this was a death at his own hands. *He* had poured that shit down his throat, not me, not anybody else. This wasn't an airplane losing its engines, or a car veering off the road, or a bunch of cancer cells out of control, or a heart attack. This was something he could have controlled, but did not.

There were days I would wait until everybody was out of the house, and then I would just throw stuff in a rage.

Or I would go to the cemetery and lie down on the soft earth and have myself a temper tantrum—pound on the ground and curse and call him a son of a bitch. Then I would start crying because I had yelled at him.

Yes, I was angry. I did not know how to deal with anger.

I knew my anger would not drive me to drink or drugs. That was not me. I just let myself feel it, anger at the situation, at Keith, at all of us for letting it happen. The anger kept me going.

I also had to deal with other people's emotions. It was only natural that Keith's family and his friends from eastern Kentucky would see his death as a Nashville tragedy, something that happened in the big city, far from his own home. I tried to bridge the huge gap between middle Tennessee and the mountains, but it was not easy.

I knew Mrs. Whitley wanted to keep as many of his things as possible in the garage where Keith and Dwight and Ricky had perfected their music years earlier. She wanted to feel that her son was still just a few feet outside the door, putting together his next song. Any mother would feel that.

I could give her Keith's performing jacket and his sneakers, but I could not give her back her son, and that made me even sadder, to see the sorrow on her expressive face.

And then the Whitleys and the Morgans had to deal with all the rumors going around.

As long as Keith was alive, his drinking was an isolated binge, here and there, mostly known only to the insiders who tried to help him. His mother says she never realized he had such a serious alcohol problem when he was growing up.

Now that Keith was gone, people began inventing stories about our marriage. They would ask how I could stay with him when he drank, and I had to remind them that he would go weeks and months between incidents. People assumed that Keith and I argued and fought, physically, but he was never abusive, not once.

He never hit me or even yelled at me. I was the one who would raise my voice, which I think is actually healthy. But Keith kept everything inside. There were few signs that others could see. Keith hurt himself, but not me. Still, you could hear rumors about fights and divisions—and, yes, inevitably, about infidelities.

There are always rumors in country music. You can hear them on radio and television, backstage at the *Opry*, whispered around Printer's Alley, and you can read them in the papers and the fan magazines. In this news-hungry society, with twenty-four-hour cable stations and gossip magazines and tabloids available at every supermarket checkout, it seems there are no limits. People can get away with writing whatever they want.

Some of the rumors started in eastern Kentucky from people who identified more closely with Keith than with me. Others circulated in Nashville from people who were jealous of me, including a few of the usual suspects with connections to Keith's band. Pretty soon, all these vicious rumors were swirling around, out of control.

One of the rumors was that I had Keith killed because I found him with another woman.

The other side to the infidelity rumor was that Keith had killed himself because he came home unexpectedly and found me in bed with another man.

The third rumor was that somebody had killed Keith, had deliberately poured stuff down his throat or injected something into him. Never mind that the police had attributed his death to an overdose of alcohol that he drank of his own volition.

The rumors had a life of their own, and they caused trouble because, sooner or later, people started believing them.

I had always been close to Keith's sister, Mary, but as the rumors kicked around, we had a raging argument over a few of the more nasty ones. She wound up saying something like, "Well, if you'd stayed home where you're supposed to be, and watched him, this would not have happened."

These words stung because I was dealing with those overwhelming feelings of guilt myself. I truly believe Keith would have died from drinking anyway, but that didn't stop me from being devasted by the fact that I had not been around at that specific moment, to stop it.

Needless to say, I had an answer for Mary: "I called you-all *how* many times when he was in the hospital? And *none* of you would come down and help me figure out anything about his past, about what was driving him to do what he was doing!"

Things were bad between Mary and me for a while. She was dealing with her grief in losing a brother, and I was dealing with my sadness in losing a husband. Things flared up that never should have been said, on both sides. But reason eventually won out, and we resolved our differences. Mary and Farrell have even taken Jesse for a week or two in the summers, which is great, because Jesse does need to know Keith's side of the family—just as Keith had asked before he died.

At first, I was overwhelmed by both my sadness and self-pity. I thought I was the only one who had ever suffered this way. But then I started to count up the people in Nashville who had died young, and the survivors who had managed to go on with their lives.

I thought about Jean Shepard, one of my best friends at the *Opry*, a woman who has befriended dozens of young singers.

Jean had been pregnant with her second son in 1963 when her husband, Hawkshaw Hawkins, died in the same plane wreck as Patsy Cline. She had to give birth and support her children all by herself, and she did it with an extraordinary spirit. I took great courage from Jean Shepard's example.

Eventually, I realized I would survive.

Keith's life had ended, but mine had not.

I had to make another decision. What was I going to do about work? Our two children needed me around, but we also needed some income. We basically had nothing. We were living day by day. It was up to me to provide for them.

For me, it was more than just that, of course. It wasn't simply a question of getting a job. There was the matter of my "career." I had been working half my life, I finally had an album out that RCA was supporting. They thought they had something good inside those little plastic cases, and so did I.

RCA was too far along in production to just casually put it off for a few months. And really, why should they? It was honest, it was good, and it had been in production long before Keith died. It wasn't as if we just stamped out an album capitalizing on Keith's death.

Part of my dedication on the album thanked "my husband, Keith Whitley, for teaching me how to sing with heart and giving me reason to." Country fans are sophisticated enough to know about production schedules. They knew I had earnestly written down those words while Keith was alive.

I was proud that other people were listening to my album, but the truth is that I could not listen to it for months after Keith died. The songs on there were all so personal. He had helped me select them. He had given me tips on how to sing them. People thought I was milking his loss for the publicity, but it was the other way around. I was spooked by anything that reminded me of Keith.

It would be easy for me to say that Keith's career mattered the most, that whatever happened to me was gravy, but I certainly admit that I had hopes and dreams for myself. Now I had two additional reasons for going out and making it big: Morgan and Jesse. Three good reasons, if you counted me.

Was it an act of ego for me to go back on the road? Or was it the most logical thing for a working mother to do?

Keith had about a hundred and forty dates booked, and I took as many as Jack and the promoters could arrange—about fifteen a month. That very next week, my band and I went out on Keith's white bus, the same one that had delivered him at the Houston airport for his last flight home.

I had a hard time getting on that bus. I kept expecting to see Keith poke his head out of the back room, and say, "Hey, come on back here—and close the door." I missed him terribly, missed him emotionally, spiritually, and I missed him physically. I could not imagine ever being with another man again.

Call it superstitious or sentimental, but I could not bring myself to take his name off the bus. It said "Keith Whitley" for the next two years. That's how we started the promotion of "Dear Me"—by going out on the road in poor Keith's bus.

It helped me to be back with the guys in my band, who loved Keith, too, but I felt terrible for the guys in Keith's band. Some of them found work right away in other bands around Nashville, but some of the others took months or even years to get settled. Even the ones who thought I was a royal bitch on wheels had loved and supported Keith, and I ached to think of them going their separate ways.

When I was doing my shows, I felt so close to him. I would be waiting in the wings, that old nervous time for me, dragging on one of those cigarettes I should not have been touching, and I would feel Keith's laughing eyes on me. It was so much easier for him than me.

I would pray to Jesus for help in stepping out on that stage. If he could go through what he did in his final hours, I could surely get out there and sing a few country songs. And then I would pray to Keith. "Be with me," I would say. I would feel him patting me on the back, telling me to get out there and to entertain the people.

As part of my show, I started singing "Faithfully," the song Keith had played for me on our first trip to eastern Kentucky. It had become "our song," the way most couples have one song that unites them. Everybody knew I was singing about Keith, and maybe some people thought I was using his death for emotional impact—but what else is country music if not opening up your emotions? We're real people, our lives are not that much different from those of the people in the audience. I wanted people to know how I felt, that my love for him was so strong that he was a presence whenever I walked out on the stage. Why pretend it wasn't?

Having seen George and Tammy become a symbol for lives and marriage in crisis, I did not want to go the same route. But I have to admit I took solace from how Tammy had survived. She had been one of my very favorite singers and people when I was younger, and now I thought of her as a kind of role model.

I would say to myself, Hell, if Tammy got through what George was doing, I can get through this stage of my life, too. I don't care who the woman is, how successful she is, she needs companionship and support. I wanted to let women know that I could survive, just like Tammy.

Keith had done a song by himself called " 'Til a Tear Becomes a Rose." I incorporated it into my show, also. His voice would be piped over the sound system and I would sing to an empty stool. Keith's fans loved it. I was being faithful to his talent. Some people thought it was corny. Only I know how I felt—and I was missing him so bad, I was able to work out my emotions by singing on a stage. It was cheaper than therapy. And more effective.

I didn't try to hide my emotions. I was deliberately trying to keep Keith in the public eye, and I couldn't help but feel cynical when people would tell me they had just discovered his music.

"My first instinct is to get up and cuss the world out," I told Jack Hurst of the *Chicago Tribune*, one of the best reporters on country music.

"I know that's a bad thing to say, but it's kind of how I feel," I said. "He waited so long, and was so deserving of every award that was passed over him, and I hurt for him many nights.

"He knew he was the best, and I think everybody else knew he was the best. For some reason, it seems like it happened the same with Dad. The nicer you are to people and the better people like you, the less thanks and awards you get."

Nowadays, people say, "Boy, I loved your dad." I just think to myself, and pardon my French, but "Bullshit!" People took Dad for granted, and they did the same with Keith.

In October of 1989, Keith's song "I'm No Stranger to the Rain" was voted the best single of the year by the Country Music Association. I had to go up onstage and accept the award for Keith, and I nearly couldn't do it, I was so choked with tears. I thought of the times he watched other people, less talented people, getting awards, and he just held his frustration inside and didn't whine about it. Now he got the award, and I had to be strong to accept it for him.

My album did very well. I was hotter than I had ever been. Suddenly I found myself planning the next steps in a revived career, including a second album for RCA.

We began assembling songs, listening to dozens and hundreds of demo tapes that circulate all over town. Just ask me. It was only four years earlier that I had been making those same tapes for aspiring songwriters. Now people tried to hand me theirs so that I might consider them for my next album.

I remembered the tape Curtis Young had given me in the

funeral limousine, the one of Keith singing "Tell Lorrie I Love Her" in our noisy little apartment.

"I want to play something for you," I told Joe.

Joe listened, and I could see him grimacing at all the noise in the background, the hiss of the tape, even the rumble of the television in the background. But he also heard Keith's hoarse, sad voice, and he knew what he had—an unexpected treasure.

As Keith's wife, I had some legal control over everything he had recorded. I talked with Joe Galante about whether it would be in bad taste to release all Keith's material so soon after his death.

"It's up to you," Joe told me. "If you're not comfortable with it, we won't release it."

My dilemma, to put it bluntly, was that Keith's backlog of great material could keep a roof over our heads.

So I made the decision.

"People need to hear what Keith is all about," I said.

Now it was time for me to record a new album, the first since Keith had passed. I was comfortable with Barry Beckett as my producer, but Joe Galante wanted somebody to try to make me sound less country, more urban. I heard they were flying in a man named Richard Landis from Los Angeles, and I feared they were all trying to turn me into a West Coast type.

Barry Beckett had been trying to get me to record a song called "Something in Red," about a woman trying to rekindle the passion of her relationship. I had resisted because I thought the first line, "I'm looking for something in red," sounded too singsongy. However, Richard urged me to listen to the whole thing, the progression, and I realized there was real strength there.

So many country songs are about wanting something that does not exist, or something that is not good for you. This was a song about having something good, and wanting to make it even better.

I figured that if Barry Beckett and Richard Landis agreed, two great minds outnumbered my own addled brain, so I recorded it. Landis called it a "career song." And he was right.

The album *Something in Red* came out in 1991, and it was huge. A year later, the song was directed for video by Jim Shea, with me wearing a black slip, trying on different outfits to rekindle the spark in my marriage, the video version of my marriage, that is.

The video certainly showed my figure to advantage. I had no problem with that. Ever since I stopped thinking I was fat and figured out that I had a good figure, I've been grateful for it and proud of it. Some people compared me to Madonna for emphasizing open sensuality on my video—I'm not sure if that was a compliment—but let's be honest. Much of music, much of entertainment, is about sensuality. We all have sex on our minds. Why not admit it?

As soon as that song was released, I began to notice women waiting outside afterward, telling me that song had special meaning to them, that it reminded them of the possibility of a strong love again.

I was glad to be bringing them that message. I discovered in some ways that I was weak, but in other ways I was strong. I had chosen to survive—and I was going to.

One of my great moments came after "Something in Red" was a big hit. I was performing for RCA people and others in the industry one night. I was running around the bus trying to get dressed, and I pulled on a pair of bright red panties. I asked Ruth to look at my dress in the light of the bus to make sure you couldn't see what I had on underneath, and she said absolutely no light got through. Fine. So I went up onstage and was performing when I bumped into one of the monitors and went sprawling, facedown. What was worse, my dress got caught under me, and it was pulled up to my waist. The band and the audience just gaped. I could see a woman in the front row that I recognized from RCA. She had her hand over her mouth, like she was in the middle of every woman's nightmare. I couldn't get up for a few moments, but finally I found the strength to push myself back to my feet.

"Well," I said, "I was looking for something in red—and now you know I found it."

As time passed, my creative side began to deal with Keith's death. One day the kids were out of the house and I realized how alone I was. It was a beautiful day, the kind of day when Keith would have said, "Hey, let's go for a ride on the Harley," but nobody was revving up his engines for me this day and I was feeling sorry for myself. I dawdled at my dressing table, putting on my makeup with nobody to see me, and I got so sad about Keith I wrote a song called "If You Come Back from Heaven."

Before long, I was performing it.

Eight months after Keith died, I made the difficult decision to stop working with Jack McFadden. Jack had been loyal and kind to us; he had rescued Keith from dozens of problems, had given up hours and days and weeks of his time to help him.

Jack and I spent a lot of time together waiting for Keith to show up or chasing after a few of his car wrecks. He did everything he could to keep Keith alive, to get him into treatment. I'll always be grateful to Jack for that.

There are people who say that Jack pushed Keith too hard, that he forced Keith out on the road, but what else is a manager supposed to do? That's the job.

I think Jack is a good guy, a family man who's been married

to his wife, Jo, for a long time. At the same time, however, I was upset because I had inherited a lot of Keith's dates—and many of them were for very little money. Often, I was performing for three thousand dollars a night—I was actually *losing* money at that price. Jack pointed out that Keith's asking price had dropped substantially because of all the shows he had missed.

"Keith was playing catch-up all the time," Jack explained. "He'd miss some dates because he was drunk and he'd have to make them up. Every time he went on a toot, he had to go to the back of the line."

Well, that was true. But I did not want to get caught in that cycle. Jack had not managed any female artists that I knew about, and I just felt there were things that could be managed better. Almost any creative person makes changes like that. I wasn't Keith, and I did not want to be playing in honky-tonks that would have worked for Keith. I wanted a tour sponsor and I wanted connections to the movies and I didn't think Jack could give me that.

It's an unfortunate part of the business. I know it hurt Jack deeply when I told him I was making a change. And when it came time to do this book, I insisted that Jack have his say:

"I felt I was the right one for Lorrie," Jack said recently. "I thought she was great. I was deeply hurt. I thought she would be a little more open with me, and the hurt will stay with me a long time."

If it makes Jack feel any better, there was hurt on my part, too.

My next manager was Stan Moress, a great guy, with connections in California, which I thought were important. He also had an assistant named Doug Casmus who went on the road with me, made me feel secure. To this day I feel close to both of them.

Stan made a great contribution to my career by introducing me to Kenny Ortega, a choreographer and director who had worked with Michael Jackson, Cher, and Gloria Estefan.

I didn't know what to expect from this first meeting. We met in Stan's office and Kenny said, "Tell me what you want from me."

"I just want to know how to be myself," I said.

Kenny stood up, clapped his hands together once and did a quick little dance step, almost a three-sixty, flamboyant, graceful, sensuous, and smart, all at the same time, accentuating the feminine moves that would work for me.

"Yesssss!" I said.

We went out for sushi afterward and talked some more, and then I began rehearsing with him. Kenny Ortega brought me out of myself. He knew I had this passion for the stage, but I did not know how to project it with feeling. He could tell of my intrigue with romance, and he taught me different moves to demonstrate it. For the first time, I was comfortable moving around the stage. I have been working with Kenny ever since, a couple of times a year, and he has become my spiritual connection to the stage.

Stan and Doug did many other things for me, but I began to feel that Stan was too close to the record companies. He was always saying, "If you don't do this, the label's going to drop you," which was true up to a point. But I didn't think he was understanding the pressure I was feeling as a single mother. I wanted stardom, of course—but not at any price. He was always telling me not to rock the boat, and soon I began to feel as if I was *owned* by the label, not just working for them.

I began to think it would be better if I had a woman managing me, somebody who would not threaten me but, instead, nurture me. Stan had hired Susan Nadler as his publicist, a very independent woman who has actually had a life *outside* Nashville. When I first met Susan, I hated her. I thought, Uh, this girl is nuts, she doesn't shut up, she's driving me crazy. But I think Susan saw more in me than I saw in myself. She used to tell me that the first time she heard "Dear Me" she pulled off to the side of the road and said, "I want to do publicity for this woman." We got to be good friends, and when she and Stan parted company, I hired her on the side to do my publicity. But I also began bouncing ideas off her, and when it was time for Stan and me to part company, Susan became my new manager.

I was discovering I could control my own destiny. I always had ideas, but I never had the leverage to carry them out. Funny what a couple of hit albums will do. In 1990, I called my friend Ruth, whose marriage was faltering down in Florida, and told her, "Okay, Ruth, it's time to come home." She said, "Well, it isn't that easy," and I said, "Yes, it is, I'm coming down there and we're coming back." So I flew down to Florida and drove her Lincoln back with Ruth and her two boys. She stayed with me for a while; then she went on the payroll, touring with me for *Leave the Light On* and when I opened for Alabama.

My first single on my new RCA contract, *Trainwreck of Emotion*, hit the charts. In 1990, my recording of "Five Minutes" hit the top ten. Later in 1990, " 'Til a Tear Becomes a Rose," my voice recorded with Keith's, also hit the top ten. And in 1993, "What Part of No (Don't You Understand?)," written by Wayne Perry and Gerald Smith, became No. 1. In May of 1996, "I Didn't Know My Own Strength" also became a bestseller.

I was getting great material, including a song called "Guess You Had to Be There," about a woman who finds out her husband is having an affair. It and the video did very well.

Joe Galante found a song called "Good as I Was to You," which I could use as a closer, after "Something in Red." In 1997, that would hit the charts.

I was nominated three straight years, 1990, '91, and '92 as the female vocalist of the year by the Country Music Association, the oldest and most important award in our business. In 1990, the duet that I recorded with Keith's voice became the Vocal Event of the Year with the CMA. In 1994, I was included on the Album of the Year for my part in *Common Thread*, songs originally done by the Eagles. And in 1994 and 1996, I was voted Female Artist of the Year by the TNN Music City News Awards.

Success is never completely smooth. Not everybody was that happy for me. Some of the new women in Nashville did not care for me. I would knock a certain song or style, and it would get back to me that some of the women thought I was a pain in the butt. Well, maybe I was, but I was an *honest* pain.

My old friends were happy for me, but many people looked at me like I should have died with Keith. I mean it. I don't have anything in common with half the women in country music. They're not from Nashville and they don't get it. I'm from the old school. I value the old traditions. I like the way things have always been done, and I don't like most of the changes the newcomers are always trying to put in. When I return to the *Opry*, I see the women, maybe a few years older than me, or maybe not anymore, who are maintaining the tradition of country. We hang out together. They're the ones I admire, the ones I can relate to. And we're the ones who'll be here ten and twenty years from now. Maybe our clothes will fit a little differently, but we'll be here.

A day couldn't pass without some reminder of the horrible end to Keith's life. I was the one who had to live with his legend—the talented mountain man who died from an overdose of alcohol.

Some days were worse than others. Weeks and weeks after the death, the Goodlettsville police sent over a package for me. Inside were the sheets from the bed the day Keith died.

They had done their tests with the substances found in the sheets. Now they were returning them to me. Unwashed.

There was probably some museum or sideshow that would have been glad to display the sheets in which Keith Whitley had lived out his last breaths. I dumped them in the garbage pail.

Through all this, I did not see a therapist or counselor. My doctor did prescribe some Valium for me, and I would take one once in a while to calm my nerves.

I'm not big in the self-help field. I don't claim to get psychic or emotional help from the television set. I admire Oprah Winfrey for what she does, but I honestly don't have time for many of the other shows that feature every problem known to humanity.

(I don't watch much television at all, actually, except for CNN and *Headline News*, some of the videos, and the great biographies on the Arts and Entertainment channel. For entertainment, I rent all kinds of movies. I particularly love the old black-and-white movies from the forties and fifties. As I keep saying, I'm a traditionalist.)

My strength came from the church. I have a strong religious feeling that I reinforce in the Catholic church. I will speak to a great priest, Father Edward Steiner, when something is on my mind. If I feel bad about something I've done, he will make me look him in the eye and he'll say, "Do you think your dad would ever stop loving you?" I'll say no, and he'll respond, "Well, what makes you think God would ever stop loving you?"

I've had times in my life when I felt like Mary Magdalene, the woman who was pardoned by Jesus for all her sins, who followed him to the cross and was one of the first to see him after his resurrection. Every time I've fallen in my life, I've been pardoned. Father Ed has helped me feel that I am a pretty good person. I feel loved and surrounded by my church and my family, and I know I have been blessed.

All the dreams Keith had for me started to come true. Out of the tragedy, my career took off.

I have no explanation for it.

Did losing Keith force me to dig deeper into my talent and resolve what was always there? Did the financial need make me work harder?

Did all the ghastly publicity make the fans and the record people and the booking agents take one more look at me?

Or was it all happening anyway?

Did Keith need to die for my career to happen? I would hate to think that.

If somebody had asked me, after all the success, if I had what I wanted, I would have said, "No, I want my marriage."

But nobody asked me.

CHAPTER TWENTY-FOUR

The hardest part of life after Keith was dealing with two children who had lost a father.

A few years after Keith's death, I took Jesse to a matinee movie. The theater was darkened, and Jesse kept twisting sideways, looking away from the screen.

"Mommy, that's Daddy over there," he said, his voice far above a whisper.

I turned my head. There was a man gazing up at the screen, oblivious to us, but with the same build, same long hair, same nose, same eyes. In the dark, it most certainly looked like Keith.

The man became aware of Jesse staring at him, and he smiled tentatively.

"Jesse, turn around, that's not Daddy," I whispered.

"Mommy, I *know* it's my daddy," he insisted.

At the moment, I was not sure he wasn't. My church has its share of mysteries and saints, and I believe God can make anything happen, but I was not expecting to see Keith Whitley sitting in the movies on a Saturday afternoon in my local multiplex.

I saw Patrick Swayze come back in *Ghost*, but I ain't Demi Moore. (Come to think of it, she ain't me.) Nevertheless, I found myself turning around and staring. What if that were an angel sitting there, keeping an eye on us?

"Maybe Daddy came back but he couldn't find us," Jesse whispered.

He had a point, since we had already changed houses.

"Watch the movie, Jesse," I pleaded.

When the lights came up, I turned to take a better look at the man, but he had moved quickly down the aisle. I never did get a good look at his face in the light.

The two children missed Keith badly. They also wondered why he had died so young. I had to find the wisdom to answer every question, to anticipate their moods.

Jesse still asks me: "Do you think I'll get to see Daddy?"

"I'm sure you will," I say, but I can't make it better; I can't take away the sadness or the pain, and as a mother, that is a very frustrating feeling.

I would find Morgan staring out the window, tears in her eyes. She was already eight years old, and she knew what death meant. We would talk about it honestly, but sometimes I had to break the mood and remind her that Keith had been a real person, not some tragic figure from a history book or an opera.

"Morgan, remember the time Keith jumped in the pool in his red silk pajamas?" I would ask.

We both could visualize his silly grin, his playfulness, and we would start laughing.

Most of the time, it was no laughing matter.

Morgan is extremely sensitive, aware of other people, very loving, very close to her family. I know she has talent for singing and acting. She's always putting on skits, doing impressions and accents, making people laugh. She wants to go to a college with a drama department, and she wants to find her own place in the entertainment business.

I have never had to be on her for misbehaving or not doing her homework. She's really in tune with me. We talk about everything from guys to makeup to clothes. We play a lot and we dance together. I don't feel there's a lot she can't talk to me about.

I keep wondering if that will change as she gets older, and I suppose it will—to some degree. For now, I tell my friends how close Morgan and I are and they say, "I wish my mom and I could talk like that."

I know she missed Keith, but like a Morgan, she kept going.

Jesse was only two when it happened. I didn't know how much he understood about death and dying. I did not want him to forget about his father, so we displayed pictures of Keith all around the house, and we still do. Jesse would ask, "Daddy coming home? Daddy come home on the bus?"

How do you tell this little guy who loved his dad so much that he is not coming home again?

"Daddy's in heaven," I would say.

And he would say, "I want to go to heaven to see Daddy."

As far as he was concerned, it was like saying, "Daddy's gone to Los Angeles to do a show."

I'd have to say, "You can't go to heaven. Not yet. But Daddy loved you, and he'd be here if he could."

I never wanted to believe that Keith wanted out of this life, but sometimes I was not so tolerant of his absence.

Out of the clear blue sky, just after we moved, Jesse blurted out, "I want to see my daddy, Mommy."

That just got to me. I started crying and I said, "You can't see your daddy, Jesse."

I realized that behind my tears there was anger—anger at Keith for putting Morgan and Jesse in that situation. I wanted to yell at him, get it off my chest. "You stupid son of a bitch," I wanted to say. "Why didn't you stop and think before you started drinking that day? Why didn't you stop?"

My silent words flew off into the atmosphere. I wanted Keith to hear them. I wanted Keith to know I was mad at him.

Other days, I could not be mad at him because the kids had such good memories.

"Remember the day Daddy got up and made me oatmeal?" Jesse asked. This was a memory I had never discussed with him. He had come up with it totally on his own. When Keith was home, I got to sleep and he would take over, do the guy thing. Keith loved to make oatmeal, and he and Jesse would spoon it down. That was one of their little rituals. They only had two years together, but the oatmeal ceremony had stuck with Jesse, without my reinforcing it.

Then there was the coffee routine. Keith loved fresh coffee, and he would drink it with great gusto, including sound effects. Jesse, when he was maybe a year old, had observed this and demanded that he have a cup, too.

So Keith had made a cup of coffee for Jesse (I like to think he watered it down and used plenty of milk and sugar). Anyway, he gave Jesse this baby cup full of coffee, and Jesse would take a nice quiet little sip, trying to have good manners, and Keith said, "Naw, man, that ain't how you drink coffee."

And Keith slurped down a big swig of coffee, let it percolate for a few seconds, then gave out this big satisfied sigh: "Aaaaaah."

Naturally, Jesse loved the slurping and the sighing. It's a guy thing.

The next day, Jesse told Keith, "I'm going to show Mommy," so he made a big show of drinking his coffee, and he went, "Aaaaaah."

His daddy was a hero to Jesse. Keith was a big kid himself, full of life, full of music. There was so much fun around the house. Now Morgan and Jesse both had to deal with the moments when it seemed natural for Keith to come bouncing around the house. Except, of course, he couldn't.

Sometimes I would wonder why Jesse had to have this connection with a father who had vanished so soon. Morgan had *chosen* Keith as her father. She had taken his name, the conscious decision of a bright and sensitive young person. But Jesse had no choice.

I truly believe that Jesse was born already knowing Keith, the result of all those times Keith talked and sang to the baby in my stomach. Everything was cool between them for months and months before Jesse was born.

Now I questioned whether that strong bond was good for Jesse.

Why did Keith have to be so good, so real?

There is another complication. Jesse knows that his father was not just Daddy, that he was Keith Whitley, a popular singer, a legend. I've got a lot of Keith's tapes, and for a long time, we used to play the videos, but I realized it might have been too much for him to see his father projected on a screen in his own house. He sees the gold records on the wall, sees the photographs, but I've made a big point that it doesn't matter whether or not his father was a celebrity. To Jesse, he is Dad, not Keith Whitley.

I did worry about whether Jesse had inherited any of Keith's tendencies for mood shifts and drinking. As he got older, I noticed that he seemed to be hyperactive, which a lot of boys are. He liked to eat a lot of sugar. He also was fascinated by alcohol. If the family was having wine with dinner, Jesse wanted a glass, too.

"What if it's hereditary?" I worried. "Is Jesse going to have to deal with this? Am I an overreacting mom?"

The pediatrician prescribed Ritalin for Jesse, and it helps calm him down, but I've seen studies that kids who need Ritalin are more prone to be chemically dependent than other kids. Jesse's doctor has said I shouldn't worry about it, but I can't help but worry.

The important thing is that we're aware of things. It's a new age, a new generation. People talk about things now that were never discussed when I was a kid. We talk about alcohol with Jesse, how it can be a good thing but does bad things to some people. You just never know. You've just got to pray about it.

Jesse is sentimental, too. Being a guy, he doesn't let it show as much as a female would, but he's a thinker.

One day Jesse came home from school and said that a kid in his class had told him, "Your daddy killed himself." Jesse wanted to fight the kid, but I told him I don't approve of fighting as a way of solving anything.

Then Jesse asked the question that was really on his mind: "Did he?"

"I promise to Daddy," I said—and that's the sacred oath in our household—"Daddy's death was an accident. He did not mean to die."

Jesse looks just like his father at times, but what I find amazing is that he has some of Keith's same mannerisms. Keith wore his shoes or boots on the wrong feet when he was a boy. And he loved to wear helmets. Now here came Jesse, walking around with his boots on the wrong feet. And wearing helmets. Jesse had six or seven favorites that he wore. The amazing thing was that he had no way of knowing that he was just like his dad. I don't know if it's an indication of things to come, or what, but Jesse reminds me an awful lot of Keith. I even had him sing one song with me on the *Greater Need* album.

It's hard for Jesse. The other kids talk about doing stuff with their dads, and that's been a sadness for him. Any time I say we're going to Grandma's, he's happy because he loves being around his uncles and his cousins and his aunts. He's a typical boy. Loves knives and guns and hunting and fishing. Baseball, football, basketball.

Keith's sister, Mary, and her husband, Farrell, have been great about taking him in the summer. They even drive both ways to pick him up, which I appreciate. They live near Grayson Lake, and they've taken him boating on the lake and camping for the first time in his life.

Mary said that Jesse seemed a little unsure about the rules of camping. She told him there was a certain amount of freedom being out in the woods, and he asked, "Does that mean I don't have to take a bath?"

"You take a camping bath by going in the lake," she explained.

Naturally, when he called home, that was the first thing he told me: "Hey, Mom, guess what? I don't have to take a bath."

You see what's important to guys.

It's very important that he be around men. He spends a lot of time with my brother, Marty, particularly when Marty's son, Nathan Taylor, is visiting from Illinois during the summer. Marty takes them out frog-gigging—going out to the pond at night with their waders on, shining a flashlight, trying to mesmerize the frogs, those little green guys, and then spearing them. The idea is to wind up with a whole meal of frogs' legs. He's been hunting and canoeing with Marty, too.

Marty is very sensitive to Jesse's moods, and will discipline him when he needs it. He also tries to tell him things Keith would have told him.

For some reason, I was afraid of storms when I was little, and it got passed along in the genes to Morgan and to Jesse, who was petrified of lightning and thunder when he was out with Marty in the country one time.

Marty told Jesse that Keith would have explained to him that storms were just nature's way of clearing the air, and that storms are relatively harmless, if you're careful.

"Your daddy would tell you not to cry during storms," Marty told him gently.

Not long after that, there was a storm in Nashville, and Marty got a call from Jesse.

"Hey, I'm not crying," Jesse told him.

I think my kids are really strong. Who knows what their lives would have been like if Keith had lived. I would not have been able to keep Keith's sickness from them, and maybe it would have affected them. Or maybe they would have affected Keith, gotten him not to drink anymore.

I think about these things sometimes. The sadness comes when I realize I'll never have the answers.

CHAPTER TWENTY-FIVE

After Keith died, I was convinced I would live the rest of my life as a widow. As far as I was concerned, there was no man who could compare to Keith, either physically or emotionally—and I didn't even think of looking around.

I still felt that way after being back at work for a few months. I would go out and do my shows, rush home to the kids, and that was that. To put it bluntly, I was physically repulsed by the thought of being with another man.

In August, I was booked on a tour with Kenny Rogers, he of the silver hair and the whispery voice and the songs that tell a story. We would perform together, and after hours we would talk together.

I was still pretty much preoccupied with Keith's death, and Kenny would talk to me about that. He would tell me I should be grateful for three full years with somebody I loved that much.

We started going out to dinner together, and of course people would talk, and the tabloids would be full of stuff, most of it untrue. Kenny became this bigger-than-life rescuer, this knight in shining armor who took me under his wing and gave me advice.

When we were back off the road, Kenny would call me

every day—that husky, confidential, I-can-help-you voice—and he sent me bouquets of flowers. I hated him at first. I kept thinking, Why is this stupid person calling me all the time? I just want to work.

Plus, he was married. Why was this married man calling me all the time?

We had some bookings in England and Switzerland, and I invited my sister Candy to go with me. One night while Candy was out sightseeing, I was alone in my room and I began having a panic attack. I got stuck on some bad thought or memory, and it started twirling around in my head. I began hyperventilating, feeling cold and clammy and experiencing a tightness in my chest, exactly as if I were having a heart attack. I'd had panic attacks before and knew what they were, but that didn't make this one any more comfortable.

At this moment, the knight in shining armor happened to knock on my door. I was so grateful to have him there that I fell to my knees, and Kenny picked me up in his arms, very gently, and sat in a big chair and rocked me. He told me to breathe slowly and relax and everything would be all right.

I felt so relieved, so reassured, with Kenny rocking me and talking to me. And I totally fell for him, right then and there. All the other times he had showered attention on me, I kept saying, "Why is he working on me? Why doesn't he leave me alone?" but Kenny suddenly became my personal salvation.

Kenny Rogers became my best friend, and more than my best friend. He flew me all over the country in his private plane. We talked for hours on the phone and never ran out of things to say. This was a totally different experience in my life. Here was this older man, a great success in show business, who knew so much and who seemed more interested in me than in himself. And he kept offering me things.

When it started, all I wanted was a pair of arms to hold me and a voice to whisper that everything would be all right. And you know what? I think all women—at least, most of the women I know—really do want a man who will support them emotionally.

Kenny was great with advice. One time I called him from the road, just totally worn down, and told him I was going crazy. He said that I just had to think things through. He was always very logical, always had analogies for things.

"There's nothing left when the curtain goes down," I told him.

Kenny responded, "Why do most entertainers get hooked on drugs?"

"Because they can't deal with things," I said.

He told me my problem was that I was too isolated on the road, that I was hustled directly from the stage into the back of the bus, so I would be out of danger until they could pack up all the instruments and get on the road again.

"You have no way to work off your energy," Kenny said. "You have to learn how to come down.

"The one thing you have," he continued, "is great friends. You have got to bring them on the road with you."

Soon after that, I started bringing Ruthie with me. She would always be waiting in the bus with fun things to eat, something to do, something to talk about. Kenny actually hired Ruth as my secretary and paid her a year's salary in cash so she would be there for me, to plan my flights, to take care of all the details.

Kenny gave me more than kind words. He lavished presents on me. He paid off the installments on Keith's Corvette. He bought me my first mink. My first diamond tennis bracelet. My first diamond earrings. My first horse. He bought a new engine for the bus. When a storm flooded my piano player's house, Kenny paid to have the house recarpeted, and bought him a new keyboard.

Kenny also told me I did not have to work if I did not want to, but of course I wanted to.

I had been making plans to move to another house out in the country. Kenny volunteered to pay the down payment so I could start all over. It was a big whirlwind, like I was above the clouds, looking down on all this. I could see my old life just floating around out there.

I knew he was married, but he said he had told his wife that he was in love with me. That brought me back to reality a bit. I had never wanted to get in the way of a marriage. But this had all happened so fast. While I was reeling from the terrible tragedy in my life, one day I woke up and found myself in a relationship I was not sure I wanted.

We broke things off numerous times, with one or the other of us saying, "I can't see you anymore." But then Kenny would show up at the door, or call me from the airport and say, "Come get me." This was nothing like what I had with Keith. This was one of those kamikaze relationships that had to end with a nosedive and a major explosion. Finally, we decided to be good friends. It was a mutual decision, but nonetheless I'll admit I was devastated.

It was almost as if that anxiety attack that I suffered in Switzerland had not ended. In retrospect, I guess I went crazy for a while. But sometimes we do some really stupid things just to find salvation or relief.

My next adventure came while I was touring with Clint Black. I developed a major crush on the man who drove the bus, a handsome Texan named Brad Thompson. He was thirty-one, exactly my age. I had my eye on him for a while, but the way things work on the road, the driver is not going to make a move on the featured female singer, so I had to ask him out. Things progressed from there.

I can see now that I was just falling in love on the rebound, probably a way to get back at Kenny.

Because Brad's previous marriage had been annulled, this was the first time I had been able to get married in the Catholic church. We had over three hundred people, with a classical music group playing at the reception. Ruth was my maid of honor and Clint Black was best man. My manager, Stan Moress, walked me halfway down the aisle where my brother Marty met him, and it was Marty who escorted me the rest of the way.

I'll admit it, I had my doubts. I once told Ralph Emery on his interview show that if anybody had gotten up in church and said, "Lorrie, I don't think this is a good idea," I might have called it off even at the altar. But nobody said anything, so I went through with it.

For our honeymoon, we went to Gatlinburg, but I got so sick that we didn't really enjoy the trip, or each other.

At first, it sure seemed like a good idea. My kids were happy to have a father figure in their lives. Brad treated Morgan and Jesse with love and respect. Jesse really needed a man around the house. He already had this image of a man bustling around the place, being loud and goofy, doing guy stuff, and I wanted this to continue for him.

But it all backfired because Brad had a drinking problem, too.

One day I came in off the road during a snowstorm and discovered Brad and Jesse getting dressed to go out and play in the snow. I asked what they were doing, and Brad said, "I'm going to pull Jesse on a sled behind my truck." I was standing close to Brad and I realized he'd been drinking.

I just flipped out. I remembered the nanny-from-hell who had wandered around the house naked when Jesse was an infant. Now I had a new husband who was going to drag my son, Keith's son, on a sled behind a truck.

"There is no way I can ever go out of town again!" I screamed.

Poor Jesse was disappointed because he thought he was

going to have some fun that day. Shirley, my housekeeper, was beside herself seeing me so angry. That was the day I realized the marriage was not going to work out. I was in a constant state of anxiety, but not all of it was due to Brad. Part of it was financial (I was so low on money, I had to file for Chapter 11 bankruptcy during my marriage). Part of it was my own body in chaos.

I didn't realize how bad it was at the time but I had endometriosis, a series of cysts on my ovaries, which was causing me terrible pain. I had had cyst problems even while I was married to Keith, but I never imagined they could get as bad as they got. I was walking around with a constant case of PMS, hurting on my right side and thinking, It's mental. Just get a grip on yourself. It's like a panic attack. But it wasn't. It was real.

Finally, the doctors ordered me into the hospital to remove a few of the cysts. While I was on the operating table, they recommended the entire uterus be removed immediately.

Because I was unconscious, my husband had to make that decision for me. Brad agreed to the hysterectomy and I didn't know about it until I came out of surgery.

When I found out, I was very depressed to think I could not have any more children. I had always assumed I would have five, like my mother. In the long run, however, I came to feel that God knew what he was doing. There was much doubt about whether I would stay with Brad, and it would not have been smart to bring another child into the world at that moment.

People close to me suggested the operation was a blessing in disguise—I would not have any more danger or pain. Because I was so young, I had to take hormone shots regularly. Candy taught Beth how to give me the shot, which she still does, regularly.

My body bounced back. My marriage did not. I filed for a divorce, and when Brad left the house, he really left. He called once from Arkansas, on his way back to Texas. I haven't heard from him since.

During the divorce from Brad, I was shooting a movie for TNN called *Proudheart*. On the last day of the shoot, there was the traditional wrap party for the entire cast and crew at the Stockyards downtown, and I asked Ruth to come with me.

There were hundreds of people milling around, and Ruth and I got separated, but soon she found me, and she had this glazed look in her eye.

"Lorrie, you are not going to believe who's here," she announced.

"Who?"

"Troy Aikman."

"Who?" I repeated.

"Just the best-frigging-looking quarterback in the National Football League," she said.

"Who cares?" I replied. I was looking forward to getting home, seeing my kids, and taking a day off.

Just then, my road manager, Jake LaGrone, came up to me and said, "Hey, Lorrie, I want to introduce you to Troy Aikman."

I looked up, way up, and said, "Hey, how you doin'?"

The best-frigging-looking quarterback in the National Football League and I soon established that I was booked to work his golf tournament in April.

"I'm looking forward to seeing you perform," he said, and that was it. There were people wanting to talk to both of us, and in a few minutes we were a dozen feet apart in a crowded room.

Ruth returned and said, "You are so stupid. Go over there and talk to him."

And I said, "Ruth, I really don't care about Troy Aikman." Which was a fact. I follow football a little, but meeting him was not one of my ambitions in life.

The band started playing, and I soon saw Troy picking his

way, politely, through the crowd. He came over and asked me to dance. Thank goodness I had on my four-inch stacked shoes or I'd hardly have reached his waist. We danced, we talked, and then he invited me out for a late breakfast. He said he had a limousine waiting outside and would give me a ride home. I gave my keys to Ruth and asked her to drive my car home.

We found some late-night pancake house over by Vanderbilt; then we got in the back of the stretch limousine, a few first downs away from the driver. Troy was being very proper, but just to make things clear, I held up my left hand and said, "You know, I'm still wearing my wedding band; my divorce isn't final." He told me he understood.

When we got to my house, Shirley was there, and my kids were asleep. I gave him a walking tour, and about two in the morning we sat down in the Red Room, where I kept my awards and posters and photographs, and I explained them all to him. Meanwhile, his limo driver was sitting outside waiting because Troy had a flight back to Dallas at eight in the morning.

I felt very comfortable with Troy Aikman. He had his own success, he was very bright and secure, and he was genuinely interested in my profession. We sat up all night in that brightly lit living room, talking about football and music and life, and around five o'clock in the morning he said he had to get going.

Then, at the front door, he gave me a kiss I will never forget as long as I live.

"Do you mind if I have your phone number?" he asked.

Mind? Heck, I would have written it on the back of his hand, like they write the plays for absentminded quarterbacks, but I managed to find a slip of paper and gave him the number. After his limousine had rolled down the hill, I thought, Well, that was interesting—but I'll never hear from him again.

Actually, I heard from him six hours later, as soon as his plane landed in Dallas. Then I heard from him some more. I could get pretty emotional about all the times I heard from him.

Very soon, I was head over heels in love with Troy Aikman. I wanted that relationship to work so badly.

We tried going out like normal people, but it isn't that easy. You don't just go out to the mall for a movie on a Saturday night. Oh, Nashville people are pretty cool about country-music performers, because we're local. You go to the supermarket or the nail salon, and people are used to seeing you. We are family. But try going out somewhere with a quarterback from the Dallas Cowboys, the organization that calls itself America's Team.

All of America recognized Troy Aikman, and there were a bunch of people who were starting to recognize me, too. And if there is one thing that people love more than an individual celebrity, it is *two* celebrities who just might be going together. The gossip magazines and the tabloids went to work on the relationship, and I don't think Troy was prepared for the onslaught.

Seeing our names in the tabloids all the time was worse than anything I had ever encountered. Somebody would ask me about Troy, and I would say something innocuous, and a week or two later there would be a screaming headline in one of those rags, something I never said. Troy and I would have to check it out over the long-distance lines.

Did you say this?

No, did you say that?

Most of it was made up. These tabloids are part of the publicity mill, more for a performer than an athlete. For better or worse, people know the score in sports, but in show business, there is more of a gray area when it comes to gossip. It's harmful, it's destructive, it's often nasty. But sometimes we need it, whether it's for validation or to just plain sell tickets. Unfortunately, no matter how many flights there are between Dallas and Nashville, the tabloids can mess up a relationship.

Our romance was a few great first downs, some great blocks and tackles, and a few memorable touchdowns, but it was only a first quarter, not a full game.

Troy was under tremendous pressure as the most important player on his team. He was also a very eligible bachelor who had succeeded in staying that way. He always said he wanted an independent woman, strong-minded, with her own career, but in the end I did not believe it. He wanted somebody around when he had a free moment. For that matter, so did I. I don't blame him for needing that. I could understand.

I've said this to Troy myself: He was so young—he's eight years younger than I am—and he just wasn't ready for a full relationship.

My hysterectomy also penalized me here. It bothered Troy that I had two children but couldn't have any more. He wanted his own children, eventually, and I couldn't blame him for that either. That was a big hurdle for a man in his mid-twenties.

I would have moved to Dallas, would have uprooted my family, would have commuted to work in Nashville, just to make it work with Troy. But it was not going to happen.

I came out of that relationship reeling from pain. I wanted to marry Troy Aikman more than anything in my life at that time. We didn't make it, but I learned something about myself. For the first time since Keith had died, I realized I could love again, passionately and openly.

After a romance in a fishbowl, I would have been very happy to meet somebody who was not in the public eye.

Instead, I met a man who was both a public official and an actor.

Fred Thompson has been seen all over the world in character roles in films like *No Way Out*, *The Hunt for Red October* and *Die Hard 2*. He's not hard to miss, at six feet, six inches. But acting is only a sideline. Fred Thompson has a quarter of a century in public service.

More important, Fred has been in the news lately as the senator from Tennessee who is investigating fund-raising for political campaigns.

I was the blond country singer who accompanied him to parties. Often they were fund-raisers for his next campaign.

Most Americans first became aware of Fred in 1973 when he was the chief counsel for the Senate Watergate Committee, helping Senator Howard Baker investigate the charges against the group that had helped reelect President Nixon.

I would like to tell you I remember watching the tall, handsome man from Tennessee on television, asking questions at the hearings. But to be honest about it, I was barely into my teens, hanging out with my father backstage at the *Opry*. Politics and current events were not my strong suit. Many people had been very impressed with the dignified, nonpartisan way these two Republicans headed an investigation that led to the resignation of a Republican president, the first time in history that an American president had resigned.

Since then, Fred Thompson has run political campaigns for Tennessee Republicans and has worked as a lobbyist for all kinds of companies. But when Senator Albert Gore Jr. was elected vice president in 1992, a Democrat was appointed to replace him in the Senate—until a special election in November of 1994. Fred Thompson was persuaded to run for the office.

About that same time, Susan Nadler and I were in Mario's restaurant, and she introduced me to Fred. He was even taller than Troy—he had been a basketball player back in Lawrenceburg, in the southern part of Tennessee—and he was a combination of friendly and sophisticated. He could chat with people in town squares all over the state, but you had the feeling he knew his way around the big cities of the world, too. He could charm voters. He could also charm me.

Fred invited me out, and I went with him to a Republican

fund-raiser. Soon afterward, he won the senatorial election in 1994. Early in 1995, he invited me to the induction of Don Sundquist as governor of Tennessee. I then flew up to Washington to meet him once, where we went to a fund-raiser for Lamar Alexander, and he came backstage to the *Opry* in March.

Fred Thompson had been married for a long time and had three grown children. Even his ex-wife seemed to have good things to say about him.

It was great to go out with an older man who was very successful on his own. I felt very secure with him, and he became a wonderful friend, a caring, inspirational man who would encourage me not to doubt myself (which, maybe you can tell by now, is one of my best things).

Fred is an extremely generous man. He wined and dined me and brought me presents—furs, earrings, Chanel shoes with real high heels.

For a while, I enjoyed my first exposure to politics. It was interesting to hear the political conversations, and people even began talking about Fred as a potential president. It was inevitable that I would be sitting at a glamorous party and would have the flickering thought, So, this is what it's like to be a First Lady. Hell, I could handle that. Then I would say, "Oops, better drop the 'hell.' "

It did not take long before I was feeling stifled at those same political dinners and fund-raisers. I could not express myself as a pungent, pithy country singer. I began to feel programmed to smile and be . . . well . . . political.

I put myself to the task of being a great companion to a stimulating and important man, and as a result I became boring. I lost my spunk, my spontaneity. I had to stop and think about the political implications of everything before I uttered a word in public. Was this a Democratic issue? Was this a Republican issue? I could not trust or use my best asset, my gut instincts. In other words, I could not be myself.

Fred let me know that it was important how I dressed. Sedate was in. Even if I felt like a little flair that night, forget it—we might be with men who had big wallets and insecure wives, wives who were a little older than I was. So get that basic black dress out of the closet. And no cleavage, baby.

Fred's senator buddies loved me, and some of my friends said they had never seen me happier. For a while, I wanted to marry Fred, but I knew he could not accept me as I am.

I had been through this with Troy. If we were seen in public, we would be in the tabloids and on six hundred cable stations, all of them with these breathless reports of what we were wearing and what expression was on our faces. It does take away the spontaneity of a relationship. I kept saying I did not want us to be like Lyle Lovett and Julia Roberts, where every question was, "Are you still together?" or "When do you find time to see each other?"

Ultimately, I decided we could have a "mature" relationship. I told Fred I'd vote for him in his '96 election. Heck, I'd even contribute to his campaign. As long as he assured me it was legal. Now that's mature, isn't it?

Chapter Twenty-Six

After nearly eight years, there were still questions about what happened those last three days of Keith's life.

I had been living with the consequences, day by day, and I knew some of the details. Now I wanted to know everything. Nothing could bring Keith back, but there were questions I had avoided much too long.

In January of 1997, I called Lane Palmer, whom I had asked to keep an eye on Keith when I went out of town on that fateful Sunday in 1989. I keep in touch with him, even though he and Beth have long since been divorced.

"I'm working on the story about Keith and me," I said over the phone. "I'd like to talk to you."

I knew Lane would not let me down. He came out to the house that night after work. Back in the old days, he was a good-time guy, but now he was sober in every sense of the word. His voice was deep, his face serious as he arrived at the front door. We hugged each other.

Part of me wanted to feel anger toward Lane. I wanted to blame him for letting Keith slip away; I wanted to despise the ugly, hard-living ways that had bonded them.

Why was Keith gone and why was Lane sitting in my house?

But I couldn't hate Lane. Lane is family. Plus, Lane loved Keith, too.

I brought him some coffee, and he lit up a cigarette. We sat down in the living room, just Susan Nadler and George, the writer, in the room.

"You and I have never had this discussion, have we?" Lane said.

We both knew the answer was no. And we both knew it wasn't going to be easy.

For a few minutes, I wasn't sure we were going to *have* a discussion. Lane sipped his coffee, dragged on his cigarette, choosing his words slowly.

"It cost me a hundred dollars to talk about this the first time," Lane said.

"Excuse me?"

"Therapy," he explained. "I talked about it in therapy. Might as well talk about it again."

He worked into it slowly, almost thinking out loud. He and Keith had shared some wild times.

"Keith was my favorite of the whole bunch," Lane continued. "It may have been that we had similar mental twists. We were both the sweetest people at times and total raving animals at other times. I don't know about Keith, but I couldn't kick a dog. But if somebody made me angry, I could club him.

"Keith was an awful lot like that. The alcohol was the most important thing to him. We didn't talk about it, but he was a different person," Lane said, meaning Keith was different when he drank.

"Keith was up for anything when he was drinking. I never *started* drinking with him. If he was drinking, hell, I'd drink with him. I was the adult. If things got out of hand, I'd be the designated driver."

Lane's words might make it sound as if he was bragging or glorifying the old days, but there was a mocking tone to his voice, as he ridiculed the mental processes of his old drunken self.

"I would cover up for him because he had a lot to lose by drinking," Lane continued. "Galante was going to ditch him, so was McFadden, so the best I could do at that time was participate and drive. See that we tried to keep him out of trouble, out of the public eye.

"There was a sweet part of Keith I really liked," Lane said. "That wild side came out when he was drinking, I was accustomed to it. Want to pitch a bitch? All right."

Lane was not apologizing to me for his subject matter or raw language. He did not have to. I had invited him out to my house to tell me the whole story. The narrative would have to come in his own language, the language he had used back before he was clean. There is no point in cleaning it up now. This is Lane's side of things. It's got to be in Lane's language, too.

"The Sunday that you left . . . ," he said to me, visibly gulping down his emotions. "I have to go slow. I put it away for a long time. After Keith died, I was going to try to get through the funeral without whiskey or dope, but I had to go to the bathroom at St. Joseph's and have some dope.

"And then I wasn't sober for fourteen months. When I sobered up I was sick, and now I've been sober for six years, six months and three days. Not that I'm counting.

"I've learned a lot about alcoholism," Lane said. Then he recalled the days before I went out on the road: "You called me over at my house. You wanted me to come over."

"That's right," I replied. "I said, 'Keith's been drinking. Would you keep an eye on him while I go on the road?' I told Beth the same thing."

"Keith promised he'd come by the shop after he dropped you off," Lane continued. "He wasn't capable of driving by that time. You remember my auto-body shop was way out in the country. I stayed there a lot. He came by. I was drinking moonshine. He was already well lit. We got going on the moonshine.

"Keith wanted to go downtown. He wanted to drive, go fast, and I said, 'Okay, I'll drive.' We left. I didn't have any particular destination; we just drove down Broadway. I was a little paranoid because I'd taken a packet of dope with me. I hadn't told anybody, but I had to have it all the time or else I'd get real squirrely. Here I am downtown, both of us drunker than a pair of shithouse rats, I'm trying to find a parking place.

"Keith jumped out and ran into Tootsie's," Lane said, referring to the classic bar on Broadway where old Tootsie Bess used to stick her hatpin into rowdy customers to maintain law and order. Tootsie's is still about the same, although Tootsie and her hatpin are long since gone.

"The streets were a little crowded, and I was concerned because he'd been drinking. I was supposed to keep him out of the public, that was my job. Do all this in private, so it wouldn't get back to Jack or you. Before I found a parking place, I'd only been gone five or six minutes, and he'd already been in Tootsie's, had a couple drinks, sang a song, picked up an old troll."

Lane looked over at me. He knew he was getting to the painful part.

"When Keith wasn't drinking, he didn't look at other women, talk about other women, even locker room talk," Lane said. "When he was drinking, he was somebody else. It ain't any less painful, is it?"

I just shrugged. This was the infamous Carmen I had learned about when Lieutenant Bell walked out to my pool.

"My job was to keep you from finding out," Lane continued. "I'd talk to Keith later and say, 'Now this shit has got to stop. You can't do this with these old yard dogs. Why are you dragging in all these trolls?' This was not a pretty woman."

Now that I thought about it, what difference did it make if

Carmen was young and beautiful, or aging and homely? But I didn't ask Lane about this.

"We left Tootsie's and went to the Hall of Shame Motel. This old gal was piled up on the console of the 'Vette. Just in five minutes on the ride, we learned she had no money, no car, was staying with friends in Franklin, and had two, three warm beers.

"I was all for ditching this old gal. I talked to Keith about it. He wanted to ditch her, too, but we may have knocked down a drink or two there. . . ."

Here Lane grew very somber, glancing over at me. I think he was hoping I would stop him from telling the next part, but I had waited over seven years to hear the full story, knowing it was probably quite ugly. We had come too far now. I wanted this insight into the beautiful man I loved, so I just stared back at Lane, which he took as a signal to continue.

"I hate this," Lane said, shuddering with apparent disgust. "Again, that's where Keith just wasn't himself. He wanted to get a blow job from this old gal before he left. At least, he had the presence of mind not to get himself a room. He wanted to do this under a stairwell. And, uh, I just wanted to get off somewhere, get away from downtown Nashville, get away from this old troll.

"She was opposed, for some reason. She wanted to know, 'What kind of person you think I am to do that?' And Keith explained exactly the sort of person he thought she was, and he was pretty accurate. Damn brutal with his description. He explained she was just a tired old road whore, out for a few laughs, and that was about it."

Keith's description matched my impression of this Carmen. I was curious whether Carmen had thought she was performing a sexual favor for a famous musician, or just doing a service for mankind in general. Lane cleared that up in a hurry.

"She didn't know who he was," Lane told me, seven years

later. "Just some funny guy who picked her up at this bar. Or she claimed not to know. We gave her bogus names. And what little time I could get Keith off by himself, he had agreed, we would just carry this old gal and ditch her. I was real satisfied with that.

"We never got to the ditching point. We just got back to the shop. I had done all the dope up and I needed some more to maintain. It had been an hour or two since I had some, and I needed some. We got back to the shop, drinking some more moonshine. This girl is getting radical on the moonshine. I had dinner guests, couldn't take Keith home, and couldn't let him drive. Couldn't take him to his house.

"He was dead set on having sex. Dead set on it. So I took him down to this old motel down the street. Got a room. Tried to control everything. Took everybody's driver's license, got their billfolds. 'Y'all just get to the motel, do your fucking; I got dinner guests, just get this out of your system, and I'll see y'all.' I delivered everybody where they needed to be delivered. I went home, ate dinner, and then . . ."

I knew the next step. I had been involved in that part.

"And then I called when I landed in Washington," I said. "Y'all told me Keith was asleep on the couch."

"I also lied to Beth," Lane assured me. "I didn't tell Beth about that old gal. I just said he was drunk and sobering up and let it go at that."

"Did you go back to the motel that night?" I asked.

"They were gone," Lane said. "Keith was really resourceful. He got a cab and went home. Bernice let him in, he got keys, came back, and got the Corvette. He came up missing. I figured he'd turn up the next day."

That brought us to Monday morning.

"Keith and I saw each other Monday at the shop. He was drinking. He was real antsy. Wanted something to knock off the edge. I didn't want to share my dope with anybody. I had to buy my shit like anybody else. It was a commodity. You don't just pass it out. I had a limit every week, and I was surpassing it. I sure didn't want to share it with anybody else. We rode around.

"That night, we got home in the wee hours of the night. I was having trouble at home explaining everything. I had to lie to Beth. McFadden was calling every fifteen minutes. I tried to placate him and cover tracks for the night before.

"I'm already hearing around campus that Keith has run amuck at the Starlite with this old troll, and introduced her as his cousin from California. He tried to sing a song or two at the Starlite and did poorly at that, but I think that was when the girl discovered she was not with Bob or Jim or whatever alias he was using."

"Do you know where he was Monday night?" I asked.

"Lorrie, I've totally lost Monday night. Something tells me I stayed up all night."

"After you lied to Beth, you met up with Keith," I said. "Was Carmen back Monday night?"

"No, Carmen was history. None of us wanted anything to do with her. By that time, he was lucid enough that I could talk to him about the problems she was causing. She had his monogrammed lighter, his drawers, and his shirt. Boy, she was a mercenary bitch. She wanted to return the stuff but she wanted some money for it to keep her mouth shut.

"You're getting the picture of me trying to put the rats back in the cage. I got this girl out there, and she won't stay put, and I got Keith rattling around and he won't stay put. Give him some whiskey to slow him down, and he gets too slow, and you give him some cocaine to bring him back, and he gets geeky and wants to go driving."

"She wanted money?" I asked.

"A plane ticket," Lane said. "It seemed so important at the time. She called me. I was a mile away from the motel. I had given her my card. Said, 'Just call, when you're all through with this debauchery, just holler.' Keith had already delivered himself, so I saw no reason to deliver this old trollop. I just blew her off and she got pissed, got demanding. She wasn't going to be treated like that. I think we hooked up that night.

"Tuesday morning. I went by early. I think he had disappeared the night before. Tuesday morning, I was at your house and Keith was up and showered."

"I can't believe it," I said. "Straight?"

I still find it staggering to think of Keith walking around, in control of himself, taking coffee with Lane, talking to his mom on the phone, at eight-thirty in the morning, and dead by eleven-thirty. I've listened to the tape I made of Lane's story and every time I wanted to stop it here, run it backward, rescue Keith from what happened next.

"He had coffee on and we talked like we talked when we were sober," Lane said.

"Did you talk about repercussions? Was he flipping out?" I asked.

"It was, like, what the fuck are we going to tell people? I had no idea how he got the keys to the car. He's got no driver's license, I've got his billfold, I think he left without money. There was no alcohol, no pills, no cash laying there for anybody to go get stuff. Everybody was going to control Keith's drug and alcohol habits."

"Did he think about repercussions?" I persisted.

"He was nervous," Lane said. "We had to be cool at all costs. Had to be cool. We were going to cover everything up real well. It was going to be as if we didn't have a drink."

"But he knew it was going to hit the fan?"

"He was worried about it hitting," Lane admitted. "He hadn't talked to Jack, and Jack was rabidly searching for him."

"Carson and Mike were looking for him, too," I said.

"We must have talked till eight-thirty," Lane said. " 'Why do we do this shit?' Talked about what a tired old sow that was he picked up at Tootsie's."

"So why did he do it?"

I think a lot of us women ask that question a lot. What makes a man want to go out and have sex with the very first woman who makes herself available?

"Alcohol," Lane replied. "We just become different people. As the disease progresses, we become more like Mr. Hyde than Dr. Jekyll."

I don't know if that was the answer I wanted, but Lane went on about the coverup he and Keith had planned that Tuesday morning, in the kitchen at our house.

"We became scared that somebody was going to take our shit from us," Lane said. "It was important to cover up. I gave him a big pep talk and all that worked fine. We were gonna ride Harleys. We were gonna con TNN into giving us money to ride around the country, live the life of Riley, have a ball. We were gonna make this grandiose start this afternoon, but right now, we were going to go all day without any dope.

"I was at my best at eight o'clock in the morning because I already had my morning drink, I wasn't shaking, I hadn't started on the cocaine for the day. That was my best thinking time, that time in the morning.

"It looked like at the last minute we had pulled the fat out of the fire. 'I'm gonna back your ass up and you're gonna back mine up, and by God, that's our story and we're sticking to it. We're going to placate Jack and you're gonna see Galante and you can rest on the bus that night.' Keith had a very important meeting with Galante that Jack was freaking about."

"At nine-thirty Kentucky time, Keith's mother said she called him, and he was fine, drinking coffee," I said. "That would be eight-thirty Nashville time."

"That was shortly after I left," Lane said. "My shop was only ten, fifteen minutes away."

"I was not going to drink anymore that day," Lane continued. "Nobody could smell the vodka on my breath and my nose wasn't running—yet. I went back to the shop, tried to do a little work. I was so grateful that we had pulled it off, done pushed it right to the limit, and backed off. 'By God, they'll never know. We're family men and let's not do this shit anymore. This is our own backyard. If were going to do this shit, let's do it in Tucson or Albu-fucking-querque.'

"Back at the shop, Jack called, real frantic. I was nonchalant. I had just left an hour ago. Jack said he had come in the house and Keith was in the bedroom, had locked himself in there, and Jack wanted to know did I know how to get in. He heard rustling. Maybe somebody was with him. Another person at the house. That's Jack's theory. Keith and I had had this agreement, we weren't going to take anything more. He was going to his meeting."

"Could he have gotten messed up from his Antabuse?"

"Naw, he was off it by then," Lane said. "Anyway, Jack had called and wanted me to get over there. I still had Keith's house keys. Still had his billfold. Keep all that shit in control. I think I drove Beth's car, but I'd have to clear that up with her. I'd like to find out more about it. There are whole Christmas seasons I can't remember. I find clothes in my closet that I can't remember. I know I bought 'em, but there are a lot of spaces in that time of my life.

"All right, I came in, let myself in the house, the door was unlocked, and Keith was laying on the bed, kind of facedown. I shook him. I thought he said something or moaned something. I couldn't wake him up. He was warm and at that point, I thought he was breathing. I didn't look for a pulse. I didn't imagine he'd be dead. I was pissed off because he'd gotten drunk again."

"Was there any vomit?"

"There was, but it was under his face. It wasn't visible. I thought he passed out but now I believe he was dying. Was in the process. After all this time, I haven't done a lot of what-ifs and if-onlys. . . ."

Lane's voice was slow and labored. A woman would be crying, sobbing, at this point, but Lane was swallowing his emotions.

"There was a little gram bag there. I don't know where it came from but at that point, the phone rang. I left everything and answered it.

"First, it was Faye calling. How foggy I was at the time. I thought I was talking to your housekeeper, Bernice. She wanted to know how Keith was. I said, tired, sleeping, didn't want to wake him up, he had big meetings that week. 'If it's all the same to you, I'd just as soon let him sleep.'

"Then I spoke to Jack. I told him, 'He's just dog-ass drunk. There's no way he's gonna be sober for a meeting.' Jack's response was, 'Well, get him dressed. We'll put him on the bus, get him out of town, blow the meeting with Galante, and make up some excuse.'

"I went over there to wake him up and he won't wake up. I roll him over and there's vomit on his face. And I noticed that the lowest part of his face is turning cold, the side that was down. And I said, 'Holy shit, what am I going to do now?' "

Lane started sniffling a little bit.

"I tried mouth-to-mouth. I can still taste the vomit. Couldn't get him to breathe. I was really, really pissed at him at that point. Tried to make him breathe and hollered at him. I yelled at him, 'You motherfucker, you can't do this, you're not allowed! This ain't in the fucking script! You ain't doing it!'

"I'd sit there for ten seconds, and then in despair I'd say, 'I'm gonna try it one more time.'

"It's fucking ludicrous to do CPR on a water bed. I really felt helpless. Couldn't help him. Couldn't do anything for him. 'Ah, fuck it, this ain't gonna work.' Dragged him over to the hard part at the edge of the bed. I was either gonna make his heart beat or break his back. It just didn't work out. It seemed forever. I didn't know the address of your house, so I called Jack and I said, 'I'm working on Keith and he's either dead or dying, and you'd better get an ambulance over here.' "

Lane took a deep breath to try to get a grip.

"It had been so frantic, all those few days. That morning we'd been all business. How it's going to be. This is what we're going to say. Cover it up. We're in control. We're active. Living, breathing. Even that morning. We were tense. We had tense lives. When he was dead, he sure looked peaceful, like a little kid.

"The ambulance came. As they came, I ate the dope. Just opened my tongue and flushed it back.

"The paramedics got there, and they weren't going to do anything except bundle him up and take him away.

"I said, 'You-all can't just take him away. You've got to do something. You're supposed to know. I believe that if somebody had some training and just worked on him, you could bring him back to life.' They were really kind. They didn't bring out all the stuff I thought they'd bring. It wasn't like TV."

I wanted to know if somebody could have run over there and given him a bag of dope, somebody he knew. If he didn't have any money, he could have promised to pay them later.

"It could very well have been," Lane said. "But I ate the dope and it didn't kill me. Hair spray. That's what killed him. That's what the medical examiner said. The bottles were in the trash can in the bathroom. Half a dozen of them."

I knew I used those hair products, but they were high quality and expensive. I bet I didn't have six bottles of them in the house.

"The police carried all the bottles out," Lane said. "I had been so diligent in trying to control everything. When I got to your house that morning, there were still three beer bottles in the 'Vette, so I put them in my car. I figured, well, maybe he'd had three beers or something. Then I called Beth. Either just before or just after the ambulance got there."

Now I understood why Lane had lied to Beth, and why both of them had told me Keith was sleeping on their couch. Keith was with Carmen. Even after Keith was pronounced dead, Lane still had to deal with Carmen.

"I was still trying to juggle the rats in the cage," Lane said. "She was in Franklin wanting to extort money because she had just figured out who she's been with, and now she reads in the newspaper that he's dead. She had fallen in love in twenty-four hours, and it was going to take a whole lot of therapy for her to get over it, and it was going to be so expensive.

"Meanwhile, Jack has found out about Carmen, and this bitch is calling me at the funeral home. I told Jack I was going to stall her, then fetch some money out to California. She was talking about the tabloids. Just as trashy a scam as you could think of. At that point, I was torn between stringing her along, sending her some money, or sending somebody out there to put an ice pick in her ear. What do you do?"

Then Lane looked me in the eye.

"Me, being in control, I needed to keep you from finding out. You didn't need to know. I could shoulder this entire burden. But then when you found out, it was a real relief. I got Carmen on the phone and, Lorrie, it was the most eloquent profanity I've ever heard. A stream. No pauses. Breath. Thirty seconds. What a low-down beady-eyed chicken-fucking whore she was. Lorrie, it actually embarrassed me—and I'm not easily embarrassed. It was great. The woman had no stick anymore. I didn't have to fool with her anymore."

So there it was. I finally knew as much as could be known.

Once again, my mind went back to the early days when I thought we could beat this thing, when we tried the non-alcoholic beer or champagne, but that just made him want the real stuff. He was getting the taste but it was the buzz he wanted. Alcohol was definitely Keith's drug of choice. I know there was cocaine around, but it was the alcohol he went for. The newspapers made a big thing about "traces" of cocaine being listed in the autopsy report as one of the substances found in Keith's body, but the death certificate said he died of acute etholism. That's what he wanted.

"Lorrie, he looked so peaceful," Lane said for the second time.

"I'm sure he was," I muttered. "He didn't have to face the music."

What was the music Keith did not want to face? I knew from my own intuition that something had happened to him when he was younger. I was hoping that was one last thing Lane could tell me.

"His mom once told me that when he was young, coming off the road, he'd be depressed, he would just sleep," Lane said. "And there was one time we talked about drinking. We were on the scooters, out at Marrowbone Lake, just sitting there smoking. He talked a lot about how some of the guys used to make him drink whiskey."

Keith had been only fifteen and sixteen when he started going out on the road. Had some of the older musicians shamed him into drinking?

"Maybe somebody in that band," Lane said. I prodded Lane about the times Keith had visited the porno shops out on Dickerson Pike.

"We never discussed those habits," Lane said. "I never could understand why Keith liked those joints. Peep shows. That would only be when he was drinking. I never went with him."

"Something that happened when he was young?" I asked.

"There was a verbal understanding," Lane now said. "You must be cool. Cool till we die. Unflappable. Handle everything that comes along. Can't admit you're scared. 'Cause they'll eat you if you're scared."

I asked Lane how he had gotten sober, and stayed sober.

"It took fourteen months after Keith died. I was drinking a quart of whiskey every day and drinking that vodka in the morning to get going. I was shooting up two ounces of cocaine a week. Eating pills at night, Valium, to go to sleep.

"Then Alcoholics Anonymous gave me the strength to stay sober ten days. God gave me ten days. I sat through one or two meetings—all those people saying it's gonna get better. I was trying to read the big book. I'd read a page and couldn't recall it. I stayed busy. Made a full-time occupation over not blowing my brains out and not getting drunk."

It was at that point that Beth had discovered she did not like being treated badly. By the time he was showing any interest in being sober, it was too late—she took their two children and left.

"That woke me up," Lane said. "I went out in the shop and detoxed myself in a truck. July of 1990. It was a hundred degrees in there, and all I remember is a lot of fear, a lot of hallucinations."

Lane said that when he was able to wobble out of the shop, nobody could tell he was sober. He had gone to see Beth to discuss a possible reconciliation but he was acting like a man who still had alcohol and cocaine in his system, a dry drunk.

"The funny thing is, I was incoherent. I had to be driven from place to place. Most people didn't know I was clean. They just thought I was a little radical for a while."

And in the end, Beth did leave him.

"I lost my family," Lane said. "I lost almost all my money."

"You've got two perfect children," I told Lane.

"That's the only thing I done right in my life," Lane said. "My children."

"Now I'm sober six years, six months, three days. And when I sobered up, I got into therapy. As long as it keeps working,

I am who I want to be. As long as it keeps working, I'll keep doing it."

I understood the concept of living day by day. Here was living proof that it could work. Lane had managed to save his life, at least this far.

"But Lorrie," Lane said, in a soft, almost plaintive voice, "if Keith hadn't died, I probably would have."

We fell silent. It was nearly midnight. Lane reached for his coat, and we stood up and gave each other a big hug.

"Lane," I said, "thanks for coming out here. We needed to have this talk."

Then he was gone, his red taillights going up the hill.

Lane had saved his own life. Help is out there. Keith never used the help that was all around him.

CHAPTER TWENTY-SEVEN

After Lane left, there was still one unanswered mystery about Keith's death. Was somebody else in the house? It seemed like there had to be. How else could that packet of cocaine have gotten there?

I still needed to talk to somebody else who might remember some extra details of what Lane—and Keith—were doing that weekend.

It had taken me months to get over being mad at Beth, my beautiful blond sister, for telling me Keith was asleep on the couch when I called from Washington. If I had known he was out on the prowl, maybe I would have jumped on the first airplane back. I certainly would have called Jack. Instead, I was lulled into a false sense of security. Now I had to talk to Beth about this.

I had to be blunt with my sister.

"Lane made you lie to me when I called from Washington," I said to her recently. "He said to tell me that Keith was lying on the couch, sleeping. Why?"

Beth had no problem with the question.

"He said, 'I promise you, this is for the best, so it won't cause problems between Lorrie and Keith.' "

"And why'd you do it?" I asked.

"Lane was so mean," Beth said quietly. "You didn't go against what he said."

I asked my sister to try to re-create, nearly eight years later, that fatal Monday, when Keith slipped away from everybody.

"I was at the shop to work with Lane," Beth said. "We were going to eat lunch and Lane said we needed to check on Keith. I said 'fine.' We got to the house and he said, 'You stay here.' He went inside, came out in ten minutes, and said, 'He's doing better, we can go to lunch.' I never saw Keith while Lane went inside. This must have been at twelve or twelve-thirty."

Since Beth never saw him, she did not actually know if Keith was in our house when Lane went in there at lunch time. Was it conceivable that Keith was not there, that he was out carousing somewhere, and Lane made up the story?

"He doesn't remember, he says. But I remember he was very persistent about my not coming into my own sister's house. Why couldn't I come in?"

Was it conceivable that somebody else was in there with Keith on Monday afternoon and that Lane did not want Beth to know?

"Yes," my sister said.

"Closure." That's the big word these days. I still needed some closure about Keith's death. I had somehow never nailed it down in my mind exactly what Keith had been drinking on that last fatal binge. I had heard rumors of a greenish tinge in his stomach; I had heard theories about his drinking antifreeze, and Lane had insisted there were six bottles of expensive hair spray empty in the bathroom.

Somehow I had not gone out and asked exactly what was found in the room with my husband.

After all these years, I called Lieutenant Bell, who has

always been courteous to me, a real professional, very respectful about not turning the case into some big media hype. I asked him to tell George the writer whatever he could about the material found with Keith. The detective said Keith had died of "alcohol poisoning," and he added "there was some controlled substance found" in Keith's system, but a minute amount.

What was found in the room? The detective did not want to rely on memory, so he went back to his records.

"There were four different bottles of stuff that were full and now they were less than full," he said, referring to the hair products in my cabinet. He said that he and I inventoried them. It's strange how I hardly remember doing that.

"There were also some beer cans," the detective said.

How many?

"Twelve-pack of Budweiser," he said. "All empty. Eleven more Budweisers. Empty. Two cans of Coors. And an empty Scope bottle."

Would that be enough to produce a lethal amount of alcohol in Keith's system?

"He'd had a pretty good night the night before," the detective said.

Were there any theories about somebody else being involved in the death? The detective acknowledged that Keith had run into "a tourist from California," meaning Carmen. But the detective gave the distinct impression that there was no ongoing investigation, because Keith had died of self-induced alcohol poisoning.

"Nobody forced him to drink all that," Lieutenant Bell concluded.

I have only slowly come to understand just how self-destructive Keith was with his alcohol.

And I have come, finally, to understand that ultimately there was nothing I could have done to stop him.

But closure?

I'm sorry to say, the answer's no.

I still have questions. If Keith had been on a two-day bender before he died, why was the house so neat and clean? How did the bed get made? What was the rustling noise Jack McFadden heard in our bedroom? Where did that packet of cocaine come from? What about the guy seen with Keith at Carrie's Corner Market the day before Keith died? Was that Keith's old buddy named Sammy? Nobody's heard from him since.

What about Carmen?

Somebody knows something.

Some day I am going to find out.

CHAPTER TWENTY-EIGHT

A few years ago, I realized I was frightened of turning thirty-five. It sounded almost, you know, middle-aged.

But one of my best friends told me, "You'll love thirty-five. You come into your own. You're not questioning so much, you're now finding the answers. You're becoming a woman for the first time. I thought it was a bunch of bull, that she was trying to psych me up, but right after thirty-five, I did indeed begin to find answers to things.

I now feel more in control than I ever have in my life. I can't help saying this: I may not have any education past high school, but I'm pretty dang smart. There is not much that gets past me.

I have thirty employees these days, and I make it my business to know what they're doing and how they're feeling. I take pride in always knowing what's going on in a room. If there are six people, I know how each one is feeling. Or I make it my business to find out.

I have questioned and thought and researched—not necessarily in books but in my heart and my mind. There are things you learn as you become a woman. You start saying to yourself, "I didn't know one-fourth of what I thought I knew."

My short time with Keith taught me a lot. I think I could actually give advice to every woman who loves somebody, who thinks maybe she can do more to help her man through a problem.

When I was in my twenties, people tried to tell me that you need help in dealing with a problem, that nobody can walk alone. I did not listen.

I said, "You don't know me. You don't know my power. You don't know what kind of love I've got."

Telling me to get some help in those days was like telling a sixteen-year-old not to smoke, not to drink. You know they are going to try it. What you need to tell them is what to do after they try it, how to keep it under control.

You know the old saying, "If only I knew then what I know now." Well, if I were faced with a man with a drinking problem today, I would go to meetings of Al-Anon on my own. I would have the right to do it—for myself, if for nobody else. My conscience is clear. Keith had the problem before we met. Others had not been able to help him.

On my own, I could not practice any form of tough love. Not at that stage in my life. I would just look at his sad face and melt. I think I'm inclined to be like that with my children, too, but after being a single mother, I learned I had to step back and be the bad guy.

Back in those days, I could not be the bad guy with Keith. It's a terrible dilemma for any woman who is madly in love with a man. But for any woman who loves, there is always something good out of something bad.

The good is that I loved like that. The good is Jesse. The good is that Morgan had a family for those years, that she loved enough to ask Keith to be her father.

The bad is what we all had to deal with after Keith was gone. There was a price for my love. You cannot give love unconditionally with no concern for the outcome, for your children and yourself.

I'm almost inclined to tell women, "If you're passionate, before you get too involved, you need to turn the other way. Run before you fall in love." And that just flies in the face of what we like to believe, that love changes everything.

Women thrive on love, we live for love. We need to be needed, we need to be depended upon. I think it is the essential nature of women. The hand that rocks the cradle rules the world.

When you feel needed, you say, "That's my husband. He depends on me. He loves me." When you feel like that, you can change the diapers and paint the house and cook supper all at the same time.

When you're in love, you overlook things. You make excuses. At least when you're young, you do.

I thought I had lucked out with my fairy-tale marriage to this beautiful man. We had two beautiful children, we were going to be even more successful, get a bigger home, and everything would be perfect.

The experience opened my eyes to life. It definitely made me more cautious, more cynical. When I first started going out with other men, after Keith died, and they would tell me how crazy they were about me, I would think to myself, You son of a bitch, you do not. You just want to fool around every chance you get.

I'm not trying to talk ugly. It's just life. At this point, I don't see that anybody's perfect. I've come to realize that we're all going to be tempted, that we're all going to be dishonest at times, at moments. It definitely changed my whole outlook on men, on commitment.

I had to ask myself, "What does it say about Keith, about all men, that I could think I knew him, but the first chance he got, my first long trip to promote a record, he went out and picked up a bimbo? And I might never have known it if he hadn't died. How can I trust anybody?"

There are days when I'm mad at Keith, but the longer time goes on, mostly what I feel is relief.

My life is different now. I don't worry about the police calling and saying, "Miz Morgan, your husband is drunk." Or that there is some girl. Or whatever.

I don't worry as much. Worry will age a woman quickly. But I do recognize that I tend toward anxieties, the occasional panic attack, that fluttery feeling. I've learned to take a deep breath and slow down, maybe take a mild pill for that occasion.

My dad used to say, "You've got to have a sense of humor." My vision of myself is, "I'm basically okay."

I had been hurt by the breakup with Troy Aikman, and was not looking for another relationship, but in 1996 I recorded a duet called "By My Side" with a talented singer named Jon Randall.

I was working on this book when we were married in November of 1996. I knew it was hard for Jon to be living in my house with the tape recorder and the notepad taking down my words, but I could not rewrite history. I could not say, "Keith is gone, take away the pictures." Keith was Jesse's father, and no matter what else, this is the man who gave him life. More than ever, I realized the hold Keith Whitley still had over me.

I'll tell you one thing that changed. I never did like to sing cheatin' songs, didn't think they were right for me. I've acted out of passion in my life, but I don't feel right in justifying cheatin' or making it part of the accepted human experience. It still ain't right.

Years ago, I used to sing "Stand By Your Man," partially because Tammy Wynette is one of my favorite singers and favorite people, and I was proud to try to match her version of the song.

You could not pay me to sing that song today. I do not believe a woman has to take everything from a man even if he is the only breadwinner in the family. I believe any woman can be successful if she wants to be, and you don't have to depend on a man to pay the bills. And you definitely do not have to marry a man to have sex.

I look at things differently since I turned thirty-five. More than ever, I came to believe in treating everybody the way they want to be treated. If men cannot do that, then leave them. We were not meant to suffer.

I'm also different in my appearance. I think I am even stronger, healthier, sharper than I was a few years ago.

I know that every woman has her own body type, and we need to be comfortable with ourselves, but I can speak only for how I feel. When I'm slim, I feel attractive, energized. When I put on weight, I don't feel great about myself.

I did not like the way I looked when I was in my teens, and I'll admit that now I enjoy seeing myself trying on a sultry red dress for a video, or wearing tight jeans offstage, or something frilly for a big show. If women admire my physical condition and men like to look at me, I'm proud of that. I work at it.

These days, my normal size-two measurements are a hundred and two pounds on a five-foot, two-inch frame, but I can go up seven to ten pounds fairly easily. I can tell when I get in my jeans, so I back off accordingly.

I am not one of those gym rats, one of the aerobics people. I do not have a personal trainer. Oh, I work on my abs a little bit—it's the rage right now—and I've got some hand weights. I might lie down on the floor and do leg raises, or if I'm cooking, I might do a few leg swings at the table while I'm waiting for the water to boil. I stretch a few times a day, but basically I just do the things I like, and I trust nature.

I'm an avid swimmer, and will go in the pool every day as

long as the weather's good—not necessarily lap after lap, but just enjoying the water. I love to work outside in the yard, pick up stuff, keep moving. Going up and down the four flights of stairs, all day.

In the winter, when I'm not getting as much exercise, I count fat grams. One big meal and little snacks during the day. Apples, fat-free caramel. I have to think about how much I'm eating because food means a lot to me—Indian food, sushi, Mexican food twice a week.

The older I got, the harder it was to take off the weight, so I paid more attention to diet. Nothing exotic. Nothing that anybody else couldn't do. Salads and fruit and pasta.

My favorite meat is chicken, and I hardly ever eat red meat anymore, although I do love hamburgers and hot dogs, so easy to grill outdoors in the summertime. If we cook out, I might eat half the fillet of a T-bone steak, but mostly potato and salad. I'm a junk-food junkie—popcorn and peanuts and cereal—but I insist on the fat-free varieties, and I try not to overdo it.

I've never been a big drinker. I like great champagne, a glass of white wine now and then, and I like a shot or two of tequila at times. My main sins are diet soda and cigarettes.

As I get older, I spend more time on what I call maintenance—sitting down, doing my eyebrows, giving myself a facial, pedicures, manicures, making sure my legs are shaved. I take time with my skin, especially during the winter when it gets so dry indoors in the heat.

I think clothes are an expression of who you are, and because I feel I'm pretty complicated, there is no one outfit or style that represents me. I love to play dress up, beads and gowns and high heels, but then I also like my sweatpants and my clogs. I like to be . . . everything.

I have this image of glamour right out of the old black-and-white movies. All those beautiful women—I would sit in the movies and imagine how they smell. I love being a woman, love wearing all kinds of clothes—cutoffs in the middle of the day, Marilyn Monroe in the evening.

My favorite color is purple, but I don't wear it well, so I tend toward the earth tones.

My mood changes even at night. At times I put on a red nightgown and high-heel slippers, and there are times I put on a pair of shorts and a T-shirt.

One of my best outlets is painting, which I started about five years ago. I had never been great at drawing, or even a prize pupil in art class in school, but I just tried it one day and discovered I liked it, and I wasn't bad at it. I love painting real-life scenes from memory, nothing abstract, but my own view of things—trees, candles, outdoor scenes. I've got a studio on the ground floor, and I usually frame the paintings and give them to family or friends.

My family is still the main focus of my life. I have such great memories of my childhood, the house packed with seven Morgans, and family visiting, friends dropping over. That is still how I think life should be.

Given the way people move around these days, it's pretty amazing that all of us still live around Nashville, not that far from Mom's house. Mom is a widow again, I'm sad to say, since the death of Paul Trainor. He died early in 1996 after brain and heart surgery.

Marty is the only one who ever lived away from Nashville for any period of time, and after he worked in advertising for a few years, he came back. It would take something drastic for one of us to move away.

It's not as if none of us has been outside Nashville. I went on the road at thirteen, and Mom has traveled all around the world. Obviously, Dad was everywhere. Even though he was brought up in Ohio, he would hit the state line and say, "There's nothing like Tennessee." We all still feel that way. We're around for each other, through good times and bad times. And there have been both sides for all of us.

Candy has been through two divorces, has three children and one grandchild. Years ago, a girlfriend of hers urged her to join her at nursing school at Tennessee State University, and Candy discovered her calling. She is now a registered nurse, working with adolescents at Vanderbilt Children's Hospital.

Beth divorced Lane after twenty-two years; then she married somebody else, basically as an escape, and they divorced after sixteen months. Now she is engaged to Mike Chamberlain.

Liana was married before, and now she's married to Billy Baltz. They live on a farm just outside Nashville and have two children, Ellis and Sarah. She's a teacher's aide at St. Pius, where her children go to school, and is also a cantor and lector during the Mass.

Marty was married once. His former wife and their son, Nathan, live in another state, but Nathan's around a lot during school vacations. Marty lives within a couple of blocks of Mom and Beth.

I've often said that Marty is the most talented of all of us, the most creative, the most sensitive. Recently he put together a children's book series that I think will sell. Also, he and I recorded one of his songs for a benefit children's CD called "Friends for Life," a celebration of global harmony. It was great fun to be in the studio with him. I think he's on the verge of something major.

As the Morgan kids get older, it's harder to get all five of us together at any given time, but we try for Christmas and Thanksgiving and Mother's Day, and we talk to each other on the phone. We keep up, and when we're together, it's as if we are kids all over again.

Food is big in our family. We love going to the Koto Sushi

Bar in downtown Nashville, where the owners give us a semiprivate room off on the side, where you take off your shoes and sit lotus-style around the low-slung table.

We met there recently, ten of us, sitting for hours and drinking tea, laughing, and talking about what kind of day we had. Morgan talked about wanting to study drama in college. She's just into her junior year in high school and has her first car, a modest Saturn, and she drives Jesse to his school before she goes to hers.

Nicknames are big in our family. They spread the message: Don't take yourself too seriously. I mean, "Fussy" and "Fussbutt" did not come from nowhere.

Liana is still Gilly, but some of us acquired new nicknames in the strangest ways. If you haven't seen us for a year, you will need a table of contents to figure out all the new nicknames.

Mom, these days, is Beezler. Explain it? We were on a trip out to Las Vegas and Mom had a bag with chips in it. Susan Nadler and I began calling her Money Bags, which became "MB," which became "Bee," which became "Beezler."

My family name at the moment is Omi, which sounds Dutch or German or something, but dates back to when Jesse was in a talent show in school. We asked if he was singing a solo and he said, "No, I'm singing backup for Omi" —a girl in his class. Everybody thought it was funny that Jesse was singing backup, and somehow it evolved to them calling me "Omi," and the name has stuck to this day.

Beth's current nickname is "Strap." This stems from Gilly's son, Ellis, wearing a tank-top shirt, holding on to the top of it and calling it his "strap hat." We were tossing the shirt around one day, and Susan began calling Beth "Strap." The name just stuck.

Dad's love of practical jokes has endured to the next generations. When I'm on the road, Beth and Susan Nadler and I will find new and devious ways to scare the living daylights out of each other, by popping out from behind doors.

After my career started to take off, I bought a house on fifteen acres up in the hills, but it was a little too secluded. My fans found it anyway, and they were ringing on the gate bell at all hours, and my kids were afraid to be there at night, particularly if I was on the road.

Also, there were no kids around for Jesse to play with. So in May of 1996, I bought a house on Old Hickory Lake in Hendersonville, with half a dozen houses in plain sight on a cul-de-sac. Jesse rides bikes with kids in the neighborhood, and there are friends and neighbors around, and we keep an eye out for each other. This is much more like the way I was raised in Madison.

I try to be home as much as possible for the children. I get up early with them, make sure they have breakfast and are dressed right before they leave for school. I want to be as constant in their lives as my mom was in mine. It's hard because I'm on the road, and I could not get by without great help around the house. My career is still important to me.

I'm still performing shows all over the United States. The research people say I am most popular in big cities, particularly in the middle Atlantic and the northeast states rather than in the rural areas. I can't explain it, although I do think I come off as independent, modern.

I had a great time on a tour with Pam Tillis and Carlene Carter, the first time three women had ever gone out on the road together on an extended sponsored tour. Obviously, the angle was that Pam is the daughter of Mel Tillis, and Carlene is the daughter of Carl Smith and June Carter, and the stepdaughter of Johnny Cash, and I am the daughter of George Morgan. But there was also the image of three strong-minded contemporary Nashville women, at home all over the country.

Sometime down the line, I'd like to try more acting. I've had just enough exposure to it to think I could be good at it. I once did the pilot for a television show which would have been called "Lorelei Lee," about a detective who is a country singer at night.

I knew I had problems with the concept when they handed me my first outfit for my singing scenes—it was hot pink and corny, the kind of thing Minnie Pearl would wear in her parody of the country bumpkin. That worked fine for Minnie—everybody knew she was a college woman, having fun playing the role—but it was not fine for me to make fun of country music.

With very few exceptions, it seems that every time television or the movies get their hands on country music, they throw in a lot of barns and hay bales and shocking pink. They must think we're all cornballs. My sense of disdain must have showed, because the show never went anywhere. I'm too proud of Nashville to dumb it down. But the right part will come along.

My friends were right. Thirty-five was just a starting point.

CHAPTER TWENTY-NINE

My life goes on, better than I ever could have imagined. At the same time, however, I owe it to Keith to keep his memory alive.

It is my responsibility to remind people that Keith Whitley was more than just a beautiful voice on a greatest-hits compact disk, that he was a man who loved, a man who felt, perhaps too strongly for his own good.

Sometimes I go over to Spring Hill Cemetery and visit Keith's grave. There are big new monuments there for Roy Acuff and Bill Monroe, who have passed since Keith did; Keith's modest tombstone is tucked away in the back, on a quiet hill.

The grave is not that easy to find, but if you ask directions of the gravediggers, they get this big grin on their faces, and they point out the landmarks—right behind that tree, right over from that big tombstone. They all know Keith, they know his music, they know his fans.

Sometimes the nuns from the St. Joseph School take their classes into the cemetery to say the rosary for all the people buried there. It was tough on Morgan and Jesse the first times their classes went, but they were proud of their dad. The nuns caught on, and would lead the whole class to Keith's grave.

Keith does not lack for company. Sometimes there are flowers there, or just cards, or even notes scrawled on scrap paper. People remember Keith. I've heard the phrase "cult figure" used, but I don't know about that. I just know that Keith lives.

He has a powerful pull on his people in the mountains of eastern Kentucky. It has been terribly hard on Mary and Dwight and particularly Mrs. Whitley, who lost two sons and a husband within five years.

My mom has lost two husbands, but she still has her five children around her, and that has kept her going. I've lost a husband, but I have Morgan and Jesse and a new life. I cannot imagine the pain of losing a child. My heart goes out to Mrs. Whitley every time I think about it.

"Mom is very independent," Mary said not too long ago. "She doesn't let on if she's in a bad mood, but sometimes I can tell by the tone in her voice that she's got the blues, and I'll go over."

A few years ago, Mrs. Whitley was in a car wreck and broke both her ankles, but she keeps going. She is the editor of the weekly paper, the *Elliott County News*, published every Friday with front-page headlines like: "Elliott County's December Jobless Rate Is Highest in State," and "Menifee Co. to Host Tobacco Workshops" and "Dwight Whitley to Perform at Mountain Arts Center."

Mrs. Whitley knows Keith is a legend. People drive dozens and dozens of miles from the interstate, from other parts of Appalachia, just to see the hometown that he loved so much.

The people in the hills are protective of their own, but in Sandy Hook, if a stranger seems sincerely interested in Keith, the people at the general store and the Frosty Freeze will direct strangers to Faye's house. They know she wants to meet people who care about Keith.

I know somebody who dropped in on her not long ago. It was a cold, sleety Sunday afternoon, and Mrs. Whitley was dressed up in good slacks and a nice sweater, as if she were expecting company. She chatted with the strangers, and gave them a little tour of the property, where there is even an old oil rig bobbing away in the backyard.

Mrs. Whitley keeps a museum of Keith's stuff in the garage—the old posters of his concerts, photo albums, a few stage jackets. She even has the heat turned on in the winter, in case anybody comes by.

Last year there was a homecoming around Decoration Day, the traditional day in the mountains for people driving back home from Detroit and Akron and Louisville, visiting the graveyards high on the hills.

Somebody told me there were five hundred people in the backyard, many of them strangers wanting to see where Keith Whitley came from. Faye's double-wide mobile home is spacious, clean, and comfortable—better than most of the world lives—but Mary said her mom heard a twelve-year-old boy, from outside the area, saying, "I can't believe Keith Whitley's mother lives in a mobile home."

Comments like that hurt the feelings of these proud people. The Whitleys have a great history. And Keith still lives among them.

Keith's music lives on, too. Joe Galante was saying recently that Keith is having the success in death that he never had in life. Joe said that going into 1997, Keith's five albums had sold a total of four and a half million copies.

"For the short period he had, Keith is one of our bestselling catalogue artists," Joe said. "But it wasn't about the money with Keith. He was one of those rare artists who come through from time to time. He loved country music. He was enough of a country singer and a honky-tonker to bring people in, a great combination of country and honky-tonk and bluegrass, all at the same time. There was that edge to him.

"He and Garth Fundis were making a second great album. He would have been nominated for all the awards. He was an heir apparent. He was just breaking through.

"Keith loved music. Certain people complain about others, they ask, 'How come that son of a bitch. . . ?' You never heard that from Keith. He was always talking about the beauty, the emotion of the music. It was sort of like being with a minister or a priest. He never felt this was about positions on the chart, or money. He was just a country singer.

"The people around him appreciated him. Ricky Skaggs, Vince Gill. People who grew up around Keith. Emmylou. You could sit in a room, listen to them, these people all would have gotten together and made a hell of a record. They had the same soulfulness."

What is Keith's legacy?

"I carry his CD, the greatest hits, around with me," Joe said. "When I start wondering what the hell I'm doing this for, I think of Keith."

Blake Mevis: "I have a theory that stars are ten percent singing and ninety percent stardust. Keith had the ten percent, don't get me wrong, but he also had the stardust. There's not a week goes by that I don't get into a big long conversation with somebody about Keith."

Don Light: "If Keith Whitley had lived, he would have been an important person in our business. He would have been Entertainer of the Year. He would have been a Hall of Famer."

Keith changed my life forever, made me understand about being an artist. After our love affair, after our marriage, I realized that my life was linked with the thrill of performing, the thrill of creating.

Because of Keith, I realized I could not live an ordinary life, or love somebody from the mainstream, from the nine-to-five world. My life could not be like Mary Smith across the street. I needed my blood boiling.

Keith never would have lived a normal life or died a normal death. He was too passionate. Passionate about everything. About Morgan, about Jesse growing in my belly. About his own mother.

Keith was an artist. I never fully understood that while he was alive, but recently I was watching a biography of Michelangelo on the Arts and Entertainment cable channel, and it reminded me of Keith.

I am paraphrasing this from memory, but Michelangelo had trouble understanding his own gifts, so he wrote a poem to God that went something like, "You put me here, you've given me the talent, and now I'm trapped within myself and I've become frail and afraid."

Another part of the poem was, "Help me be free of my mind."

The analysts on *Biography* were saying that Michelangelo's outlet was his work, his expression. I had this searing realization that Keith must have been like a latter-day Michelangelo, searching and talented, scared of the feelings within him, not understanding the power and the beauty of his own voice, his own words, the impact he had on others. And so frail inside.

At times I've said that just being with Keith always would have been good enough for me. I tell myself that I probably would not have put so much effort into my career, that I could have run the house and supported Keith's art, because I believed in him so much.

Lately, I do not know if that is true. It's easy to say at thirty that you are dedicated to somebody, but how long do you put up with destructive behavior? These days I'm just not so sure about what would have happened.

I'm not trying to stir things up, but I still feel there was something Keith could not handle, whatever it was. He had so much going for him. A wife, children, a career, a loving mother, great fans. But something drove him to those binges.

Lately, I have come to think that Keith was looking for a way out, that maybe it would not have mattered what I did.

I have got to be honest with myself. I don't know if I could have stuck it out. I might have had enough. I might have delivered some ultimatums. It just never came to that.

When I visit his tombstone, the anger is gone, the tears are mostly gone.

Poor Keith. He loved to smoke so much. I always smoke a cigarette for him, right down to the butt, and then I gently place the butt right by his tombstone.

I tell him what's going on. How the kids are. Who's making good songs, who's making garbage. I tell him about my life, how I keep searching for a love that will match what we had. I don't think he's jealous. Keith knew that life must go on. For my part, I've got to stand by Keith Whitley's memory, forever and faithfully.

ABOUT THE AUTHORS

Lorrie Morgan, daughter of *Grand Ole Opry* star George Morgan, has sold more than seven million records. She lives with her two children, Morgan and Jesse, in Hendersonville, Tennessee.

George Vecsey has written eleven adult books and six children's books, including *Coal Miner's Daughter* with Loretta Lynn, *Martina* with Martina Navratilova, *Get to the Heart* by Barbara Mandrell, *Five O'Clock Comes Early* with Bob Welch, and *Troublemaker: One Man's Crusade Against China's Cruelty* with Harry Wu. Mr. Vecsey has been a sports columnist with *The New York Times* since 1982. He lives in Port Washington, Long Island, New York, with his wife, Marianne, an artist.